DATE DUE

The l Life

The Trajectories of Rural Life: New Perspectives on Rural Canada

Edited by
Raymond Blake and Andrew Nurse

Canadian Plains Research Center
and the
Saskatchewan Institute of Public Policy
2003

UNIVERSITY OF
REGINA

Saskatchewan Insitute of Public Policy
University of Regina
Regina, Saskatchewan S4S 0A2
Canada
Tel: (306) 585-5777
Fax: (306) 585-5780

National Library of Canada Cataloguing in Publication Data

Main entry under title:
The trajectories of rural life : new perspectives on rural Canada / Raymond B. Blake, Andrew J. Nurse, editors

(Saskatchewan Institute of Public Policy publications, 1499-6693 ; 2)
Co-published by : Saskatchewan Institute of Public Policy.
Includes bibliographical references and index.
ISBN 0-88977-152-9

1. Canada—Rural conditions. 2. Rural development—Canada. I. Nurse, Andrew, 1966- II. Blake, Raymond B. (Raymond Benjamin). III. University of Regina. Canadian Plains Rsearch Center. IV. Saskatchewan Institute of Public Policy. V. Series.
HN103.5.T73 2003   307.72'0971   C2003-910291-2

Cover design: Brian Danchuk Design, Regina
Cover illustration: "Towers and Sky," by Julian Forrest (2000)

Printed and bound in Canada by Houghton Boston, Saskatoon
Index by Patricia Furdek, Indexing and Abstracting Services
Printed on acid free paper

— Contents —

Acknowledgements

Saskatchewan remains one of the most rural provinces in Canada, and it should not be surprising that the Saskatchewan Institute of Public Policy at the University of Regina is particularly interested in challenges facing rural Canada. Yet, the Institute wanted to organize a conference that went beyond the myths of rural Canada's past to develop a clear picture of its present reality from all perspectives—demographic, social, economic, political, cultural and ecological. Moreover, the conference wanted to explore the evolving relationship between urban and rural Canada and the significant ways in which they depend on one another. The conference's underlying objective was to promote understanding and dialogue among all Canadians—urban and rural—about the contribution that rural Canada makes to the life, identity, and prosperity of the country, and about the measures that might be needed to secure a sustainable and dynamic future for Canadians in rural communities.

In organizing such a conference, the Institute partnered with the Centre for Research and Information on Canada/Centre de recherche et d'information sur le Canada (CRIC), the Canada West Foundation, and the Association for Canadian Studies/Association d'études canadiennes, the Canadian Plains Research Center, and the Center for Canadian Studies at Mount Allison University.

Of course, from the time an idea for a conference is first discussed to the time a collection of essays is finally published, one incurs many debts. The support for the conference was overwhelming, and the Institute would like to acknowledge the financial support offered by a variety of interested and committed groups, including the Council for Canadian Unity, Agriculture and Agri-Food Canada, Western Economic Diversification Canada, the Government of Saskatchewan, the Social Sciences and Humanities Research Council of Canada, SaskPower, the Privy Council Office, the University of Regina, Farm Credit Canada, Agrium, the Canadian Wheat Board, Canadian Pacific Railway, Canadian National, Scotiabank, Enbridge, Mr. Allan P. Markin, CIBC, CrownLife, SGI Canada, Dow AgroSciences, Saskferco, Canadian Western Bank, SaskTel, SaskWater, and Big Sky Farms. Their contributions made the conference and this book possible.

As well, we are indebted to several people who helped to make this book possible. Harold MacKay, the conference chair and chair of the SIPP Board of Directors, helped in a number of ways, as did Brian A. Johnson of Crown Life and Michelle Stanners of the Council for Canadian Unity. While his name does not appear on this book, Andrew Parkin, the co-director of the CRIC, played an important role in shaping its contents, and Kathryn Curran and Erna Pearson of SIPP can take credit for the success of the conference and for what success this book might enjoy.

Raymond B. Blake and Andrew Nurse
May 2003

The Rural Problematic:
An Introduction to *The Trajectories of Rural Life*

Raymond Blake and Andrew Nurse

This is not another collection of essays romanticizing rural Canada. Nor does it offer yet another prescription for effective rural economic development. Instead, the goal of this collection is to both resist the seemingly persistent urge to romanticize and prognosticate about rural Canada and the people who live geographically outside the urban environment and suggest different ways of looking at rural life. In this sense, its goal is to build upon an increasingly strong base of research and writing on rural Canada to suggest different perspectives on the countryside, the small town, the environment, and the landscape. The important element of this perspective, in our view, is not to think about rural Canada in isolation; rather we feel that it should be clear to everyone interested in the past, present, and future of rural Canada that its symbiotic relationship with urban life needs to be placed in the foreground. A primary objective of this collection is to suggest ways in which such a conception of rural Canadian life can be productively developed from a variety of perspectives: demographic, social, economic, political, cultural, and ecological. This brief introduction will highlight some of the key themes addressed here.

Change and Continuity in Rural Life

Rural communities have been profoundly affected by late-modern processes of political-economic, demographic and cultural change. In Canada, the impact of these changes are all about us: in the absolute population declines in Saskatchewan and Newfoundland noted in the last federal census, in the crises of the east and west coast fisheries, in the farm crisis covered almost daily in the news, in serious ecological problems, and in the reorientation of rural social services (epitomized by the problems experienced by many small communities securing effective medical care). There is a tendency to view these problems in stark terms: as part of a qualitatively new era in Canadian history triggered, perhaps, by the forces of "globalization" or "urbanization" or the rise of the "service sector economy." In important ways, however, the problems of rural Canada are not particularly new. Rural migration, pollution, wildlife conservation, and other matters have been long-standing persistent concerns of rural Canadians. It has, in fact, never been particularly easy to be a farmer or a fisher or a business person in small-town Canada, and urbanization and economic change have been long ongoing historical trends. What, then, makes the early twenty-first century different for rural Canadians? Why should the problems and concerns of rural Canada merit particular attention if, for instance, so much of the Canadian population is now urban? How can we approach a consideration of the problems and prospects for rural life in Canada in the twenty-first century?

Hard and fast answers to these questions are difficult to specify in a short introduction, but several matters are important to note. First, the problems and concerns of rural Canada need to be looked at in terms of their historicity. In the past, urbanization and socioeconomic crises have tended to promote nostalgic images of rural life as the font on community, caring, and a simpler way of life. Nostalgic ideals of rural Canada do a remarkable disservice to rural life and culture in that they reduce the lived experiences of rural Canadians to a bare and one-sided essence that cannot approximate the complexity of gender relations, work routines, family connections, economic processes, and the hopes and aspirations of rural Canadians. Nostalgia, in other words, has not served rural Canadians well in that nostalgic images of rural life as somehow less complicated than urban life mystify the concerns and experiences of rural Canadians. One important element in contemporary discourse on rural Canada—epitomized by the essays in this collection—is that realistic conceptions of rural life, its past and its future, have challenged nostalgic ideals in ways that permit a more effective and useful dialogue about the challenges of twenty-first century living outside the urban environment. Such a perspective elides the ideal of rural life as static and simple, replacing it with a focus on on-going historical change as a fundamental hallmark of the rural experience.

Second, a cogent understanding of the ongoing historicity of rural Canada is particularly important in the contemporary context of "globalization." Exactly what globalization is can be a matter of considerable debate. Certainly, the Canadian experience of globalization differs from that of other countries, owing to the strong economic, political, and cultural ties that bind Canada to North America. For rural Canadians, the more important consideration might be trade liberalization and its potential impact on rural communities and industries. Recent trade disputes relating to softwood lumber and to grain and other farm production illustrate this point. In this regard, the significant issue is less trade liberalization than a failure of it. Canada's rural industries, for instance, are shockingly efficient and this efficiency is one of the reasons that other countries attempt to deflect the logic of trade liberalization to place limits on imports from Canada. If rural Canadians are most directly affected by duties placed on softwood lumber or agricultural subsidies, urban Canadians cannot dismiss this concern as parochial. Forest and agricultural products remain important elements of the Canadian economy; lost or foregone markets affect the economy as a whole. As a result, there is every reason to see the problems of rural industries—whether triggered by trade disputes, droughts, over-fishing or any other causes for that matter—as pressing national concerns. Here the key question is: how will Canada fit into a liberalized international trade order?

Third, contemporary research indicates that the problems and prospects of rural Canada are also connected to urban life in other ways. On one level, this statement is self-evident and obvious. Markets for rural industries are found, primarily, in urban centres either in Canada or the United States. In another way, this point requires clarification. The lived experiences of rural Canadians, their social and political views, can bear marked similarities to urban Canada if we consider issues such as job insecurity, family incomes, the politics of gender, and pollution. The work of rural and urban Canadians, for instance, may differ (or, it may not!) but the need for job security, effective social services, good public and post-secondary education are all examples to illustrate this point. When one considers issues such as health care, employment, violence against women, the rapidly rising costs of a university education, and other matters of this sort, it becomes clear that rural and urban Canadians must confront some issues together. Said differently: the process of making Canada into a better country should not isolate rural from urban Canadians. Instead, their shared concerns should bring them together as they look for ways of building a vibrant and dynamic society north of the United States/Canadian border.

Complementing this process is the blurring of the distinctions between rural and urban lifestyles. It would be incorrect to look on rural and urban life in Canada as basically the same. But, in the same way that there are similarities in social concerns, there are similarities in other realms of life. Throughout Canada, rural people travel to urban centres to work or to shop. Importantly, this trend is not one-sided. Urbanites work and shop in rural communities as well. This movement of people on a weekly or daily basis has been facilitated by the creation of transportation systems that link communities together and provide for rapid travel. Beyond this, however, new technologies of communication link Canadians together and with the wider world in historically unique ways, at least in terms of speed. The internet may or may not revolutionize culture, but it does provide a means for people living just about anywhere to communicate and it does provide potential access to a wider range of cultural, social, economic, political, and other news, images, ideals than hitherto. Better transportation, e-mail, chat rooms, and the web will not collapse geographic distinctions, but they will serve to blur boundaries that before were treated as hard and fast.

Fifth, changes in the demographic character of Canada will affect the perceptions and realities of rural life in Canada. As Manju Varma notes in her discussion of multiculturalism in Atlantic Canada, ethnic diversity is frequently geographically polarized in Canada. Rural Canada, it is important to note, is far from ethnically and culturally homogeneous, but the most diverse human geography in Canada is found in the country's large cities. In considering matters of ethnic diversity, it is similarly important to resist the image of rural Canadians as backward, purely white, or representative of an older ideal of Canada. With the exception of First Nations, the people who live outside Canada's cities are, themselves, the descendants of immigrants. Their families came from Germany and Holland, China and the Ukraine, the United States and India, and many other countries. The relative levels of ethnic diversity in urban and rural Canada, however, do raise important issues for public education, for understandings of multiculturalism as public policy, and the availability of services that can support an ethnically diverse population. All of this makes rural Canada demographically different from urban Canada, but this difference does not mean that rural Canada is isolated from the need to consider diversity issues or that urban Canada is somehow better than rural Canada. The ethnic diversity of urban centres has not eliminated the need for cultural, social, and economic policies that can support a diverse population outside of Canada's cities, nor will it for the foreseeable future. The specific concerns of rural Canadians with regard to diversity, in this sense, can also be part of a wider Canadian dialogue on this subject. As with other social issues, the concerns and hopes of rural and urban Canadians may be closer than common stereotypes make them seem.

None of this should be taken to indicate that rural Canada is the same as urban Canada. The fact that there are similar concerns, interests, problems, and aspirations in rural and urban Canada does not mean that rural Canadians lived experiences are the same as the lived experiences of urban Canadians. Technology can blur cultural and contextual differences between rural and urban life, but it does not eliminate them. The most effective means to engage current discourse on rural Canada is to look at its connections to urban life in ways that both recognize differences but elide stark oppositions. There are differences—demographic, economic, political, etc.—between rural and urban Canadians that make the experiences of life for those living outside the city different from those living within it. Today, rural Canada does confront new challenges—particularly with regard to new communications technologies, international trade liberalization, and social services—but the fact of these new challenges should not lead one to assume a hitherto static quality to rural life. Moreover, the differences between rural Canadians themselves—in terms of gender, class, ethnicity, geography, social views and political allegiances—need to be recognized. What all of this suggests is that research on rural Canada needs to be attuned to the dynamics of difference and similarity. Concerns similar to those of urban Canada exist in the countryside, but the way one addresses these concerns may need to be different.

The Boundaries of Policy

The essays presented in this collection are intentionally suggestive rather than definitive. The problems and prospects of rural Canada are neither simple nor self-evident. In considering the state of rural Canada today, the essays in this collection work with several important themes. One central theme that needs to be explored is the definition of what actually constitutes rural Canada. As the essay by Doug Ramsey, Bob Annis, and John Everitt indicates, rurality is amenable to both cultural and empirical definitions. Many Canadians, for example, might see themselves as living in a rural community even while Statistics Canada definitions deny that such a community is actually rural. Andrew Nurse's essay explores this issue further by looking at the ways which definitions of rural culture have changed over time and how urban conceptions of rural cultural differences have affected understandings of country life.

Another important theme in contemporary research on rural Canada is gender. Here, researchers are increasingly focusing their attention on gender dynamics in the countryside. The essays by Jennie Hornosty and Deborah Doherty, Wendee Kubick and Robert Moore, and Louise Carbert illustrate this point. Hornosty and Doherty's essay discusses the extent of spousal abuse in rural Canada. Their essay indicates a potential connection with urban life in that violence against women is shockingly prevalent across Canada, but they go on to look at the ways the characteristics of rural communities make it more difficult for women to report abuse and to leave abusive relationships. Likewise, Carbert looks at the under-representation of women in rural politics. A stereotyped ideal of rural Canada might view this under-representation as part of a rural social conservatism, but as Louise Carbert's essay suggests, a variety of factors are likely at play, including: the prominence of patron-clientele relations, heightened concerns with economic as opposed to social issues, political patronage, and what might be thought of as community dynamics. As Kubick's and Moore's essay shows, under-representation in politics should not be taken to signify a lack of pressing issues for rural women. As they point out, rural women have to cope with a wide range of different lifestyle dynamics and issues that point to broad social concerns and political views.

A third key theme of current research is culture. Robert Wardhaugh provides a different side of rural life in his discussion of "bush parties" and "booze cruises." His essay shows how considerations of popular culture can also shed light on the changing dynamics of class, gender, and ethnicity in small town Canada. Manju Varma's essay indicates that diversity remains an important consideration for rural Canada today. Exactly how rural Canada can integrate itself into the multicultural matrix of urban Canada is a consideration that merits attention particularly in a time of regionalized rural population decline. By itself, immigration is not a solution to stagnating rural economies, but it is one potential issue that could be explored in a consideration of workforce redevelopment. To attract immigrants, however, rural society will need to address diversity issues. The key, as Varma suggests, is to understand that it will not be possible to address diversity in the countryside in the same way as in the city. Instead, differently contextualised policies are needed.

A final important theme addressed in this collection is sustainable development. As the recent work of the Canadian Plains Research Centre indicates, rural dislocation has become a pressing reality in some parts of the country. The essay by David Gauthier and his collaborators looks at rural social cohesion in order to define sustainable development in a multifaceted way. Taking the terms to mean more than ecologically sound industry or effective longer-term economic development, Diaz et al. look at a range of social, economic, and environmental factors that they feel should inform the policy-making process if meaningful social communities are to be maintained into the future. June Carmen explores the historical dimension of development of sustainable communities in rural municipalities in Saskatchewan by focusing on rural schools and teachers. As the one public-use building in rural municipalities, schools provided a space for the gathering of farm families and helped to make a community. The closure of schools and selling them for other purposes often left farm communities without a space for community gathering and, in the process, weakening the communities affected by such changes.

Bruno Jean's postscript on rural Canada returns to the issue of the importance of rural Canada. For Jean, a strong rural Canada is essential for a strong Canada. Much ink and countless dollars have been spent on research on rural sustainability and strength. Yet, if we look at the fishing communities of the east coast or the farms of Saskatchewan, it is not at all clear that this ink and money has produced effective results. Both Michael Rushton and Roger Gibbins wonder about the efficiency of this spending in their contributions to this collection. They both contend that hard-headed policy decisions need to be made and that the opportunity cost of sustaining rural communities needs to be front and centre in any policy discussion. Should governments, Rushton wonders, provide social services and goods to rural areas in an effort to stem migration if the rural population is not economically sustainable? Should not, in other words, more emphasis be placed on market-based decisions even if these decisions would, ultimately, witness a decline in the quality of rural life and the rural population. Jean's essay does not suggest that Rushton and Gibbins are wrong, but he looks at this point from a different angle, drawing other concerns into the policy formulation mix. In the short term, these different views cannot be merged into one but their interchange, one might hope, will lead to a better understanding of exactly what is at state in rural communities throughout the country. John Roslinski makes a similar point in his essay on Aboriginal peoples, noting that the discussions around self-government must involve Aboriginals living in both rural and urban parts of Canada.

Final Considerations

At the end of the day, the essays in this collection will likely not change anyone's strongly felt views about rural Canada and its importance. By definition, strong views are difficult to change and that is not the objective of this collection anyway. Instead, the contributors to this collection look to advance research on rural Canada, to suggest new and more effective ways of studying rural life, and to promote a different type of discourse about rurality in Canada. They look, in other words, to engage issues, rather than stating the "final word" on them. This is, one hopes, a particular strength of this collection. Definitive statements are always appealing. The security and certainty they provide can be comforting. Our view, however, is that this is not the time for definitiveness. What is needed, we believe, is a new discourse about rural Canada, its past, present, and future. We hope that this collection contributes to this discourse.

CHAPTER ONE

Rural Community in Westman:
Theoretical and Empirical Considerations

Doug Ramsey, Bob Annis and John Everitt

Introduction

One of the difficulties in assessing the state of rural Canada relates to a poor understanding of what rural is or is not. Debates and discussion regarding the notion and definition of rural have been ongoing in the social sciences for decades (Hillery, 1955; Hoggart, 1990; Halfacree, 1993). The health sciences, particularly due to the difficulties in providing health care services to non-urban areas that tend to have scattered, sparsely populated, aging populations fueled in part by the out-migration of young people, have weighed into the debate more recently (Rourke, 1997; Leduc, 1997; Buske et al., 1999). The purpose of this paper is to address the definitional question of what is rural. In doing so, the notion of community is addressed within a rural context. Following a review of the literature regarding conceptual and empirical descriptions and classifications of rural, two empirical exercises conducted for Manitoba are illustrated. First, the standard Statistics Canada classification of rural is applied to the Regional Health Authority (RHA) district boundaries. Second, the results of focus group analysis conducted in southwestern Manitoba in early 2001 are highlighted. The paper concludes by offering a number of research questions that require attention if rural health, and therefore rural health care issues, are to be adequately understood. public opinion polls, among other sources, continually illustrate the importance of health care to Canadians. In assessing whether rural Canada is "moving forward" or being "left behind," understanding rural health care issues is pivotal. In order to understand whether rural health care issues are distinct from urban health care issues, a clearer notion of what rural means to people is required.

Describing Rural

Descriptions and definitions of rural vary from the broad and conceptual to the narrow and empirically specific. Basic descriptions include features such as size, population density, and location. More comprehensive descriptions account for the economic, social, and ecological attributes which are argued to be distinctly rural. Cloke (1994) recognizes such an array of attributes in a definition of rural which includes extensive land uses, attachment to the environment, and cohesive social structures. This definition recognizes the physical attributes of what has been traditionally viewed as rural, the living condition, and the spatial degrees of rural as it relates to urban. It is the latter which has caused a blurring of distinction between what is truly "rural" and what is truly "urban." Defining rural as a comparison to urban is not new—a prime example being the sociological constructs developed by sociologists based on the "rural-urban continuum" which extended from "truly rural community" to "truly urban society" (Pahl, 1966). Identifying clear distinctions between rural and urban becomes even more problematic in what is known as the "rural-urban fringe," an area which is located between urban centres and their suburban surround and the rural hinterland (Pryor, 1968; Bryant et al., 1982; Beesley and Walker, 1990; Beesley, 1999).

While some argue that "rural" has become an irrelevant descriptive term (Hoggart, 1990), others make the case that rural can be expressed as "social representation" (Halfacree, 1993). The notion of social representation relates to the sociological framework of "rurality." Clarke and Miller (1990), for example, suggest that rural is a feeling which is distinct from urban in adopting a definition of rurality based on "the residents, their values, and their lifestyles, as well as by the geography and density" (p. 76). This definition recognizes both the qualitative (values, lifestyles) and quantitative (people, space, density) dimensions to rural. This leads to the distinction between "space" and "place," the latter being the social dimension in defining community (Kearns and Joseph, 1995).

Bealer et al. (1965) suggest that in order to develop a conceptually and analytically sound definition of rural, one needs to first identify clear definitions of the three elements of "rurality" comprising rural (occupational, ecological, and sociocultural). Miller and Luloff (1981) adapted the Bealer et al. (1965) framework by extending the occupational dimension to include, beyond agriculture, a range of rural resources such as mining, fishing, and forestry. Further, Miller and Luloff (1981) offer a cultural typology based on attitudinal structures that included views on a range of social issues (e.g. civil liberty, abortion, and racial segregation). It was argued that distinctions in views between urban and rural areas could be ascertained.

Beyond conceptual descriptions and applied indices of rurality are more specific definitions of rural which attempt to place spatial boundaries based on specified criteria. Statistics Canada, for example, defines rural as that which is not urban. Thus, rural areas are those which have fewer than 1,000 people living within a population density of less than 400 people per square kilometre (Statistics Canada, 1991). A slight variation based on density has been adopted by the Organization for Economic Cooperation and Development (OECD) which defines "predominantly rural regions" as those with population densities of less than 150 persons per square kilometre (OECD, 1994). Rural has also been described based on a combination of size, density, and location; labour market definitions that account for commuting patterns; and Metropolitan Influence Zones (MIZs) (Beshiri et al., 1999 and 2000). Mendelson and Bollman (1998) have combined both rural and small towns into a Statistics Canada–based definition of "populations living outside the commuting zones of larger urban centres—specifically, outside Census Metropolitan Areas (CMAs) and Census Agglomerations (CAs)."

Accepting that a distinction between rural and urban exists, Humphreys (1998) argues that from a health perspective, in order to address and resolve health problems in rural areas, the distinction needs to be better understood. In the health context in rural Ontario, Rourke (1997, 113) defines "isolated communities" as those with "fewer than 10,000 people, greater then 80 kilometres from a regional centre of more than 50,000." Thus, in providing health care services it is not enough to accurately reflect what is truly rural but it is also necessary to relate this rural distinction to distance from urban centres. Leduc (1997) extends this notion in developing a rurality index designed to measure the level of health services in rural Canada based on six categories or variables: health care facilities, staff and equipment; number of physicians; remoteness and availability of transportation; paramedical support; social factors; and population. Based on these categories, Leduc proposes a "General Practice Rurality Index" (GPRI).

Related to indices of rurality is the development of typologies which place rural populations within the context of other populations. Frameworks developed for Canada include simply distinguishing between urban and rural/small town (Mendleson and Bollman, 1998) and three categories on a continuum: rural, semi-rural, and urban (Pitblado et al., 1999). In a study of non-metropolitan counties in the United States, Flora et al. (1992) adopt a framework that includes three categories: rural, less urbanized, and urbanized. Each of these categories is then subdivided based on adjacency to urban areas. Adjacency reflects the importance placed on "isolation" when defining degrees of rurality. Urbanized areas are those which contain at least 20,000 people, less urbanized areas are characterized by populations of between 2,500 and 19,999, and rural areas are those which had populations of fewer than 2,500 people.

Flora et al. (1992) then develop a typology of non-metropolitan counties based on their economic and social character. Economic activities include farming, manufacturing, mining, and specialized government. Social character designations included counties with persistent poverty, based on per capita income, and counties classified as retirement destinations. A final category was based on counties in which at least one-third of the land was federally owned. This typology may have utility in a Manitoba context given the manufacturing and agricultural economies of the south compared to mining economies in the north. A category based on First Nations communities could be included in place of the federal land categories. A range of social indicators, including per capita income, could also be identified for measurement.

From the perspective of how populations grow numerically and expand spatially, Bollman and Biggs (1992) utilize a classification system which looks at rural, urban and "fringe," or near urban and near rural, areas. This is similar to the framework adopted by the OECD which looks at rural as it relates to, or borders on, metropolitan areas. The OECD framework has the added dimension of "northern" which acknowledges the distinction between rural and remote. Bollman (1994) takes this distinction further by recognizing five categories of rural: rural nirvana, agro rural, rural enclave, resource areas, and "Native" north. This classification could be applied to Manitoba; however, there would be difficulty in distinguishing between resources areas and "Native north."

In a health context, Goins and Mitchell (1999) identify five residential categories, including two urban categories (towns, cities) and two rural categories (farm/non-farm, crossroads). The fifth residential category, communities, could hold attributes of both rural and urban. The inclusion of community as a separate category, in comparison to the two urban and two rural categories illustrates a dilemma in applying such classifications to regions. The following section is a first introduction to applying rural and urban distinctions to the health regions in Manitoba. One of the difficulties in applying this framework to Manitoba is the simplicity of the two rural categories. That is, while "southern" Manitoba is characterized by agriculture and "northern" Manitoba is not, "middle" Manitoba includes a mixture of farm and non-farm areas.

Statistics Canada's Statistical Definition Applied to the Health Authorities of Manitoba

Eleven Regional Health Authorities of Manitoba are in place to administer health care. As illustrated in Figure 1, there is a direct correlation between size and location—with smaller RHAs located in the more densely populated southern region of Manitoba and larger RHAs in the remote and more sparsely populated northern regions. That is, there is a

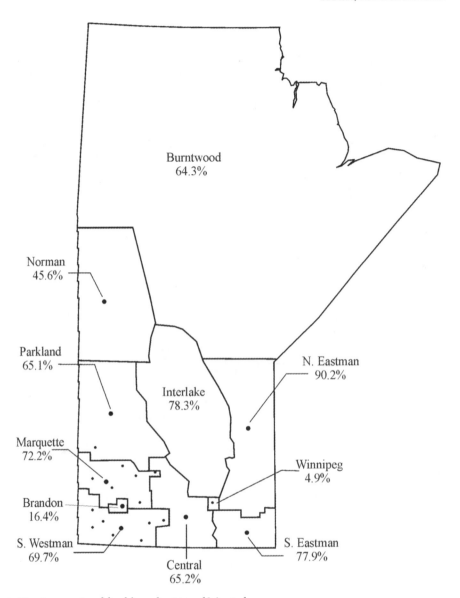

Figure 1. The eleven regional health authorities of Manitoba.

concentration of people in southern Manitoba and in particular, in Brandon and Winnipeg. As one moves northward, the regions become larger in area but serve smaller numbers of people. In terms of the percentage of the urban population in Manitoba, only five Census Divisions (CDs) in the province claim a population with more urban residents than rural (Table 1). Not surprisingly, the CDs which include Winnipeg and Brandon, the only "statistical" cities in the province, have high proportions of urban residents (99.9% and 75.9%, respectively). Consequently, the boundaries of the Winnipeg and Brandon Health Authorities are small in area.

Less clear however, are the distinctions between urban proportions of the total population in other health regions. Burntwood and Norman Health Authorities, for example

Table 1. Urban-Dominated Census Divisions of Manitoba, 1996

Census Division	Communities	Health Authority	% Urban
11	Winnipeg	Winnipeg	99.9
7	Brandon	Brandon	75.9
21	Flin Flon, The Pas, Snow Lake	Norman	59.5
9	Portage	Central	56.4
3	Altona, Carmen, Morden, Morris, Winkler	Central	50.8

Source: Statistics Canada, 1997. Regional Health Authorities, 1998.

Table 2. Ranked Classification of All Urban Centres in Manitoba

Name	Type	Population	Health Authority
Winnipeg	Primate City	614,740	Winnipeg
Brandon	Regional City	39,175	Brandon
Thompson	City	14,385	Burntwood
Portage	City	13,077	Central
Selkirk	Town	9,881	Interlakd
Steinbach	Town	8,487	S. Eastman
Dauphin	Town	8,266	Parkland
Winkler	Town	7,241	Central
Flin Flon	Town	6,572	Norman
The Pas	Town	5,943	Norman
Morden	Town	5,689	Central
4 Communities	3 Settlements 1 First Nations	3,000–4,000	Various
8 Communities	6 Settlements 2 First Nations	2,000–2,999	Various
30 Communities	16 Settlements 14 First Nations	1,000–1,999	Various

(Figure 1), while having lower percentage rural populations than South Westman, South Eastman, and Central, must serve larger areas and therefore, dispersed populations. The concentration of residents in the urban centres of Thompson (Burntwood) and Flin Flon, The Pas, and Snow Lake (Norman) create a deception that the regions on the whole are "less rural" (Table 2; Figure 1). While the issues associated with providing health care services to rural residents within the Norman and Burntwood Health Authorities may be similar to the North Eastman Health Authority, rural and urban proportions of populations as the baseline are too simplistic. Further, while residents in the southern health authorities may be statistically "rural," they have greater access to primary and specialized health care services given their proximity to Winnipeg and Brandon. In fact, one could argue that the dispersion of residents throughout the Burntwood Health Authority, that is, the larger area of the region, results in the greatest challenges in providing rural health care services in the province. Thus, statistical definitions of rural are not entirely reflective of the situation when one applies Statistics Canada's data to the health authorities of Manitoba. It was to this point that a need for a better understanding of rural in a Manitoba context was recognized.

Focus Group Study

Methodology

Qualitative methodologies have become increasingly accepted in the social sciences in recent years (Berg, 1998; Limb and Dwyer, 2001; Kitchen and Tate, 2000). Among qualitative methods, focus groups have been employed as stand-alone approaches as well as a technique for either providing background to a particular research question or to reinforce findings from quantitative analyses (Morgan, 1997; Stewart and Shamdasani, 1990; Berg, 1998). In order to gain rural residents' perceptions of rural, community, and health, fifteen focus groups were held in rural communities throughout the Westman region of Manitoba between January 23, 2001, and April 19, 2001 (Table 3). They were arranged and organized by a local health contact. These contacts were instructed to invite members of the community and to reflect youth, farmers, health professionals, the clergy, business leaders, and seniors. The meetings were held at a range of sites, including health centres, church halls, and community centres. Each focus group was framed based on seven questions:

1. How would you, as a rural resident, describe community?
2. What do you consider to be your community?
3. What is unique about your rural community?
4. How would you, as a rural resident, describe rural?
5. How would you describe health?
6. How would you describe a healthy rural community?
7. How do you know when you live in a healthy rural community and how is it measured?

Table 3. Rural Health Focus Groups, Manitoba, 2001

Community Name	Date Held	Number of Participants	RM Population, 1996	Settlement Population, 1996
Strathclair	January 23	4	1,030	377*
Miniota	January 29	6	1,025	217*
Minnedosa	February 5	15	665	2,440
Virden	February 7	10	1,840	2,955
Russell	February 15	16	550	1,605
Carberry	February 27	12	1,900	1,490
Hutterite Colony	February 28	16	na	100**
Rivers	March 1	13	895	1,120
Deloraine	March 5	11	620	1,040
Treherne	March 7	9	1,275	670
Glenella	March 12	15	555	130
Souris	March 14	8	710	1,615
Killarney	March 20	10	1,175	2,210
Melita	April 17	5	530	1,155
Glenboro	April 9	9	860	665

Source: Focus Groups, 2001
* 1991 data; ** estimate for each colony

Following the discussions describing the particular community, participants were handed a letter-sized photocopy of their particular region based on 1:50,000 topographic maps and asked to draw the community boundary. While these results are discussed in detail elsewhere (Ramsey, Annis, and Everitt, 2002), it is important to note that the size, shape, and context of individual definitions of community ranged from small nodal areas to arrows that extended beyond the map area provided.

Community

The notion of community has been described in essentially two distinctive ways: the geographic (spatial) community and the community of interest (socioeconomic) (Goldschmidt, 1947, 1978; Kearns and Joseph, 1995; Ramsey and Smit, 2002). The descriptions of community provided in the focus groups have been classified based on these two dimensions. In terms of the geographic community, participants noted connections to land, patterns of interaction and business trading areas, and lack of population diversity. Feelings ranged from the simple ("a bunch of people living together in one spot") to the more complex as noted by the following participant: "there is some connection to land… geography is part of that, but there is also the spiritual connection in terms of people that have lived their whole life in one area and have a deep sense of connection to the land itself. It's not just livelihood." To many, community extends beyond the immediate jurisdiction in which they live. To some, communities crossed municipal, provincial, and even national borders. To most, however, the scale of community was more local, and as described by one participant, "community is sort of like family, where people you know, will stop and talk."

The community of interest is a more subjective or qualitative entity, including such descriptions as a place that provides a sense of belonging, exhibits common beliefs, loyalty, dependency, trust, common bonds, roots, and feelings of security. Participants also mentioned qualities of community such as being a good place to raise a family and a place that is based on relationships and unique interpersonal connections. As noted by one participant, community is "where you get a lot of support. A comfort zone." Not all descriptions were positive, however, such as the lack of privacy that was mentioned in a number of meetings.

While for the most part clear distinctions can be made between the spatial and nonspatial descriptions of community, many comments were difficult to categorize. For example, one participant noted that because rural people tend to think of community "more broadly than town people," that a series of "overlapping communities" can be identified in a physical sense, but based on communities of interest (e.g., schools, work, recreation, social networks).

Rural

A similar distinction can be made with rural, that is, a spatial notion versus a qualitative construct based on social and economic considerations. Rural as a spatial entity was described in varying ways, including anything outside of the city with less population density and more open space than its urban counterpart. Others noted that rural can be measured based on distance to obtain services which are often located in urban centres. Similar to the notion of community, in terms of isolation, comments such as "you need a lot of gas money" were made. Participants noted that in rural areas there is generally a low population over a large land mass. There was general consensus throughout most meetings that while Winnipeg was clearly urban, Brandon, with a population of approximately 40,000, was not purely urban. That is, Brandon exhibits rural characteristics, such as its role as an agricultural service centre. A number of times in different focus groups the term "rural city" was used to describe Brandon. One participant described Brandon as follows: " I consider Brandon to be rural. It still seems like a small town. I guess there wouldn't be the gossip knowledge, but it's ten minutes across town."

Rural can also be described as "place" as illustrated in comments such as having feelings of isolation, albeit with people who are friendly. Participants noted that in rural areas people volunteer their time freely (which is not to say that urban people do not). Rural areas tend to offer a slower pace of life. There was a feeling in many meetings that in rural areas one does not generally need to lock one's doors. However, in a number of instances comments were made acknowledging that this lifestyle was changing. A number of comments about rural are difficult to classify. These range from the mention that rural areas have slow inter-net access to participants who made such statements as: "I think rural is rural," rural "is a state of mind," and that rural is "quiet and dark at night." Each of these statements, while not offering specific details, illustrate a qualitative notion of rural areas that participants feel are distinct from, if not positive in comparison to, urban areas. For example, one individual stated that while having lived in both Brandon and Winnipeg in the past, that he would always be rural. That is, rural was a state of mind or a feeling. These descriptions of rural and community illustrate, albeit in a cursory way, some of the difficulties in reaching a clear dis-tinction between rural and urban.

Summary

While perceptions and descriptions of both rural and community have changed from Hillery's (1955) review to the present day (Ramsey and Smit, 2001), some similarities remain. First, there are both spatial and non-spatial attributes of community and rural. In making these delineations, distinctions between rural and urban can be made. Whether rural is accu-rately reflected in Statistics Canada's definition is debatable. Certainly, at least in a Canadian context, rural does exist. As with urban areas, rural areas face changes in economy, society, environment, institutions, and polity. However, it would be difficult to argue that changes in both urban and rural, and points on the continuum in between, were the same. The simple overlay of RHA boundaries to rural population proportions illustrates that there is no one "rural solution" to providing health care to rural Manitoba. Making this provision more dif-ficult is the dominance in the "rural south" of Brandon and Winnipeg, southwest and south-east, respectively. In northern Manitoba, while the population appears statistically either "less rural" or similar to the proportions in the southern Manitoban RHAs, the health care needs are very different. As mentioned, the urban centres of Thompson in Burntwood RHA and Flin Flon, The Pas, and Snow Lake in Norman RHA create a deception that those RHAs are "less rural." Further, an argument could be made that the health care issues are different between the north and the south, as well as between urban and rural. For example, the north is characterized by mining and forestry economies, colder climate, and remoteness, whereas the south is characterized by farming and an aging population. In these respects it appears that a distinction needs to be made between whether one is analysing health of rural people and/or analysing whether there are distinctly rural or regional health issues.

One area of change relates to the human condition, including quality of life, well-being, and health. The proportion of statistically urban in Canada has risen throughout this centu-ry and now represents approximately 80 percent of the total population. Many rural areas, and therefore communities within these areas, face issues such as youth out-migration, loss of services, and redundant economies. With these losses and redundancies is a resultant aging population. This, compounded with issues of distance and fewer people, presents many difficulties in providing adequate health care services. While this paper focused on the need to understand rural before attempting to analyse rural health, one substantial question was raised. As the demands for health care services are increasing, and will continue to do so as the population ages, how can adequate health care services be provided to rural areas in Manitoba? In order to answer this question, a next-step project has been identified whereby a survey will be administered to health care providers in each of the communities included in the focus group analysis. The purpose of the survey will be to ascertain gaps in health care services across southwestern Manitoba, to identify possible efficiencies that could be achieved, and to assess future scenarios regarding rural health care provision in southwestern Manitoba.

References

Bealer. R., Willits, F. and W. Kuvlesky. 1965. "The Meaning of 'Rurality' in American Society: Some Implications of Alternative Definitions." *Rural Sociology* 30: 255–66.

Beesley, K. 1999. "Living in the Rural-Urban Fringe: Toward an Understanding of Life and Scale." In N. Walford, J.C. Everitt and D.E. Napton (eds.), *Reshaping the Countryside: Perceptions and Process of Rural Change*. New York: CABI Publishing.

Beesley, K. and G. Walker. 1990. "Local Satisfactions and Concerns in Urban Fringe Areas." *Ontario Geography* 34: 23–36.

Berg, B.L. 1998. *Qualitative Research Methods for the Social Sciences*. Boston: Allyn and Bacon.

Beshiri, R., R. Bollman and H. Clemenson. 1999. "Alternative Definitions of Rural." Draft paper prepared for Statistics Canada, Ottawa.

Beshiri, R., Bollman, R., Clemenson, H., Mogan, A. and A. McDermott. 2000. Defining Rural. Draft paper prepared for Statistics Canada, Ottawa.

Bollman, R. 1994. "A Preliminary Typology of Rural Canada." In J. Bryden (ed.), *Towards Sustainable Rural Communities: The Guelph Seminar Series*. Guelph: University of Guelph, University School of Rural Planning and Development.

Bollman, R. and B. Biggs. 1992. "Rural and Small Town Canada: An Overview." In R. Bollman (ed.), *Rural and Small Town Canada*. Toronto: Thompson Educational Publishing.

Bryant, C., L. Russwurm and A. McLellan. 1982. *The City's Countryside: Land and Its Management in the Rural-Urban Fringe*. London: Frances Pinter.

Buske, L.M, S.N. Yager, O.B. Adams, L. Marcus, L. and F. Lefebvre. 1999. "Rural Community Development Tools from the Medical Perspective: A National Framework of Rurality and Projections of Physician Workforce Supply in Rural and Remote Areas of Canada." A Report Prepared for the Canadian Medical Association for Health Canada, April 1999.

Clarke, L. and M. Miller. 1990. "The Character and Prospects of Rural Community Health and Medical Care." In A. Luloff and L. Swanson (eds.), *American Rural Communities*. Boulder: Westview Press.

Cloke, P. 1994. "Rural Community." In R.J. Johnston, D. Gregory and D.M. Smith (eds.), *The Dictionary of Human Geography*. Oxford: Basil Blackwell.

Flora, C., J. Flora, J. Spears and L. Swanson. 1992. *Rural Communities: Legacy and Change*. Boulder, CO: Westview Press.

Goins, R. and J. Mitchell, 1999. "Health-Related Quality of Life: Does Rurality Matter?" *Journal of Rural Health* 15: 147–56.

Goldschmidt, W. 1947. *As You Sow*. New York: Harcourt, Brace and Company.

———. 1978. "Large-Scale Farming and the Rural Social Structure." *Rural Sociology* 43, no. 3: 362–66.

Halfacree, K. 1993. "Locality and Social Representation: Space, Discourse, and Alternative Definitions of Rural." *Journal of Rural Studies* 9: 23–37.

Hillery, D. 1955. "Definitions of Community: Areas of Agreement." *Rural Sociology* 20: 111–23.

Hoggart, K. 1990. "Let's Do Away With Rural." *Journal of Rural Studies* 6: 245–57.

Humphreys, J. 1998. "Delimiting 'Rural': Implications of an Agreed 'Rurality' Index for Healthcare Planning and Resource Allocation." *Australian Journal of Rural Health* 6: 212–16.

Joseph, A.E. and A.I. Chalmers. 1995. "Growing Old in Place: A View from Rural New Zealand." *Health and Place* 1, no. 2: 79–90.

Kearns, R. and A. Joseph. 1995. "Restructuring Health and Rural Communities in New Zealand." *Progress in Human Geography* 32: 18–32.

Kitchin, R. and N.J. Tate. 2000. *Conducting Research into Human Geography: Theory, Methodology, and Practice*. Harlow, Essex, UK: Prentice Hall.

Leduc, E. 1997. "Defining Rurality: A General Practice Rurality Index for Canada." *Canadian Journal for Rural Medicine* 2, no. 3: 125–31.

Mendelson, R. and R. Bollman. 1998. "Rural and Small Town Population is Growing in the 1990s." Working Paper #36. Agricultural Division, Statistics Canada, Ottawa.

Miller, M. and A. Luloff. 1981. "Who is Rural: A Typological Appoach to the Examination of Rurality." *Rural Sociology* 46, no. 4: 608–25.

Morgan, D.L. 1997. *Focus Groups as Qualitative Research*. Thousand Oaks, CA: Sage.

Organization for Economic Cooperation and Development (OECD). 1994. *Creating Rural Indicators for Shaping Territorial Policy*. Paris: OECD.

Pahl, R. 1966. "The Rural-Urban Continuum." *Sociologia Ruralis* 6: 299–327.

Pitblado, J.R., R.W. Pong, A. Irvine, K.V. Nagarajan, V. Sahai, J. Zelmer, L. Dunikowski and D.A. Pearson. 1999. "Assessing Rural Health: Toward Developing Health Indicators for Rural Canada." A Study Prepared for Health Canada. Centre for Rural and Northern Health Research, Laurentian University.

Pryor, R. 1968. "Defining the Rural-Urban Fringe." *Social Forces* 47: 202–15.

Ramsey, D. and B. Smit. 2001. "Impacts of Changes in the Flue-cured Tobacco Sector on Farmers in Ontario, Canada." *Applied Geography* 21: 347–68.

——. 2002. "Rural Community Well-being: Models and Application to Changes in the Ontario Tobacco-belt." *Geoforum* (accepted, final revisions submitted, January 2002).

Ramsey, D., B. Annis and J. Everitt. 2001. "Definitions and Boundaries of Community: The Case of Focus Group Analysis in Southwestern Manitoba." *Prairie Perspectives*.

Rourke, J. 1997. "In Search of a Definition of 'Rural'." *Canadian Journal of Medicine* 2:113–15.

Stewart, D.W. and P.N. Shamdasani. 1990. *Focus Groups: Theory and Practice*. Newbury Park, CA: Sage.

Statistics Canada. 1991. *Profiles*. Census Division, Ottawa, Canada.

——. 1997. *Canada Census of Population—Manitoba Profiles*. Census Division, Ottawa, Canada.

CHAPTER TWO

"The Varying Moods of Country Life":
Marius Barbeau, Folklore, and the Cultural Reconstruction
of Rural Life in Quebec

Andrew Nurse

The development of folklore studies, Marius Barbeau explained to his future biographer, Laurence Nowry, in 1965, marked an important development in Canadian cultural history. To be sure, the creation of folklore studies had not been an easy task. As a "pioneering" folklorist working first for the Anthropology Division of the Geological Survey of Canada and then (after a reorganization of government anthropology) the National Museum, Barbeau battled the indifference of his bureaucratic superiors, limited resources and perhaps most importantly, in his view, time. The on-rush of modernity, he explained, threatened folk traditions even in the rural hamlets where he conducted his research.[1] Ultimately, Barbeau's efforts met with success. By the end of World War II, he had convinced the Museum to establish an extended folklore research programme while he himself collected thousands of legends, songs, recipes, arts and crafts, dances, and a myriad of other cultural practices and objects, now preserved in the Canadian Museum of Civilization.[2]

Barbeau's formative role in the history of Canadian folklore has been acknowledged. Celebratory studies have examined his work creating folklore as a field of scholarly enquiry and research,[3] while more critical studies focus on the ways in which Barbeau's ideological predisposition affected his research programme and structured the nature of the archives and museum collections he created.[4] What has received less attention is the way in which Barbeau's folklore developed as a point of cultural interaction between rural and urban life in Canada in the first half of the twentieth century. It is precisely this issue I will address in this essay. The argument I will make is twofold. First, I will contend that the development of scholarly folklore studies helped to reconstruct the image of rural life in the twentieth century. In Barbeau's case, his understanding of traditional folk culture constructed rural Quebec

---

1. "Marius Barbeau, interviewed by L. Nowry at the National Museum, 1965," transcribed by R. Landry (1982). Copy on file at the Canadian Museum of Civilization [hereafter CMC].

2. For a discussion of Barbeau's work collecting traditional material culture, see: Pascale Galipeau, *Les paradis du monde: l'art populaire du Québec* (Hull: Canadian Museum of Civilization, 1995).

3. Laurence Nowry, *Marius Barbeau, Man of Mana: A Biography* (Toronto: NC Press, 1995).

4. Galipeau, *Les paradis du monde*. For an effective critical study discussion of Barbeau's ethnographic filmmaking, see Lynda Jessup, "Tin Cans and Machinery: Saving the Sagas and Other Stuff," *Visual Anthropology* 12 (1999): 49–86.

—his primary research field—as a liminal space within which different, more intense, and more authentic cultural experiences could be found. Second, I will argue that the process of folklore as a field of scholarly work helped to transform the very rural culture it sought to preserve.

To illustrate these points, this essay will begin by tracing the ideal of traditional culture to Barbeau's immediate predecessors in the mid-nineteenth century in order to highlight the different signifiers mobilized by his discourse of tradition. Next, it will examine Barbeau's work as a folklorist from the perspectives of both ideology and cultural practice. Finally, this essay concludes by looking at the implications of Barbeau's folklore specifically and the diffusion of folkloric conceptions of rural Canada more generally. Here I will argue that story of Barbeau's folklore has broader implications for contemporary discussions of rural Canada than as a particular case study in cultural history. In particular, it highlights both the ironic implications of folklore studies and helps to historically situate current discourse on rurality. Understanding these implications and this discourse, I would contend, is important for a critical and fruitful discussion of the future of rural Canada.

A Genealogy of Tradition

On a number of occasions Barbeau claimed he was a pioneer in the study of folklore in Canada.[5] For French Canada this claim is technically incorrect. When Barbeau began to study and preserve folk traditions in the late 1910s and early 1920s he was already working within a cultural tradition which stretched back into the mid-nineteenth century and encompassed authors like J.C. Taché, who published the first significant collection of French-Canadian legends, and musicians like Ernest Gagnon, who first collected and published a selection of French-Canadian folk songs in the 1860s. When Barbeau began to study French-Canadian folklore, Gagnon's *Chansons populaires du Canada* was still popular, having run through a considerable number of editions. The literary and musical work of Taché and Gagnon was not ideologically neutral. They each were important individuals in a tradition of cultural expression that emphasized the unique, stable and religious character of French-Canadian rural life.[6] Within this discourse, tradition and rural life were not separated from a broader dialogue on French-Canadian culture. As the Abbé Casgrain explained: "the history of Canada is, for all intents and purposes, the history of religious life and civilization on the banks of the St. Lawrence."[7] The key feature of French-Canadian culture lay in its spirituality, institutionalized in the Roman Catholic Church, and the religious manners and customs of the populace.

A religious and nationalist conception of traditional French-Canadian life found expression in a series of texts published from the mid-nineteenth century to the first decades of the twentieth. J.C. Taché, for example, organized *Forestiers et voyageurs*, his collection of French Canadian oral traditions, within precisely this framework. In the legends he collected from voyageurs and lumber workers, Taché found a reminder of the historical accomplishments of French Canadians and an indication of the importance of religion. Declaring himself to be "avant tout catholique," Taché was careful to explain that "le voyageur canadien est catholique et français." The culture of the voyageur and woodsman incorporated these two dynamics.[8]

---

5. For one instance, see Marius Barbeau, *I Was a Pioneer* (Ottawa: National Museums of Canada, 1982), 6.

6. For a discussion see: Réjean Beaudoin and André Lamontagne, "French-Language Literature in Canada," in Kenneth G. Pryke and Walter C. Soderlund (eds.), *Profiles of Canada* (Toronto: Copp Clark Pitman, 1992).

7. Abbé Casgrain, *Histoire de la Mère Marie de l'Incarnation, première superieure des Ursulines de la Nouvelle-France, précedée d'une equisse sur l'histoire religieuse des premiers temps de cette colonie* (Québec: 1864), 31. Cited in ibid., 249.

8. J.C. Taché, *Forestiers et voyageurs* (Montreal: 1946), 16.

In Taché's view, these legends were notable for their "gaité [et] naïveté charmante," but he found in them other qualities that merited attention. Through the contemplation of the elaborate and often mystical events they presented, one became aware of greater spiritual powers:

> l'homme a besoin de se souvenir de ce qui a été ou de ce qu'on a cru, et encore parce que l'esprit de l'homme, à le considerer comme intelligence exilée loin de l'essence du vrai, du bon et du beau, ne peut plus vivre de réalisme que son âme des vérités naturelles qu'elle perçoit: il faut d'un voyageur dans l'inconnu, à l'autre se reposer dans la foi à des mystères.[9]

For the musician Ernest Gagnon, the important feature of traditional French-Canadian music lay in its moral purity. Gagnon collected traditional music in the vicinity of Quebec City for which he supplied the score and published.[10] The music he collected illustrated a particular cultural character. "Dans tout les cours de mes recherches, je n'ai guère raconté que deux chansons vraiment immorales," he explained. This, he contended, made traditional French-Canadian music different from that of France: "[p]lusieurs de nos anciennes chansons se chantent encore aujourd'hui en France," he noted, "avec des variants lascives que nous ne connaissons pas en Canada."[11]

By the first decades of the twentieth century, the equation of traditional French-Canadian culture with a Catholic moral purity had hardened into a formula that found its fullest expression in the cultural work of the Abbé Lionel Groulx. Writing in the twentieth century, Groulx was more preoccupied with modernity than his predecessors because, he felt, it presented particular problems for French-Canadian culture. Urbanization and economic development brought with them cultural changes that threatened religious devotion and morality. A deeply religious man, prodigious author, and influential historian, Groulx drew little distinction between Catholicism and French-Canadian nationalism. For him the traditional culture of French Canada and Catholic devotion were inseparable.[12]

The discourse of Taché, Gagnon, and Groulx, then, constructed traditional culture as an essential element of the French-Canadian national character. While this discourse focused on rural life as the site of tradition, it did not confine tradition to a rural locality but instead constructed it as a basic defining feature of the nation as a whole. Rural life, in this sense, epitomized the broader Catholic culture that defined French Canada. The landscape of tradition created by this discourse acknowledged its gaiety but privileged its spirituality making traditional culture a sign of upstanding moral practices and spiritual devotion.

The Parameters of Tradition

Barbeau's understanding of traditional French-Canadian culture developed along very different lines. An anthropologist by training, Barbeau represented a new type of researcher —the professional scholar—who brought recognized training and state sanction to his engagement with the rural life and culture of modern Quebec. Born in the Beauce in 1883, Barbeau grew up in a middle-class family where he early distinguished himself as an able scholar. After attending a local commercial school, he moved on to classical college and then the Université Laval where he initially intended to pursue clerical studies. A loss of faith

---

9. Ibid., 16–17.

10. For an assessment of Gagnon's cultural work see Gordon E. Smith, "Ernest Gagnon's 'Chansons populaires du Canada': Processes of Writing Culture," *The World of Music* 37, no. 3 (1995): 36–65.

11. Ernest Gagnon, *Chansons populaires du Canada* (Québec: 1968), 314–15.

12. Susan Mann Trofimenkoff, *Action français: French Canadian Nationalism in the Twenties* (Toronto: University of Toronto Press, 1975).

caused him to shift his scholastic focus to law but, it seems, left in his mind unresolved questions about the nature of humanity and culture. His successes at Laval led to a Rhodes scholarship, Oxford and then the Sorbonne where he abandoned law to study anthropology with R.R. Marrett and Marcel Mauss. After completing his degree, Barbeau returned to Canada in 1910 to take up a position with the newly established Anthropology Division of the Geological Survey of Canada.[13]

Barbeau's initial work for the Anthropology Division focused entirely on First Nations. In the course of his early research, however, he became interested in the degree to which First Nations culture had been affected by interaction with French Canada. Encouraged by other anthropologists, he began to study and collect French-Canadian traditional culture in 1914 in order to provide a research base that would permit an investigation of cultural interaction. Very quickly, Barbeau's scholarly interest in French-Canadian culture expanded beyond this narrow objective and he began to see the study of folklore as a scholarly project in itself. Over the next two decades he worked extensively across rural Quebec—in the Gaspé, on the north shore of the St. Lawrence, on Île d'Orléans, and Île-aux-Coûdres—collecting and preserving a diverse array of cultural practices and objects from orally transmitted legends and songs to recipes to handicrafts and furniture to clothing and ordinary household objects.[14]

In addition to collecting culture, Barbeau wrote extensively. Including book reviews, essays, song collections, and a myriad of other texts, he penned literally hundreds of works on French-Canadian folklore and life.[15] He gave dozens of public lectures, organized exhibition displays, and spoke on radio and later television. During and after World War II, he lectured at the Universities of Ottawa and Montreal and at the Université Laval helping to create the first Canadian post-secondary educational programme in folklore. His career as a folklorist, in other words, was partly of his own making but also animated by broader institutional processes and cultural developments. Barbeau represented a new social type in Canada in the first half of the twentieth century: a professional scholar whose authority and legitimacy supplanted that amateur men-of-letters and clerics who had previously dominated the collection and study of traditional French-Canadian culture.[16]

As a field of scholarship and research, folklore studies appealed to Barbeau for a variety of reasons. On the most immediate level, he felt a personal connection to traditional culture. At least some of the legends he collected, he later recalled, reminded him of stories he had first heard as a child in the Beauce.[17] The idea of collecting and studying a culture he viewed as part of his personal history clearly had a significant appeal. Deepening this appeal was Barbeau's conviction that traditional culture was disappearing before the on-rush on the modern age. The development of mass media was a particular problem. Listening to radio or watching television, he later explained, was like getting culture from a faucet. "People turn the tap and they have the thing flowing there [and] this makes them silent and from that time on they don't remember or they don't learn from their own past."[18] For Barbeau, the intrusive power of modern commercial culture made the preservation of traditional culture a

---

13. Nowry, *Marius Barbeau*.

14. For a fuller discussion, see Andrew Nurse, "Tradition and Modernity: The Cultural Work of Marius Barbeau" (Queen's University, Ph.D. dissertation, 1997), chapter 4.

15. Mario Béland, "Marius Barbeau et l'Art au Québec: Bibliographie analytique et thématique," *Outils de recherche du Celat* 1 (1985) and Clarisse Cardin, "Bio-Bibliographie de Marius Barbeau," *Les archives de folklore* 2 (1947): 17–96.

16. For a discussion of the professionalization of scholarship, see Carl Berger, *Honour and the Search for Influence: A History of the Royal Society of Canada* (Toronto: n.p., 1996).

17. Marius Barbeau, "Why I Publish Folk Songs," *Canadian Author and Bookman* 37, no. 4 (1962): 9.

18. "Marius Barbeau interviewed," 79.

race against time.[19] Without collection, preservation, and publication, traditional culture would eventually be lost.

For Barbeau, the personal appeal of folklore was complemented by the ideological dynamics of what the American historian Jackson Lears has called "antimodernism." As Lears explains, antimodernism is a cultural recoil from the cultural, economic, and social processes of modernity: urbanization, industrialization, the development of mass media, and consumer culture. Antimodernism could take a variety of forms but at its heart lay a retreat from the ideal of progress that animated western political and economic thought throughout much of the nineteenth and twentieth centuries. Driven by a variety of factors, antimodernists looked on modern culture as artificial, eclipsing the authentic and grounded cultures of the traditional past.[20] In Barbeau's treatment of folk culture, one can see the mobilization of a standard series of antimodernist motifs: an appreciation of traditional arts and crafts, a disdain of mass media and consumer culture, and a concern with the perceived homogenizing effects of modern social and cultural development.

In his various writings on folk culture, Barbeau made these points explicit in ways that led him to define traditional culture in markedly different terms from his predecessors. According to Barbeau, several factors defined traditional folk culture. First, he held that the folk culture of rural Quebec was distinctly different from the modern culture of urban North America. Modern culture, he argued, was a culture of homogeneity. Against this foreground of essential similarity, the traditional culture of rural French Canada became both unique and unusual. Barbeau likened this unusuality to a mystical return to a child-like sense of wonder. "When I was a little boy," he once recalled, "I grew fond of folk tales and songs. The world around me was new, and I was all eyes and ears to grasp it." Later, when he began to study and collect folklore, this child-like sense of newness and wonder remained firmly established in his mind: "I had never forgotten the enchantment of my father's fairy tales."[21] The folk culture of rural Quebec recalled this wonder and enchantment. "Something in them," Barbeau wrote of the inhabitants of Charlevoix country, "makes one think of ... ancient wonderland. For two hundred years they have lived by themselves and the spell of fairy-like enchantment is not quite broken yet."[22]

Second, Barbeau argued that by listening to folk music or appreciating folk art, one encountered a world of heightened emotion and adventure. For example, Barbeau once introduced an Acadian folk song recital in the following manner: "the folk-songs of Acadia, as those of all other countries, express the varying moods of country life ... the loneliness and humour, the weariness and the love of the peasant for his land."[23] In the preface he wrote for another concert programme, Barbeau noted that the modern representation of folk songs still retained "[i]ts flavour ... of the past, of the colourful, adventurous days when explorers and fur-traders first penetrated the American wilderness." "Their presentation here," he continued, "is a symbol ... of an age of high adventure and romance."[24]

19. Ottawa *Journal*, 25 April 1929.

20. T.J. Jackson Lears, *No Place of Grace: Antimodernism and the Transformation of American Culture, 1880–1920* (New York: n.p., 1981). See also Leo Marx, *The Machine in the Garden: Technology and the Pastoral Ideal in America* (New York: Oxford University Press, 1964) and Christopher Lasch, *The True and Only Heaven: Progress and Its Critics* (New York: Norton, 1991).

21. Barbeau, "Why I Publish Folk Songs," 9.

22. Marius Barbeau, *The Kingdom of Saguenay* (Toronto: Macmillan, 1936), 89.

23. Ottawa *Journal*, 10 November 1945.

24. Marius Barbeau and Graham Spry, "Songs of Old Canada," preface to *Songs of Old Canada: A Concert by Madame Jeanne Dusseau* (Association of Canadian Clubs in cooperation with the National Gallery of Canada and the Toronto Conservatory of Music, n.d.).

Said differently: traditional culture functioned as a form of liminality that suspended the normal operation of modern life and culture and called forth different and more intense emotions. At the time he made this point, Barbeau was speaking to an urban concert audience, but his discourse had clear geographic implications. For Barbeau, and for his audience, the true folk were found beyond the boundaries of urban life, in the small towns, fishing villages, and on the farms that served as the locus of his research. This discourse constructed rural life as a mystical and "fairly-like" geography that offered a type of intense experience now lacking in the city. It made the countryside itself a liminal space, at least for the urban audience to whom Barbeau spoke. The difference between Barbeau's geography of tradition and that of Taché, Gagnon, and Groulx is also clear. For his predecessors, the geography of tradition was animated by the metaphysics of Catholicism; the countryside was a place of devotion and morality. Barbeau's metaphysics cast rural life in a mystical light, promising adventure and liminality instead of devotion.

Finally, Barbeau believed that folk culture was superior to modern culture in that it emphasized the significance of the spiritual and mental elements of human life as opposed to what he conceived as the modern focus on material development. "Our admiration for the unparalleled development of industry and machinery," Barbeau noted on one occasion, "and for all things that are practical has indeed tended to discredit the older culture of our forebears, the culture that was more of the mind and of the heart."[25] "Progress," he explained, "is often toward improvement, but sometimes it is the other way. We have advanced to success in many things, but I think the question of making progress in a cultural way and in the improvement of the soul, the mind and art, would be one that brings doubts to the minds of many. Don't think that because you enjoy the results of civilization that you are more cultured."[26]

In this sense, the folk traditions of rural Quebec deserved appreciation by virtue of their very backwardness. By eschewing modern developments thanks to some measure of geographic isolation, rural Quebec retained a set of values that did more than link it to the past. For Barbeau, rural Quebec constituted the geographic location of traditional cultural practices and crafts and maintained values that had been lost in the modern city. Despite his views on the geographic expansion of modern culture, Barbeau's discourse constructed stark divisions between rural and urban life. Unlike the earlier discourse of tradition, Barbeau's treatment of folk culture constructed rural and urban cultural geography as starkly different and valorized rurality precisely because of this. In other words: rural life and culture gained value to the degree that it differed from its urban counterpart. To the degree that it did not, its value diminished because it, too, lost contact with its heritage and in the process lost its cultural authenticity and vibrancy.

Strategies of Preservation

Barbeau did not believe that rural folk culture could survive much longer. The force of modern culture was simply too strong. His work as a folklorist was intended to address this problem, to ensure the continuity of tradition into the future, to preserve the moribund past, and to diffuse the values, practices, and arts of traditional culture into modern society. His work as a folklorist, however, served other functions and affected the rural culture he sought to preserve in, at times, ironic ways. In effect, Barbeau's work as a folklorist itself became part of a cultural dynamic that transformed the very culture it sought to save from time. Several elements of Barbeau's cultural work are important in this regard.

25. Ottawa *Citizen*, 25 April 1929.
26. Ottawa *Journal*, 25 April 1929.

First, the work of preservation was important in itself. Barbeau encouraged folklorists like himself to scour the countryside recording legends, songs, saying, dances, and recipes, and purchasing all matter of material "artifacts" for preservation or display in museums across the country. In Barbeau's case, this work produced an impressive archive—literally thousands of transcribed texts—and an unknown number of artifacts that still constitute a core element of museum collections in Canada. For Barbeau, collection was important because it provided a defense against what he saw as the inevitable processes of economic and cultural modernization. Even if the remaining enclaves of tradition succumbed to modern culture and economics, the museum and archives ensured the survival of traditional artifacts, legends, and practices.

The irony of this collection process is that the very act of collecting and preserving traditional culture served to recontextualize traditions in ways that fundamentally altered their meanings. In the first instance, the publication of traditional music and legends drew these cultural practices out of the sphere of popular community use and oral transmission and into the matrix of modern property relations and copyright laws. In published form, the "author" of, say, a collection of traditional legends gained copyright over them. The net effect of this work was to establish a new process of ownership with clear legal implications.[27]

In Barbeau's case, this process was complicated by the fact that he worked for the federal state. As a state employee, he did not own the material he collected. Even if he had it copyrighted in various publications, the culture he collected remained public property under the control of the state and available for public examination (as it is today). This did not mean that Barbeau exercised no control over the material he collected, particularly if it was published. When dealing with other folklorists, Barbeau could be generous, supportive, friendly, and encouraging, but he could also insist that he be acknowledged as co-author of collections in which his collected material was published. If he were acknowledged as a collector only (perhaps in source attributions), he would, he explained to one folklorist looking to use some of the songs he had collected, be deprived of authorial status. The fact that much of this material had not been previously published, he continued, made the matter even more pressing because, he wrote, "my claim … for authorship hasn't been placed before the public."[28] In a similar way, material taken from his published works without due acknowledgement, particularly upset him and here Barbeau did use copyright laws to press his case. In the 1930s, he sued a newspaper that had reprinted a popular piece he wrote without permission or payment.[29] This issue continued to trouble Barbeau; as late as 1959 he complained to the Composers, Authors, and Publishers Association of Canada about what he viewed as the unauthorized use of songs he had copyrighted.[30]

The exact specifics of these cases might be less important than the overall principle being established. The question is not: should Barbeau have received credit for his work collecting traditional culture? Instead, the important issue is: how did the collection and publication of traditional culture alter its legal standing and diffusion in society? Barbeau deserves credit for his folklore work, but in a very real sense he was not the author of the material he collected and published. The exact author of oral traditions, in fact, remains a contested issue. What is important here is that the people from whom Barbeau collected

---

27. Ian McKay, *The Quest of the Folk: Antimodernism and Cultural Selection in Twentieth-Century Nova Scotia* (Kingston and Montreal: McGill-Queen's University Press, 1994), 139.

28. CMC, Barbear Fonds, Marius Barbeau to Harold Boulton, 15 March 1929 (copy).

29. "M.M. Barbeau Réclame des Dommages" *Le Devoir*, 30 aout 1933.

30. Archives nationales du Québec, Barbeau Fonds, micro 5084 #M699.4, Marius Barbeau to Composers, Authors, and Publishers Association of Canada, Ltd., 11 February 1959 (copy).

this culture were not considered authors, but sources. By collecting this material and publishing it, Barbeau drew its disposition under the rubric of copyright law that, for the first time, established legal sanctions for its unauthorized use. In effect, this work turned rural culture into a legally sanctioned good over which individuals who had little or no connection to the communities in which this culture was collected could establish a legal claim to control it.

In the second instance, collection and preservation also established new meanings for traditional culture by removing this culture from its original location and relocating it to museums and archives. In this context, traditional legends, songs, and artifacts ceased to be part of an existing culture and became static signs of the past. In the museum or the archives, a song or artifact was made to signify its own demise. It became a remnant of the past to be appreciated on exactly this ground, instead of an active part of an ongoing community practice.

Barbeau's folklore work did not involve simply museum collections and archives. Through his efforts, rural culture was also moved to art galleries, private collections, and other venues. The relocation of traditional culture to art galleries of private collections reconstructed rural culture in a different way. In the course of his work as a folklorist, Barbeau discovered that some art galleries, such as the National Gallery of Canada, proved interested in developing folk art collections. The concentration of the National Gallery, however, was not on the systematic preservation of traditional material culture, but on the purchase of something that could be considered a genuine work of art. During his fieldwork in rural Quebec in the 1920s and 1930s, Barbeau secured a number of art objects for the Gallery, including a crucifix, two gilt figures (one the Virgin and Joseph with baby Jesus and the other the head of an angel) and a variety of smaller pieces. Barbeau also purchased a number of blankets and bedcovers from Île-aux-Coûdres and secured two altars from the Seminary of Quebec.[31]

In addition to art galleries, Barbeau discovered that private collectors were interested in developing modest collections of folk arts. Several of Barbeau's acquaintances outside of Quebec found the catalogne rugs of Île-aux-Coûdres, for example, attractive home decorations. E.A. Corbett, Director of the Department of Extension at the University of Alberta, ordered an Île-aux-Coûdres rug through Barbeau in 1933. After he received a request for a particular item, Barbeau wrote to a woman he had met during fieldwork and asked if she would be prepared to make whatever article might have been requested. "Should friends of yours like to have rugs of this kind [i.e. catalogne] or other bright homespuns ... for home decorations," Barbeau told Corbett after he had arranged his order, "I would be glad to order them for you."[32] At times, Barbeau involved himself more directly in the sale of folk crafts: he purchased folk crafts himself and then resold them. This seems to have been Barbeau's approach if he encountered older crafts that seemed of particular beauty. "In the course of my trip [across lower Quebec]," he told one correspondent in 1932, "I have acquired several beautiful old bedspreads from Île-aux-Coûdres. These were made fifty or sixty years ago. They have beautiful designs with vegetable dyes.... . Would you be interested in seeing any of them?"[33]

Occasionally some individuals wanted to accumulate larger collections that included folk arts as well as homespun cloth, rugs or bedspreads. Charles S. Band, for instance, relied on Barbeau to provide advice on what types of folk crafts he could purchase to decorate a new

31. CMC, Barbeau Fonds, Eric Brown (Director, National Gallery of Canada) to Marius Barbeau, 11 September and 3 October 1928; 17 February 1931; 10 March 1933.

32. Ibid., Marius Barbeau to E.A. Corbett, 12 June 1933 (copy).

33. Ibid., Marius Barbeau to Charles S. Band, 8 November 1932 (copy).

house he bought in 1932.[34] In 1935 Band again asked Barbeau's assistance to decorate his log cabin. For the log cabin, Band asked Barbeau if he might know of a carved-wood angel about 2'6" high.[35] Band, in fact, seemed particularly fond of angels, because Barbeau attempted to interest him in two angels he had discovered on the Île d'Orléans: "I know of two angels (wood carving) in the neighbourhood of Quebec which I would buy," he told Band in 1933. "One is a splendid piece from the old church of St. Laurent." "It is," Barbeau concluded, "one of the finest Quebec carvings I have seen." The price at the moment was $200 but Barbeau promised to try to secure it for less.[36] Barbeau also arranged for the purchase of chairs, antique boxes, weather vanes, crucifixes and medallions.[37]

The effects of this type of recontextualization were different in each instance. In the art gallery, as National Gallery Director Eric Brown explained to Barbeau, the focus was on beauty. Unlike the Museum, whose location transformed traditional culture into a sign of its own demise, relocation to the art gallery transformed it into an aesthetic object now cast as a work of art that stood on its own as a thing of beauty to be appreciated on exactly these grounds.[38] The exact meaning of folk art in a private collection is difficult to determine because it depended on the idiosyncrasies of the collectors themselves. Quite possibly, different collectors understood the meaning of catalogne rugs, homespun bedspreads, or colonial furniture in different ways. The rugs, bedspreads, and wooden angels Barbeau secured for Charles Band's log cabin were intended to complement the rustic retreat from modern life Band was constructing for himself.[39] Here, rural arts and crafts took on aesthetic and ideological meanings to become at once objects of aesthetic contemplation and signs of a purer and simpler time.

Each of these possible recontextualizations involved both a revaluation of traditional arts and a concomitant de-contextualization of the original meaning (or meanings) of the folk art object. In his discussion of folklore, Barbeau had emphasized the functional utility of folk arts. Folk songs were the one example on which he wrote at length but Barbeau did indicate that all folk arts were generally functional in some capacity.[40] As part of a fine arts collection or as home decoration, the functional elements of traditional material culture were effaced. In one form or another, it became the exact opposite of what had attracted Barbeau to folk culture in the first place: an aesthetic display with little functional utility. Put another way, Barbeau's folklore helped to transform folk arts into the very luxury items he claimed they were not.

Among the most significant people with whom Barbeau worked to promote the traditional culture of French Canada was T.R. Enderby, president of the Canadian Steamship Lines (CSL). Barbeau became acquainted with Enderby through his publisher, Hugh Eayrs, general editor of the Macmillan of Canada. In the interwar years, Barbeau and Eayrs worked together on a number of successful and critically acclaimed projects. By the late 1920s, Barbeau was looking to publish an extended scholarly collection of French-Canadian folksongs and turned to Macmillan as the company to see his collection into print. Eayrs liked Barbeau's idea, but felt it was not financially viable and asked Barbeau to see if support for publication could be secured from the Quebec provincial government.

34. Ibid., Charles S. Band to Marius Barbeau, 2 December 1932.

35. Ibid., Charles S. Band to Marius Barbeau, 25 October 1935.

36. Ibid., Marius Barbeau to Charles S. Band, 1 November 1933 (copy).

37. Ibid., see, for example, the list enclosed in J.B. Bickersteth to Marius Barbeau, 23 March 1934.

38. Ibid., Eric Brown to Marius Barbeau, 11 September 1928.

39. For an effective discussion of the interwar back-to-nature movement see Douglas Cole, "Patrons and Public: An Enquiry into the Success of the Group of Seven," *Journal of Canadian Studies* 12, no. 2 (1978): 69–78.

40. Marius Barbeau, "Survival of French Canada," *Canadian Forum* 15, no. 176 (1935): 313.

The Quebec government was not immediately able to support the project but Eayrs had given Barbeau another idea. In a conversation in early 1932, Eayrs mentioned that Macmillan had recently published a book on the Great Lakes in which the CSL had taken an interest as part of a program to encourage tourist travel on their lines. During the conversation it occurred to both Eayrs and Barbeau that the CSL might be interested in a similar type of book, which Barbeau would write, on the lower St. Lawrence where the company also ran cruises.[41] The book would be called *In the Heart of the Laurentians* and would be specifically designed for the tourist market. "Les touristes de la Mailbaie et de Tadoussac que le Manoir Richelieu seraient des clients pour ce volume," Barbeau told one correspondent.[42] Eayrs agreed to bridge the idea to Enderby: "[s]uch a book as we propose," he told Enderby, "would, I think, do a good deal towards bucking up holiday travel in the section of the country in which you are particularly interested."[43]

Enderby was impressed with the idea and suggested that Barbeau write a book along the lines of tourist books in current use in Great Britain. Barbeau had few difficulties with this idea and agreed to tailor the book to the needs of the CSL. He used "old people" who had been in the employ of the CSL for information and explained that he could modify some of the folklore he had already collected to suit the routes of company cruises. "You may note," he told Enderby, "that the legends are localized in various places down the Saint-Lawrence [sic]. If you were interested in the book from the point of view of publicity, I may localize most of the legends at various points of Charlevoix and Chicoutimi [counties]. The stories lend themselves to arbitrary localization. For instance in the Witch-canoe story, I could make the lumberjacks start from a camp on the Saguenay and travel along the coast in Charlevoix. That would at the same time give an idea of location around there."[44] For his part, Enderby agreed to place the services of the CSL at Barbeau's disposals. The only difficulty he had with the book was the proposed title, *In the Heart of the Laurentians*, which he felt more suggestive of skiing than a boat cruise.[45] Barbeau agreed to change the title and in 1936 the text was published as *The Kingdom of Saguenay*.

The Kingdom of Saguenay was not Barbeau's sole venture into tourist promotion. In fact, his work as a folklorist became intricately intertwined with tourist promotion in the interwar years and after. He published a number of articles that were specifically designed to attract tourists to Quebec City and agreed to allow some of his shorter more popularly oriented folklore pieces to be reprinted as tourist publicity.[46] He also actively supported the development of rural Quebec tourism and encouraged the use of traditional arts and crafts as tourist souvenirs, the market for which, he felt, was wide and under-appreciated. For example, he felt that folk cuisine could be profitably integrated into the menus of tourist-oriented restaurants. "In recent years," Barbeau noted in 1941, "I have collected hundreds of recipes of old French Canada, from Island-of-Orleans pea soup, pancakes or crepes suzettes with maple syrup, to audorilles and cretons. Yet virtually none of these many items is available in Canadian tourist hotels."[47] He also felt that it might be possible to develop a gourmet tour, similar to ones in France, where people would travel about the country sampling different—and unusual—types of food, wines and liquors.

41. CMC, Barbeau Fonds, Marius Barbeau to Hugh S. Eayrs, 4 February 1932 (copy).

42. Ibid., Marius Barbeau à E. Desrocher, 5 février 1939 (copy).

43. Ibid., Hugh S. Eayrs to T.R. Enderby, 13 February 1932 (copy).

44. Ibid., Marius Barbeau to T.R. Enderby, 16 March 1932 (copy).

45. Ibid., T.R. Enderby to Marius Barbeau, 6 December 1935.

46. Ibid., Marius Barbeau to T.R. Enderby, 24 March 1933 (copy) and Marius Barbeau à Sylvio Brassard, 26 février 1940 (copy).

47. Barbeau, "Backgrounds in North American Folk Arts," Queen's Quarterly 48, no. 3 (1941): 288.

During World War II, Barbeau worked with his colleague Douglas Leechman as an advisor to the YMCA War Service Educational Exhibition program. Educational exhibitions of arts and crafts were common occurrences during the war years. Most of these exhibitions were designed to bolster home-front patriotism,[48] but the exhibition designed by Leechman and Barbeau was intended to illustrate the economic potential of a handicrafts industry geared to the tourist market. It was, in modern parlance, an historical resources study. Their exhibition plan covered an extensive range of folk arts and crafts from native silver to French-Canadian cuisine. It noted the profitable uses to which certain handicrafts were already being put as collectors' items or tourist souvenirs and recommended an extension of this use. Hunters' decoys, for instance, the exhibition plan noted, were "no longer made extensively for the hunters as their use ·has become illegal, [but] they might very easily be made into souvenirs and tourist articles." Weather vanes, model sailing ships and hooked rugs, Barbeau and Leechman noted, were other successful tourist commodities. The list of successful items, they felt, might be extended to include pottery (currently being developed as a tourist enterprise in the Chicoutimi region of Quebec by the provincial government) as well as lace, embroidery, and cuisine.[49]

Barbeau's ventures into tourist promotion, his association with the CSL, and his advocacy of traditional crafts as tourist souvenirs indicate a third trajectory of modern engagement with rural life. Here the transformation of rural culture took on perhaps its most extreme form. In *The Kingdom of Saguenay*, and through his other efforts to illustrate the potential uses of traditional culture for the tourist industry, folk culture—and the folk themselves—became commodities. They became, as it were, an unusual experience that could be purchased for the relatively brief period of a St. Lawrence cruise or a vacation in rural Quebec or preserved for a lifetime in the pages of one of Barbeau's books. The culture of rural life became not simply a display but a good to be bought and sold by a geographically, socially, and often ethnically foreign industry and audience.

The irony of this cultural process is evident: in transforming the folk and folk culture into commodities, Barbeau contributed to the intrusive, commercialized modernity that he felt led to the destruction of traditional culture. His work aided the expansion of a commercial consumeristic market into the countryside albeit, perhaps, not in ways Barbeau had imagined when he foresaw the demise of traditional life and culture. On its most basic level, the logic of tourism was the logic of consumerism. Its development absorbed and redefined objects that, in some cases (such as decoys), had completely lost functional utility. On a deeper level, however, the logic of consumerism was not simply about commodification. It transformed household objects, crafts, songs, and stories not simply into commodities, but also into mnemonic devices whose primary function was to signify rest and relaxation and the experience of cultural difference as a diversion from modernity. The logic of this practice served to again resignify the cultural geography of tradition and rural life. In this instance, the logic of a folkloristic tourist promotion reconstructed the countryside as a place of leisure that complemented the liminal intensity of Barbeau's folklore. This logic remade the material culture of rural life at the same time that it represented the rural folk (the fishing and farming families and others who lived outside urban centres) as charming and enchanted.

Lessons of History

Marius Barbeau's work as a folklorist was not unusual. As a "pioneering" and publicly

---

48. For example, see: R.S. Lampert, "Ontario Artists Paint War Effort," *Saturday Night*, 20 March 1943, 2 and 20.
49. CMC, Barbeau Fonds, Marius Barbeau and Douglas Leechman, "Plan for an Educational Exhibition of Handicrafts for the YMCA War Series," nd.

prominent Canadian intellectual, he played a key role in creating folklore as a field of professional enquiry and scholarly analysis, but his work was broadly similar to that of other Canadian folklorists who came after him or who were influenced by the same ideological currents that drove his fascination with tradition and rural life.[50] Barbeau's honesty, scholarly integrity, and commitment to his ideals need to be openly acknowledged. He was a man of remarkable energy and caring who gave openly of his time and whose work ethic should not be questioned. He sincerely believed the arguments he put forward and was more than willing to help the literally hundreds of people who asked for his assistance. He deserves all the credit he has been accorded for his work establishing folklore at the National Museum.[51] The story of his work as a folklorist, in other words, should not be taken as an indictment of his personal character or professional ethics. In fact, if it were, there would be little reason to recount this history.

Instead, what makes Barbeau's folklore culturally important is the way in which it illustrated the broader cultural trends that served to redefine the importance of rural life in twentieth century Canada. The work of folklorists cast rural Canada in a historically new and different light. Through the work of folklorists (and historians as well as a range of other professional cultural producers), rural life took on a new significance as a site of historical continuity whose value lay in its cultural geography. Rural Quebec, in Barbeau's case and, more generally, rural Canada, were reconstructed as sites of tradition and enchantment to which one could turn to find cultural colour, authenticity, and unusual experiences now supposedly alien to modern urban life. In effect, an urban world of scholars, art collectors, museum professionals, tourist promoters and others redefined the meaning of rurality as an antimodern space.

The restructuring of the meaning of rural life is only part of this cultural history. By its very activities, folklore dramatically altered rural culture. As Barbeau's folklore demonstrates, the reconstruction of rural culture moved in several directions simultaneously remaking some traditional crafts as consumer goods and others as works of art, some as museum objects and others as private luxury items. At the same time that Barbeau worked to preserve what he viewed as the remnants of dying past, his folklore facilitated the expansion of modern commercial and legal relations into the space of traditional culture.

In the early twenty-first century, Canadians live with both the reality and the legacy of these cultural processes. The legacy of this process is all about us: in tourist development strategies, country homes, antique hunting at country auctions, rural retirement villages, and the new semi-rural subdivisions that have developed around urban centres. The transformation of rural life of which Barbeau's folklore was part has had a significant effect on the demography of the countryside and what people expect to find outside the city. Drawn by the promise of rural and small-town otherness, cottages, rural vacationing, country homes, and rural retirements have become a part—certainly not all, but a part—of the rural composition of Canada today. Exactly what this means for rural Canada is not completely clear— and certainly requires further study—but it is one result of the cultural processes with which Barbeau worked in the interwar era.

This history also offers a warning for current projects designed to "redevelop" a countryside now already dramatically transformed, as the essays in this volume indicate, by mass media, new communications technologies, demographic shifts, transportation systems, and capitalist economic development. In the face of a crisis in rural primary commodity industries,

---

50. For a discussion, see McKay, *The Quest of the Folk*.

51. See: Norwy, *Marius Barbeau*, for a fuller description of Barbeau's importance and his work.

tourist promotion is still viewed as a viable alternative development strategy. Some forms of tourism remain similar to those Barbeau promoted, but today rural tourism also takes on new forms, such as eco-tourism. Whether or not eco-tourism or tourist promotion in general can be tied to successful new rural redevelopment programmes should be an open question. As the history of Barbeau's folklore indicates, tourism does not just develop a new visibility for existing cultural practices and objects; it redefines those objects and restructures cultures. The story of Barbeau's folklore should lead to a cautious approach to eco-tourism that takes into account the realities of rural life and environment and not simply an approach which is developed and designed elsewhere.

The implications of this story are particularly relevant for eco-tourism, an important new development in tourism in a number of provinces in Canada. In some ways, the environment constitutes the antimodern "other" of late-capitalist society in a manner similar to the way the rural "folk" became the other of twentieth-century urbanites.[52] But, is it possible to promote ecological tourism and not further advance the commodification of the environment? In odd and potentially ironic ways, might not eco-tourism work with a logic similar to that of earlier economic developments in that it could serve to reinforce the commercialization of nature[53] and solidify its transformation to commodity status? If this were true, eco-tourism might indeed serve as a rural economic development strategy, but its implications for the environment could be profound.

I will freely confess that I have no ready answer for these questions. Certainly, the implications of any rural development strategy need to be carefully assessed before any policy can be formulated. A final important lesson of Barbeau's folklore, however, is that assessment may not be enough. The future of rural Canada needs to be understood as part of an historical process and assessments of future programs to change rural Canada need to be made within this framework. The issue for this type of assessment is not necessarily the positive and negative elements of any particular course of action (although these are important), but the potential results of historical changes introduced with, potentially, the best of intentions. Understanding policy options as part of an historical process, the story of Barbeau's folklore suggests, should shift attention away from the shorter-term strengths and weaknesses of any particular policy and toward a consideration of its long-run effects. The ironic results of different actions need to be considered as well because, as we have seen, objectives and implications are not necessarily the same thing. By thinking about the present and the future in this historical sense, a new light can, I feel, be brought to the problems and the prospects of rural Canada. And, that is precisely what is needed.

---

52. Frederic Jameson, *Postmodernism, or the Cultural Logic of Late Capitalism* (Durham: Duke University Press, 1991).

53. William Cronon, *Changes in the Land: Indians, Colonists, and the Ecology of New England* (New York: Hill and Wang, 1983).

CHAPTER THREE

Changing Roles of Saskatchewan Farm Women: Qualitative and Quantitative Perspectives

Wendee Kubik and Robert J. Moore

Introduction

Over the past three decades, farming in Canada has been characterized by economic uncertainty, rapid technological change, and massive restructuring, fundamentally altering the economic, social, and personal circumstances of farm families at both the production and household levels (Gray, 1997; Winson, 1992; Lind, 1994; Lawrence, 1987). The impact of these changes is especially stressful for farm women and has repercussions for their health and well-being (Kubik, 1996; Alston, 1995; Walker & Walker, 1987). Lowe (1989) states that for women, stress is largely derived from an unequal division of labour between men and women in society and as such, the gender-based division of labour seems to be responsible for many of the observed sex differences in health and illness (p. 36).

Several authors (Alston, 1995; Buttel & Gillespie, 1984; Ghorayshi, 1989; Leckie, 1996; Rollings-Magnusson, 1999, Shortall, 1996) have consistently shown that work on the farm is divided by gender. Alston (1995) notes, "Farming families are not undifferentiated sites where all members share equally: they are structured around gender relations which allow men to be dominant both within the family and within the production sphere... Further this gender division of tasks devalues women's work both within the family and the community, while men's work is accorded greater prestige and value" (p. 51). The prevailing ideology of farming as a man's occupation perpetrates women's traditional role as "farmwife," "helper," or mother or daughter of the "principal operator," roles that enshrine women's dependence. In spite of being crucial to the survival of their enterprises, their work goes unrecognized because they do a variety of jobs daily which does not fit into any specific "occupation." This means the contributions of farm women are only recognized within certain limited parameters, and their work is given little public value despite their enormous contribution both to the farm and home. Often, the "invisibility" of the work performed by farm women and the lack of recognition they receive for their work perpetrates the myth that they do not contribute to the farm or are not farmers in their own right (Shaver, 1996).

Several issues that influence women's lives and health have added concerns for farm women because farm families have special characteristics that differentiate them in various ways from non-farm families (Walker & Walker, 1987; Martinez-Brawley & Blundall, 1991). The intertwining of home, work, and community contexts, the not infrequent isolation, and the long hours of work[1] are some of the ways women's roles on the farm are distinctive (Gordon, 1987). Farm families on the Canadian Prairies are a kinship and economic unit whose members not only live together but must, by necessity, work co-operatively in order that their means of subsistence—the farm—remains viable in a context of rapidly changing market conditions. Given this unique fractionated experience of overlapping domestic, production, and community roles and the inherent structural undervaluing of their contributions, what are the effects of this reality on the physical health and psychological well-being of farm women?

Research Method

To begin answering some of these questions, we felt it was necessary to employ a participatory research strategy focusing on both qualitative and quantitative aspects of farm women's lives. It was our intent to involve farm women and groups reflecting the interests of farm women in the research process, rather than view them simply as objects of the research. Our partners in this research were the Saskatchewan Women in Agriculture Network (SWAN) and the Farm Stress Line. SWAN is an educational and advocacy support network for farm women with members throughout the province of Saskatchewan. Part of their mandate is to study how various policy issues affect women farmers and to lobby the government regarding these issues. The Farm Stress Line is a unit of Saskatchewan Agriculture and Food in the Saskatchewan Government. It provides a confidential peer counselling service for farmers by men and women who have practical farming experience and are trained in crisis counselling. The counsellors are the frontline workers on the toll-free telephone service covering the province, who come into daily contact with farm men and women trying to cope with the stress of farming. These two groups and various farm women were involved in the planning and implementation of the research design, the development of the questionnaire, the analysis and interpretation of the results, and the dissemination of the findings.

Preliminary Interviews

To begin, 18 preliminary interviews were conducted in order to find out the broad issues affecting farm women. Informed opinion was sought from a number of individuals working with and representing farm women. These interviews were conducted with SWAN, women counsellors from the Farm Stress Line, Saskatchewan Women's Institute, The National Farmer's Union, the church, Saskatchewan Rural Municipalities, Saskatchewan Wheat Pool, Saskatchewan Health Boards, The Task Force on Balancing Work and Family, Prairie Women's Health Centre of Excellence, Saskatchewan Agriculture and Food, Saskatchewan School Board trustees, a film maker, a Head of Patient Services and a nurse in a rural hospital. Most of these women were also farmers as well. The intention was to provide an opportunity for people knowledgeable in the area to express in their own words what they believe to be the important issues in the lives of farm women, their health and well-being.

Questionnaire

From these interviews a 20-page questionnaire was developed, pre-tested first by SWAN members and female Stress Line Counsellors, and then it was pre-tested on farm women from various parts of the province. The 10 areas that the questionnaire focused on were: Health Care, Health Status, Social Support, Well-being, Life Style and Activities, Stress, Work, Male

---

1. A 1988 survey of Saskatchewan farm women by The Women's Legal, Education and Action Fund (LEAF) documented that farm women worked, on average, 96 hours a week: 19 hours of farm work, 30 hours at household tasks, 8 hours gardening/canning, 26 hours in active childcare, 9 hours of off-farm work (41% of the cases), and 4 hours of community service.

and Female Roles, Demographic Information and Farm Issues. One Rural Municipality Administrator in each of Saskatchewan's 20 crop districts was asked for the names of all the farm women in their RM. Approximately 3000 questionnaires were sent out and we received 717 back for a return rate of about 22%.

Interviews with Farm Women

On the last page of the questionnaire, we asked women who would be interested in being contacted for an interview to write down their names and phone numbers. Two hundred and thirty-four of the women said they would be willing to be interviewed; however, because of time and money constraints we chose only one woman out of each crop district. The women were selected in terms of different demographic characteristics such as age, off-farm work, number and age of children, type of farm, income, etc.

Sample of Farm Women

The average age of the women was 50 years, with women born as early as 1913 and as late as 1979. The majority of respondents (57%) were between the ages of 41 and 60 years. Of the respondents, 70% of the women reported spending their childhood growing up on a farm. Of the farm women, 94% indicated they were either married or living with their partner, 94% reported having children, 47% reported that they owned or rented land in their own name, and 24% indicated that they had their own membership in a farm organization and this was most likely to occur in women under the age of 40.

Results

Work

In terms of work on the farm, the farm women reported on average that they did over 80% of the work associated with a variety of household tasks while participating in 37% of the farming work. Of the farm women, 40% reported that their average work day was over 13 hours, 54% reported off-farm work, with the majority holding jobs in health services, education, and clerical, 60% indicated that their off-farm money went to cover household expenses, and 67% reported that their farm operation could only continue with difficulty (perhaps not at all) without their off-farm income.

Many farm women, themselves, are not aware of how much work they do or the importance of their contributions are to the farm:

> "I'll sit down with a farm woman sometimes and I'll ask her, you know what all she does and she says, 'Oh, you know, I just kind of look after the house and the kids.' And then when you quiz her a little more deeply you find out that she's also, you know, running into town for parts, she's doing all the bookkeeping, she's dealing with all the creditors on the phone. She's, you know, cooking extra big meals for, for harvest and seed-cleaning crews and she's dealing with chemical-sprayed clothing in the laundry which requires special handling and she's doing all sorts of things which is really farm work and she's probably doing them at the same time as she's looking after the kids which means that she's really doing two jobs at once but she doesn't think of it that way. And her husband very often doesn't think of it that way and sometimes even if she does, she may not feel comfortable putting something like that onto a census form reporting her as a farm operator because her husband may not see her that way and she doesn't feel comfortable putting herself down as that if her husband doesn't see that. And that's certainly the kind of traditional division of roles which is in people's heads but which isn't in people's actual day-to-day work life."

Farm Women's Physical Health and Psychological Well-being

In the survey, 74% of the farm women rated their general state of health as good to very good; only 14% viewed their health as fair to poor. A majority of farm women reported that they were happy and interested in life (64%) and satisfied with their lives at the moment (74%). Such ratings were more likely in women 60 years of age and over and less common in women under 40 years. Over 95% of the women reported that they had someone who made them feel loved and cared for.

When asked about stress in their lives, 54% of the farm women found their lives "somewhat stressful," 29% labelled their lives as "very stressful," and 16% "not very stressful." Farm women under 40 years of age were more likely to report their lives as being stressful.

Not surprisingly, the farm women reported "financial problems" (61%) as the most stressful events they encountered. Forty-two per cent indicated that they had experienced conflict in their household over sharing available financial resources. Approximately 48% of the women indicated that they had been involved in the care of someone in the past year.

However, even though they had a great deal of stress in their lives, 90% of the farm women indicated that their ability to handle the day-to-day demands in their life was good to excellent. The most frequent coping strategy to "try and figure out how to deal with the situation" and then "do something about it" (41%), "asking for help/talking to others" (28%), "withdrawal" (21%), "exercise/walking" (16%), "getting angry" (15%), and "praying" (10%) were responses that were also not uncommon:

> "Coming out of the income shortfall very directly, of course, is the excess of work because farm couples are having to seek off-farm employment just to pay the grocery bills let alone keep the farm afloat. That has a spin-off into the community in that there are not as many people in the community to operate the community as there used to be, so you're finding shortfalls in the people needed to operate church events. It's getting harder to find people to run the rink, it's getting much harder to get people out to farm organization meetings because people are just too tired at the end of the day and may not have the time. Plus the off-farm work will often take them out of the community so that the basic sense of belonging to a community gets less."

> "One of the best ways of coping with stress is to reach out and talk to others. Farming is a solitary independent profession and farmers are not used to talking to others about their problems. They have a great sense of independence and are used to doing things themselves. They are used to fixing things and feel they can fix themselves. When it happens that they can't, they feel helpless, often a breakdown occurs. Men and farmers are not brought up to look for help."

Issues

In terms of the farm, the major issue facing farm women today is the lack of financial resources. This situation is linked to almost every other aspect of their lives right now. When asked to identify issues that they believed women living on a farm had to deal with in their lives, 68% of the farm women reported "financial problems," 50% the "lack of/juggling time," 38% "raising children," 38% the "dismal/unsure future," 25% the "distance from/travel time to everything," 14% the "lack of government support," and 8% the "erosion of health services."

Of the farm women, 55% believed that there are particular expectations placed on women in rural communities. The expectations that were most frequently expressed included being a traditional woman (33%), involved in the farm (14%), a volunteer (12%), and doing with less (12%). Younger farm women were more likely to express the view that there were expectations/pressures placed on women living in a rural community:

"A traditional farm wife would have three meals on the table. Big hearty meals, breakfast, dinner, supper and she would have spent her whole day cooking, baking bread and you know, the house would be perfect. She would have this huge, weed-less garden. She would can all this food for the winter and her chickens would be fed and they would never be forgotten about. That picture of perfectness would be there and the responsibility, you know, to not let any of it fall and to keep going day after day after day. That's how my mother did it, that's how his mother has done it … and, I haven't."

"It's still treated as really exceptional when a woman is, is responsible for farm work publicly. People may say it approvingly, 'Oh, how nice, you're, you know, you're hauling grain, you're really into this farming thing.' But just the fact that it's treated as something exceptional, whether it's positive or negative it's still like an idea where you feel as if she's sticking out."

Of the farm women, 19% believed family violence/abuse was an issue in their community; 17% reported that it was an issue for them "sometimes" while 79% indicated that it was "never" an issue in their family; 42% of the women believed that there were "accessible services" available in their area for those experiencing family violence/abuse and 44% indicated that they didn't know:

"Violence, it's hard to admit you are battered—you ask yourself what is wrong with you? What have you done wrong to make it happen? Your husband is in control of the vehicle, phone... isolation and distance are issues. There is a shame in letting people know your family is not doing well. There is no support when a woman tells her story because she's the 'import' and her husband's family has been in the district running the farm for decades. In rural areas violence does not have as much exposure, in urban areas it is discussed more and they are more open to discussing it."

When asked about social issues, over 90% of the farm women agreed that "elected politicians soon lose touch with the people"; 77% indicated that "people like me don't have a say in what the government does." They tended to believe that "most people try to be helpful" (88%), that "most people are fair" (82%), and that "most people can be trusted" (73%). But they also indicated that "people are more competitive today" (84%) and that they "only look out after themselves" (70%). Finally, many felt that "there is a downward shift in people's values" (83%).

Access to Heath Care System

When farm women were asked how easy it was for them to access health services 40% of the women reported that it was "easy" to get the health care services they needed; 12% "very easy." The absence of difficulty was promoted by ease of access to doctors (21%) and the presence locally of a hospital, clinic, or specialist services (21%). Reports of difficulty were most likely prompted by restrictions on access to doctors: lack of appointment times and waiting lists (45%), and travelling time/distance to access specialists (24%). Of the farm women, 16% reported they, or a family member, did not receive health care in the last 12 months that they viewed as needed. The major reasons being "waiting time too long" (24%), that the service was "not available in the area" (20%), or that the service was "not available at the time required" (21%).

Of the respondents, 21% believed that support services for dealing with personal, social, or financial services were adequate in their area, 35% thought they weren't. Of farm women, 41% indicated that they "didn't know" whether the availability of such services was adequate or not!

Some form of mental health/counselling services to deal with stress, family problems, children and youth was frequently mentioned as needed (62%). The need for more health services, especially doctors and nurses was often reported (21%), as well as services to assist in the management of finances (15%).

Evaluation of the Health Care System

In the majority of instances, the greatest number of individuals interacting with the health care system was in the 40–59 age group. Farm women below 40 years of age tended to participate in the health care system less frequently. Only in the instance of flu shots did respondents 60 years of age and over report a higher participation rate.

Of the farm women, 42% viewed the quality of the health care system in Saskatchewan as "fair," 27% saw it as "good," 24% as "poor," and 3% indicated it was "excellent." The avail-ability of health services in their community was rated as "fair" by 37% of the farm women, 35% perceived availability to be "good," 21% viewed availability as "poor," and 5 % as "excel-lent." A more positive rating of the quality/availability of health services in their local com-munity occurred in farm women 60 years of age and over. Those under 40 years of age more often indicated a rating of fair.

The positive feature of the health care system in their locale that farm women most fre-quently cited was access to doctors and services (hospitals, clinics, home care, ambulance) in their community (61%). Quality health care (22%) (e.g., "Good" doctors and facilities) and the caring and dedicated people that they encountered (19%) were also features that were appreciated.

Respondents most often reported the lack of services in their community (50%) as the worst feature of health care in their area. The lack/loss and overworked status of health care professionals in their communities was mentioned by 39% of the farm women. Long waiting lists (34%) and the distance needed to travel to reach a hospital or to see a specialist (28%) were also mentioned as negative features of health care in rural communities.

Conclusions and Implications

The Health of Farm Women

A wide range of physical, socio-cultural, and psychological factors affect women's health and the health of farm women today would appear to be especially sensitive to issues in the broader social context. They report that the main factors they are dealing with in their lives in Saskatchewan at this point in time are financial difficulties, overwork, and the resulting stress. More specifically, on the farm they contend with financial problems, seeding/harvest, and too much work. At home they have to deal with "just balancing everything," finances, raising children, and marital problems.

Many of the farm women, in their spontaneous writings on the survey questionnaire and in the face-to-face interviews argued that the government was responsible for the recalcitrant problems in their lives:

> "I have been involved in farming for 37 years, working alongside my husband as we farmed and raised a family of four children. It has been such a wonderful life with many ups and downs, good times and bad, sacrifices and rewards. We reach our retirement years with a feeling of such uncertainty as we see our rural communities disappearing, poor access to health facilities and such a severe devaluation of our farm land and other farm assets we have worked a lifetime to attain. As our federal government continues to ignore the crisis in rural Sask. and the drastic need for the feds to support us in this global price squeeze, our optimistic attitude toward "next year" is dwindling. We can no longer control our own destiny and this is why we are witnessing increased depression, addictions (to drinking and gambling), suicides,

divorce, family abuse, etc. Even children in schools are concerned that Mom and Dad argue more and there is a decrease in harmony in rural families. The bottom line—farm crisis because of low commodity prices. Rural Sask. needs help."

The vast majority of farm women in the sample rated the state of their physical health as good to excellent. However, at the same time, nearly half of the sample reported that they have received treatment for "long-term" health problems and were concerned about the effects of their work on their health. Furthermore, about half of the farm women considered themselves overweight while around one third of the farm women perceived their fitness level as being "fair" to "poor."

In terms of their sense of well-being, the farm women rated themselves high on self-esteem, were for the most part happy and interested in life, and gave themselves elevated marks on their ability to handle the day-to-day demands in their life. In addition, they believed others viewed their capabilities positively as well. This speaks to their resiliency in the face of their hardships, a quality that is an important in maintaining good health.

The farm women enjoyed a high level of social support reporting that they had someone who made them feel loved and cared for and that they had people they could talk to about private matters if they needed help. A large number were also regularly involved in some group, organization, or activity.

Documented in both the survey results and the face-to-face interviews was the omnipresent experience of stress in the lives of the farm women. Farm women not only had to cope with stress resulting from their own lives but also took on responsibility for the well-being of their families. They often indicated that it was their responsibility to help their families cope, many times sacrificing their own psychological health in the process:

> "I am concerned that farm women are the 'Silent Sufferers,' given the farm crisis. As the financial crunch of the farm escalates, they take on more roles than they can handle. Eventually this results in health and relationship problems. These women are still expected to "stand by their man" in spite of how much it may adversely affect their own well-being."

Having trouble relaxing and experiencing feelings of anxiety and depression, as well as frustration and anger, were reported by over half of the farm women. There was often a sense of not being in control of their lives accompanied in many instances by feelings of helplessness and worthlessness.

Implications for Program/Service Development

Farm families and farm women have special concerns that differentiate them in various ways from non-farm families. The factors that appear to be impinging most upon farm women's health at the moment are financial considerations, overwork, and stress. Governments, service providers, and health professionals need to acknowledge that the health of farm women is not solely a product of life on the farm but is also governed by the larger social-political context in which that life exists. This is the context in which programs or services must be developed. Many women in the interviews stated that, if their financial situation would improve, a large number of their other problems would disappear.

Farm women appear to be more traditional and conservative regarding the roles of men and women. Consequently, programs and services established in rural areas need to be sensitive to the often unarticulated needs of farm women.

In addition to being overworked and experiencing work-related stress, a large proportion of farm women are also involved in caregiving roles in rural areas. Programs and services that would ease the caregiving burden (e.g., more homecare services, child care supports) would more than likely improve the quality of life for many farm women.

Access to Health Services

Overall, a large number of farm women found it difficult to access health services in their area because of restrictions on access to doctors/specialists, long waiting times to get appointments to see doctors and specialists and long waiting lists to receive health services. Travelling time and the distance to access specialists were also barriers. Often the services needed were not available in the area in which the women lived. When asked what concerned her most about health care, one of the farm women interviewed stated:

> "Access to services. Finding out in time to do something about it if somebody has an accident. Partly because when something happens it's going to take a long time for the ambulance to arrive. It's going to take a long time for them to get into a facility where the difficulty can be dealt with. Also, if you get sick on the farm, you have to make that determination, well, do you drive into town to get a prescription, or will that just make you sicker? Access to services, health services is a big one. That's kind of the extreme situation. The whole range of health services is a major stressor. You lose a lot of time because you have to go to the city for most things or you have to go to a community that's even more distant than the city."

Living on a farm in Saskatchewan means that it is necessary to travel to reach most health services, often in poor weather, from isolated regions, on bad roads. There is great variability across the province in terms of the location and kinds of health services offered; hence, depending on what area of the province you live in, access can be easy or very difficult. Distance and travelling was mentioned over and over again in the interviews as one of the constants in the lives of farm women. This was an overarching dimension in the lives of farm women. Accessing health care and emergency services, participating in community events, having children involved in activities, attending off-farm work, getting supplies, and taking part in recreation all involved time and travel and its associated costs. When the distance that farm women and their families have to travel is substantial and they need to stay overnight, additional associated costs, such as meals and hotel rooms in cities, gas and car upkeep, and perhaps babysitting are incurred. Such costs are an added financial burden for many farm women and their families, many of whom are experiencing economic difficulties:

> "But the problem for a lot of farm families is, and this is very much women's concerns, is that, it matters where the service is in terms of proximity to your household. Take here in terms of emergency care, you know how far is it to the hospital when you need to have your baby. And how far is it to the hospital when your kid has had an injury. This is the proximity we worry about and we've got good transportation systems etc. but sometimes the timing is of the essence and the proximity. And the other part is that a lot of our families have older members, seniors in them in the rural communities and it's very often women who worry about proximity again of service for the care of them, how far do you have to go for the weekly care that your parent might need? So proximity of service and, I guess in general in a lot of rural communities the sinking feeling that we're getting less and less as there are fewer and fewer of us here."

Over one-third of the farm women did not believe that there were adequate support services for dealing with personal, social, or financial problems in their area. The kind of assistance they desired involved counselling services to deal with stress, family problems, children, and youth. In discussing these needs many noted that in rural areas, more so than in the cities, there was a stigma attached to using mental health and counselling services. As a result, there was a reluctance to use these services because they believed that others in the community would be aware and that they would be "labelled." Thus, while the farm women wanted more counselling and support services in their area, they argued strongly that such services must be provided in a way that people do not feel shamed:

"Yes, we've talked about that at our group a lot, how if you have a broken arm or a broken leg, you go to the doctor, that's fine. But if you have a mental problem, if you're depressed with something, then everybody says 'oh, look at her, she's there,' and it's very hard to get people to admit they need help. If your car was in front of there, probably nobody would go by that even if they knew it was your car (in the city). Where out here, everybody knows your rig and if they come in and see you sitting in the waiting room, everybody knows who you are, you know, there's no secrets. So you have to get to that point, sort of found that you've hit rock bottom before you go and admit that something's wrong. And it's even harder for the men than the women, I think."

A considerable number of farm women indicated that they were not aware of the availability/accessibility of support services in their community for personal, social, or financial problems.

Implications for Program/Service Development

A relatively high number of farm women indicated access to health and support services was difficult. Obviously, easier and more timely access to general practitioners and specialists and a reduction in waiting lists for specific procedures would address this difficulty. This may require hiring more physicians and surgeons in both rural and urban areas (where the majority of farm families have to travel to access these services). Novel incentives to entice more professionals into rural areas may be needed. A more viable and practical option would be to increase the use of nurse practitioners and other qualified service providers in rural areas.

Services that could travel to rural communities would be a way of ensuring that farm women had greater access to health services with less inconvenience and at a lower cost. Easy access and reduced expenses would likely have the effect of increasing the participation rate of farm women and their families. For example, the breast screening program in Saskatchewan that travels to rural areas to administer mammograms is a model that could serve for other programs. Women can conveniently access such a service, without having to travel huge distances and incur the associated costs. Such services would particularly be of benefit to senior women, especially those who do not want to drive long distances or deal with city traffic or have to rely on others to transport them. Such services could be advertised as a community event and be promoted by various local groups and organizations previously made aware of the visit. This would be a way of encouraging women who might not ordinarily do so to become actively involved in their own health care as well as reaching women who otherwise might not be aware of the service.

The need for some form of mental health/counselling service to deal with stress, family, children, and youth problems was indicated by a majority of farm women. Making these services available across the province within easy access would help farm women and their families cope with many of the problems they reported they are faced with today. Suggestions were made in the interviews of having one location where there were many different kinds of services available, ranging from counselling, to child care services, to educational services (e.g., resume writing). It was mentioned that this type of format would also bring a degree of confidentiality about the type of service being sought that might facilitate use. It was also argued that if women knew various services were available under one roof, they would more likely access services that they might not normally consider because of inconvenience or cost.

The finding that a large percentage of farm women were not aware of services in their area is an issue that needs to be addressed. More effective dissemination of information regarding the availability of and access to health and support programs is needed. In addition to the acknowledged information provided by doctors, nurses, and pharmacists, increased advertising in the local media and use of the Internet would facilitate the awareness by farm women of services that are locally available.

Finally, making services accessible for farm women demands taking into consideration time and location. Seasonal demands upon the time of farm women (e.g., seeding, harvest) means that they are not always in a position to readily access such services. Program offerings should take such factors into account.

Quality of Health Care

Many farm women in the sample rated the quality of health services/care in their community as "fair" or "poor." It is very likely that such evaluations reflect to some extent the lack of consistency in the quality of health services across the province in rural areas, i.e., some areas simply have better quality and more services than others do. What was very much appreciated by the farm women in their communities was having easy access to doctors and services and the presence of caring and dedicated health professionals.

The absence or loss of health care professionals and the overworked status of many of these individuals most frequently prompted negative evaluations by the farm women of the quality of health care in their community. The long waiting lists and the distance needed to travel to reach a hospital or to see a specialist were other features of health care in rural communities that were criticized.

When asked to appraise the quality of health care in Saskatchewan, almost two thirds of the farm women rated it as "fair" or "poor." Of the women who had gone to a hospital emergency department in the last 12 months, over half evaluated the emergency services as "fair" to "poor."

One of the criticisms mentioned frequently by the farm women was the lack of recognition by health professionals of the issues that farm women and their families face in their lives. This was consistent in the survey results and reiterated again and again in the face-to-face interviews. Not only was there the feeling that urban dwellers do not understand or care to understand what is happening on the farm, but also that the politicians who make decisions and the professionals who design programs were out of touch with the cares and concerns of farm people:

> "Many doctors are from urban backgrounds and not familiar with rural culture. Stresses are not dealt with because they don't understand the issues. The doctors think you are complaining—they really don't get it. Tell you to relax, rest, get away—don't understand you don't have money to get away and you can't leave if you have animals, the work has to be done, cattle and crops won't wait, it is hard to relax when you have collection agencies calling you, no money coming in and you can't make payments, or the weather isn't co-operating. Added on top of that is the workload on small town doctors—they've got to see so many people, they've got such a backlog. You've got your 15 minutes and he writes you a prescription. There are a lot of problems with revolving doctors that aren't encultured to rural life or women's roles on the farm."

Implications for Program/Service Development/Delivery

The obvious answer to improving access to health care for farm women would be to increase the number of professionals and services available in their communities. Since at this time in Saskatchewan it is difficult to recruit health care professionals into rural areas, alternative solutions to overcoming this problem need to be forthcoming. Setting up, staffing, and strategically locating across the province more integrated health and educational service centres would increase the number of services available to a greater percentage of farm women.

The increased use of nurse practitioners is another viable alternative. Mobile services that would tour the province would be another option towards improving access to and the quality of care for farm women. Increased education about the problems and issues that face farmers, particularly women on the farm, need to be addressed in the education of today's health care professionals.

Farm families and farm women have special concerns that differentiate them in various ways from non-farm families. The intertwining of home, work, and community contexts, the not infrequent isolation, and the long hours of work are some of the ways women's roles on the farm are distinctive. Many farm women are economically dependent on a notoriously unstable farm income, even though they may be working double or triple workloads to try to keep the farm viable:

> "How economically vulnerable farm families feel has a big thing, a big impact on their sense of well-being and their sense of good health. Every time the minister of agriculture in this province says something to the effect that the trend of farming is towards corporate farms and the big hog producers are much more competitive than the rest of us, there is a decline in the health and well-being of family farms and it has nothing to do with having closed the local hospital; it has everything to do with farm families feeling that they are no longer of value in this society and that they have to be defensive in public. They have to remind people, 'We grow what you eat,' in a querulous way. They are no longer valued, and they have really no future. They're a dying breed. That's extremely stressful for people and it leaves you in a place where you think not only are you vulnerable but any sort of counter-measure you might take is in fact backward. It's, you know, you're standing in the way of progress and so that it leaves you helpless by way of helping yourself."

Farm women make very important contributions to the province of Saskatchewan. By beginning to make their lives and the work they do "visible," a better understanding of their work, problems, changing gender roles, and rural communities will hopefully aid in the formulation of relevant social and economic policy in this sector of the population. A goal would be to reduce the negative impact of the many distressing forces related to these changes that impinge on the lives of these very significant people who produce one of our most important and necessary commodities: food.

Acknowledgements

This project was supported by financial contribution from the Health Transition Fund, Health Canada and the Health Services utilization and Research Commission, Saskatchewan. The views expressed herein do not necessarily represent the official policy of federal, provincial or territorial governments.

References

Alston, M. 1995. *Women on the Land*. Kensington, Australia: UNSW Press.

Buttel, F. and G. Gillespie, Jr. 1984. "The Sexual Division of Farm Household Labor: An Exploratory Study of the Structure of On-farm and Off-farm Labor Allocation Among Farm Men and Women." *Rural Sociology* 49: 183–209.

Davis, F. 1988. *The Social, Economic and Legal Equality of Saskatchewan Farm Women*. Saskatoon: LEAF.

Ghorayshi, P. 1989. "The Indispensable Nature of Wives' Work for the Farm Family Enterprise." *The Canadian Review of Sociology and Anthropology* 26: 571–95.

Gordon, E. 1987. "Stress in the Farm Family." *Canadian Home Economics Journal* 37, no. 1.

Gray, I. 1997. "Rural Restructuring in Australia: Contradictory Futures Under Economic and Managerialist Policies." Paper presented to the Canadian Sociology and Anthropology Association, Congress of Social Sciences and Humanities, St. Johns, Newfoundland, June 1997.

Kubik, W. 1996. "The Study of Farm Stress: A Critical Evaluation." M.A. thesis, University of Regina.

Lawrence, G. 1987. *Capitalism and the Countryside: The Rural Crisis in Australia*. Sydney: Pluto Press.

Leckie, G. 1996. "'They Never Trusted Me To Drive': Farm Girls and the Gender Relations of Agricultural Information Transfer." *Gender, Place, and Culture* 3: 309–25.

Lind, C. 1994. *"Something's Wrong Somewhere": Globalization, Community and the Moral Economy of the Farm Crisis.* Halifax: Fernwood Publishing.

Lowe, G. 1989. *Women, Paid/Unpaid Work, and Stress: New Directions for Research.* Ottawa: Canadian Advisory Council on the Status of Women.

Martinez-Brawley, E. and J. Blundall. 1991. "'Whom Shall We Help?': Farm Families' Beliefs and Attitudes About Need and Services." *Social Work* 36, no. 4: 315–21.

Rollings-Magnusson, S. 1997. "Hitched to the Plow: The Place of Western Pioneer Women in Innisian Staple Theory." M.A. thesis, University of Regina.

Shaver, F. (ed.). 1996. *Women in Agriculture.* Brandon: Canadian Rural Restructuring Foundation.

Shortall, S. 1996. Training to be Farmers or Wives? Agricultural Training for Women in Northern Ireland. *Sociologia Ruralis* 36, no. 3: 269–85.

Walker, James L. and Lilly J. Walker. 1987. *The Human Harvest: Changing Farm Stress to Family Success.* Winnipeg: Agricultural Canada, Manitoba Agriculture, and Manitoba Education.

Winson, Anthony. 1992. *The Intimate Commodity: Food and the Development of the Agro-industrial Complex in Canada.* Toronto: Garamond Press.

CHAPTER FOUR

Responding to Wife Abuse in Farm and Rural Communities: Searching for Solutions that Work

Jennie Hornosty and Deborah Doherty

"Rural life is great. You know your neighbours and who to trust. You have privacy, no traffic ... you get help from others and it's cheaper to live. The kids are happy."

"My husband said if I left he would kill the dog or let the calves die and it would be my fault. When he threatened to kill me, I thought, who would know—the farm is so isolated."

A Snapshot of Rural New Brunswick

In order to understand wife abuse in a rural context, it is important to recognize the nature of that context. New Brunswick is a largely rural province with 51% of its 738,133 inhabitants living in areas defined as rural. According to the 1996 Census, rural means living in small towns, villages and other places with populations of less than 1,000 (Statistics Canada 1996). Only Prince Edward Island and the Northwest Territories have a higher percentage of their population living in rural areas. By comparison, 22% of Quebecois and 17% of Ontarians live in rural areas. Even provinces with considerable activity in the areas of farming, fishing and agriculture have a greater proportion of urban dwellers. For example, the rural population of Manitoba is 28%, Saskatchewan 37%, British Columbia 18% and Newfoundland 43%.

Although family violence is often characterized as a problem that takes place in the privacy of the home, clearly families do not live in a vacuum. Family violence must be seen in relation to a broader framework of social, political and economic factors that impact on all aspects of rural life. Moreover, the shifting constellation of such factors directly relates to how policy makers, crisis workers or various service providers recognize and respond to family violence issues in a rural context.

The farm and rural women we interviewed for our study shared many general concerns relating to life in a rural area. These included, to mention a few, fears associated with an uncertain future relating to the decline of the family farm, the lack of alternative rural employment especially full-time jobs, increasing poverty, the lack of access to education, daycare and health services, as well as inadequate transportation, housing and social services. As a result, the underlying fabric of rural life was seen to provide rather tenuous support to residents generally, while creating significant obstacles for victims of abuse. Moreover, many of the systemic issues identified by the rural women we interviewed are barely reflected in economic development plans. Most rural development initiatives tend to prioritize industrial development and infrastructure improvements such as the provision of safe drinking water and sewage systems. While no one would argue that ensuring safe drinking water is not of paramount importance, ensuring safe families has not received the same attention.

Many of the barriers confronting rural residents, such as those identified above, are systemic in nature. Some are imbedded in institutional frameworks and societal attitudes that have fostered a number of related systemic problems such as gender inequality, sex-role stereotyping, racism and so on. Others relate generally to larger economic situations such as trade barriers. As a result, many of these issues must be addressed at a provincial, national and even global level. As such, we recognize that it will take more than the enhancement of individual crisis interventions to change the lives of rural women living with abuse. Nevertheless, the strategies and solutions put forward in this paper must be seen as part of the solution.

Before presenting our findings, we shall provide a brief overview of rural New Brunswick. According to Census data (Statistics Canada 1996, tables 15 and 16), 11 of the 15 counties in New Brunswick may be characterized as predominantly rural in nature. Only four counties have greater numbers of urban dwellers than rural dwellers and these counties surround the three largest cities, namely Moncton, Saint John and Fredericton. With more than half the inhabitants residing outside of urban centres, it is not surprising that many people in the rural areas of New Brunswick are involved in jobs in agricultural, fishing, fish processing, logging, mining and forestry, and tourism.

The 1996 Census of Agriculture reported 3,206 farms in New Brunswick with the largest average farm size of all the Atlantic provinces. The New Brunswick Department of Agriculture, Fisheries and Aquaculture indicates that 1,200 of the farms produce beef and most of these are "small family operations or complimentary enterprises on large diversified farms" (2000, p. 21). The Northwestern Region and the Western Region of the province are involved predominantly in the potato, poultry and hog industries while the Central Region is fairly diversified with dairy, beef, fruit and vegetable farming and harvesting of wild blueberries. The Southern Region also supports diversified operations with about 600 farms producing vegetables, berries, poultry, dairy and beef. The agriculture and agri-food industry is a major contributor to the provincial economy.

Many would describe the forest as the backbone of New Brunswick with over 600 million hectares of productive forestland. The New Brunswick Department of Natural Resources and Energies reports on their website that 16,000 individuals obtain their wages and salaries directly from work in the forests. In addition, the value of jobs related to the forest and pulp production is valued at more than $1.5 million. The fisheries are an important activity in certain areas of the province, along with major fish processing plants.

Men and women living in rural communities, whether coastal or inland, tend to rely heavily on employment associated with natural resource-based industries. These primary industries (agriculture, fisheries, forestry), along with the secondary industries of manufacturing and construction, comprise the goods-producing sector and account for about 25% of all jobs in the province and a significant percentage of the seasonal jobs (LeBreton, L'Italien, and Grignon 1998). In fact, 20% of all workers in New Brunswick are seasonally employed and most of them are men. A significant portion of these live in the rural areas of the province (LeBreton 1999).

Both men and women take jobs as seasonal workers, although there are a higher proportion of men (63%) than women (37%). Statistics indicate that "a large proportion of seasonal jobs,

43%, were for 12 weeks or less in 1996" (LeBreton, L'Italien, and Grignon 1998, p. 8). Indeed, only a quarter of seasonal jobs lasted more than 26 weeks. The length of seasonal jobs, in combination with the generally lower hourly wages paid for seasonal work, has direct and serious consequences on the income levels of seasonal workers, many of whom live in rural areas. Many rural workers are unemployed for part of the year and there are few employment opportunities for women.

Labour market specialists point to a shift in New Brunswick over the past decade towards an economy based more on the tertiary sector and an emerging communications technology. In fact 73% of New Brunswickers are now employed in the tertiary sector in retail and whole-sale, as well as health, social services and government. This shift has been accompanied by an increasing emphasis on the service sector and economic development in urban centres. However, rural areas have not benefitted to the same extent. Data show that the unemployment rates in New Brunswick tend to be below average in urban areas and higher than average in rural areas (LeBreton 1999). This is reflected in the rural/urban migration and employment patterns for young people in the province.

Trends in urban/rural residency also show some differences with respect to gender. Although there are more women than men living in the province, Census data show that more men than women live in the rural areas. Of the total male population, significantly more (191,240) live in rural areas compared with the city (171,250). Women are concentrated slightly more in the urban centres. However, for both genders there is a similar pattern of migration to cities in the late teens and early twenties and back to rural areas during the childbearing and middle years, returning to urban centres later in life (Statistics Canada 1996). This pattern is significant since many studies indicate that wife abuse often commences or escalates during the childbearing years, the very time when families tend to migrate to rural areas.

Literacy is another concern in New Brunswick. In an exhaustive study of literacy skills in New Brunswick, it was discovered that 60% of New Brunswickers over the age of 16 years (approximately 300,000 people) do not meet the minimum desirable standard for literacy (Statistics Canada 1998). This compares to 45% of Canadians overall who do not meet minimum desirable literacy standards. Moreover, Census materials reveal that many New Brunswickers have dropped out of school, and a high proportion (42%) of the potential labour force (the employed, unemployed and people not in the labour force aged 15 to 65 years) do not have a degree, certificate or diploma (Statistics Canada 1996).

Inadequate literacy and numeracy skills can have devastating consequences on the ability of an individual to find employment, care for a family, shop, look after health care needs, or leave an abusive relationship. While not restricted to rural areas, the Report finds that low literacy is connected with a number of economic consequences that are characteristic of many rural communities. For example, people with the lowest literacy level are seven times more likely to hold primary or industrial jobs, and work fewer hours per week and fewer weeks per year, than those with higher literacy skills. They are also five times more likely to be unemployed. Indeed, 75% of those at the lowest literacy level earn wages below NB's mean wage rate.

In light of this mix of factors relating to rural employment, incomes, education, and literacy, it is apparent that poverty is a reality for many rural families. Census data (Statistics Canada 1996) show the median income in New Brunswick was $15,200. While urban dwellers received the greatest portion of their incomes (between 73% and 77%) from employment, those in the rural areas received a significant portion of their incomes from transfer payments (LeBreton 1999). Other differences relating to income disparities exist between the various regions of the province. The mostly rural counties of New Brunswick have median incomes well below average. This is consistent with the experience of the rural women we interviewed who spoke not only about their own suffering, but of the chronic stress experienced by families faced with unrelenting job losses and poverty.

Finally, a picture of New Brunswick would be incomplete without some attention to its linguistic makeup. New Brunswick is largely comprised of French- and English-speaking populations. Approximately 65% of the population (473,260 people) have English as a first language, while 33% have French as their mother tongue (239,730 people). The remainder of the population, 10,295, have some other language as their first language. This mixture of languages adds another dimension to the challenge of responding to family violence in rural areas.

Family Violence in a Rural Context

Over the past 20 years, issues of wife abuse and family violence have come to the foreground, both for researchers and policy makers. There now exists a voluminous body of research literature that provides different theoretical and empirical models for examining the nature and extent of family violence,[1] and this information continues to grow. At both the federal and provincial levels, governments have established committees and policies that explicitly address issues of family violence prevention.

While researchers have documented that wife abuse cuts across all ethnic, socioeconomic and religious groups (DeKeserdy and Hinch 1991), scant attention has been paid to the situation and needs of abused women in rural communities (Canadian Farm Women's Network 1995; Epprecht 2001; Jiwani 1998; Logan, Walker and Leukelfeld 2000; Van Hightower, Gorton and DeMoss 2000). The dearth of information about abused women in geographically isolated communities may be due, in part, to an urbocentric bias among social researchers and/or an assumption that few differences exist between the experiences and needs of abused women in rural and urban areas. There is also a tendency to idealize rural life and ignore the extent of social problems, including family violence, in rural communities (Martz and Sarauer 2000; Websdale 1998).

However, there is reason to believe that wife abuse is as prevalent in rural communities as in urban areas. Statistics Canada's Violence Against Women Survey (1993) found no significant differences between rural and urban areas in the incidences of wife assault. Saskatchewan researchers, Martz and Sarauer (2000), report that the women they interviewed believe that wife abuse is common in rural areas, although because of fear and isolation that rural women experience, there may be fewer reported cases. Earlier, McLeod (1980), in a groundbreaking report for the Canadian Advisory Council on the Status of Women, noted that wife abuse is not less of a problem in rural communities, but may be more hidden. Survey research in the United States also demonstrates that the prevalence of wife abuse in rural regions is similar to that of urban areas (Bachman and Saltzman 1995, cited in Websdale 1998; Websdale and Johnson 1997).

There are, however, other compelling reasons to focus on family violence in rural communities. Rural communities, although not identical in their social structure and values, do share important cultural, social and physical characteristics that distinguish them from urban environments. Rural communities, for example, are more physically isolated; poverty rates and unemployment tend to be higher. Rural communities generally have fewer resources and services available. This means that access to health care, education, counselling, affordable housing and other social services may be minimal. Public transportation and licensed childcare is

---

1. In this paper, we are using the terms wife abuse and family violence interchangeably. While the term "family violence" can imply that violence within the family is committed by both husbands and wives towards each other (see Straus et al. 1980), in much social science discourse the term family violence is understood as husbands abusing their wives.

often inadequate or non-existent. Another dimension is the socio-cultural aspect. Researchers have found that traditional norms around marriage and the family are more prevalent in rural communities, as are patriarchal attitudes that devalue and objectify women (Gagne 1992; Jiwani 1998; Websdale 1998). Websdale uses the concept "rural patriarchy" to refer to "a cluster of collective values, beliefs, and ideas that deem rural women to be subordinate to rural men" (1998, p. 93). Patriarchal attitudes are not absent from urban communities but rather co-exist with a wide array of other competing values. While rural communities are not monolithic, researchers have found that they are generally more socially cohesive, have greater value consensus and have less tolerance of diversity.

We are not suggesting some sort of essentialist dimension to rural life, but rather argue that rural and farm communities[2] do share certain characteristics that make them different from urban environments. Taken together, these structural characteristics make it more difficult for abused women to "name" the abuse, report it, seek and get help or leave abusive relationships. Geographical remoteness means families are more isolated which may make it easier to hide abuse (Chalmers and Smith 1988). It also can mean that it takes police longer to respond to a call for assistance. Lack of public transportation is an impediment to women seeking help or wanting to leave the abusive home. Lack of affordable housing or employment prospects makes it more difficult for women to survive without the abusive partners' wages. Patriarchal values and beliefs legitimate male social control over women; thus women who seek support in dealing with abuse may be perceived as violating community norms about appropriate gender roles. These obstacles can reinforce women's fear and isolation and make them more vulnerable to abuse (Doherty and De Vink 1995; Hornosty 1995).

That is to say, the forms of abuse—physical, emotional, sexual, economic—suffered by rural women may be similar to that experienced by abused women in urban areas; however, the community context in which the abuse occurs can be dramatically different. Our research findings, like that of other researchers (Jiwani 1998; Logan, Walker and Leukelfeld 2000; Martz and Sarauer 2000; Websdale 1998), suggest that understanding the social and cultural context in which abuse occurs is essential in order to both fully understand the subjective experiences of abused women as well as to design appropriate and effective programs for helping abused women. The abuse of women in their homes cannot be divorced from the broader social-cultural setting in which it occurs.

Methodology

The findings we present are based on interviews with over 50 abused farm and rural women and discussions in community focus groups in New Brunswick. The data gathered is in conjunction with research initiated in 1994 by the Family Violence on the Farm and in Rural Communities Research Team, one of the original five teams of the Muriel McQueen Fergusson Centre for Family Violence Research.[3] This multi-disciplinary team,[4] which included both academic and community researchers, had the following research objectives:

---

2. There is an important distinction to be made between farm and rural (non-farm) communities especially in the context of looking at wife abuse. While farm communities are, by definition, rural, there are unique aspects to farm life that need to be considered in examining the reality of abused farm women.

3. The Muriel McQueen Fergusson Centre for Family Violence Research is located in Fredericton, New Brunswick. It was one of five national Centres established in 1994 as part of the federal government's Family Violence Initiative.

4. The original team included an RCMP officer, a public health nurse, a farm woman, the executive director of a public legal education service, a counselor and academics. Specific membership has fluctuated over the years. Original members included: Jennie Hornosty (team co-ordinator), Deborah Doherty, Pat Hayward, Kathy Long, Margaret McCallum, Floranne McLaughlin, Susan Nind, Sandra deVink.

a) to understand how rural women talked about their experiences of abuse; b) to understand how these women came to define such behaviour as no longer tolerable; c) to identify the social and cultural aspects of rural life which women felt make it especially difficult for them and other abused women to seek help or leave such relationships; and d) to identify remedies and resources for improving community responses and eliminating violence and abuse in rural regions.[5]

One of our main goals was to understand how rural and farm women living with abuse made sense of their lives in the context of their rural environment. We wanted to capture women's experiences of and thoughts about abuse in their own words. We therefore used qualitative methodology, informed by feminist perspectives, and a commitment to action-orientated and collaborative strategies. Qualitative research methods are the most appropriate means of exploring people's views of their experiences and reality. Unlike quantitative studies that are concerned more with issues of frequency and distribution, qualitative research is rooted in the perspective of participants and their subjective meanings. Making sense of the data involves using inductive strategies that are sensitive to the social contexts in which behaviour occurs. In according authenticity to women's experiences in their everyday lives, our research is within a feminist tradition of giving voice to those whose views have historically been marginalized.

Prior to beginning our main interviews, we had a number of open-ended discussions with several abused rural women who had left their abusive relationships.[6] These women assisted the research team by sharing their life stories and helping us better understand what types of questions we should be asking, how to ask them and what to be sensitive to. They made us aware of different socio-cultural barriers women faced when confronting abuse and the subtle ways in which language can hide the reality of abuse. They helped us develop a framework of issues to be explored in interviews and made suggestions for specific questions we should ask. Using a qualitative approach allowed us to modify our questions and issues as we gained different insights into the problem.

The participants, largely farm and rural women from central and northern New Brunswick, were recruited through advertisements in local newspapers, postings in public places, word of mouth and referral from service providers, and by direct and indirect contact by members of the research team. The in-depth, semi-structured interviews we conducted lasted between one and a half to five hours each. Given the linguistic composition of the province, we conducted interviews in both English and French. With the permission of the participants, most of the interviews were taped and later transcribed for analysis. In addition to the interviews, we held three community focus groups in Northumberland County; two were conducted in English and one in French.

The interviews began by explaining to the women that we were interested in their stories and their experiences. In the interviews, we asked background-type questions pertaining to their childhood experiences, the community in which they grew up, the length of time they had been in a violent relationship, the nature of abuse, the role of religion in their lives, the number of children etc. We asked them to tell us about their experiences of abuse in the family, how they defined wife abuse, and what factors they felt contributed to the perpetuation

---

5. This research is still going on. In an earlier report (Family Violence on the Farm and in Rural Communities Research Team 1997), we explored some of the barriers victim's of wife abuse face in accessing support services, including transition houses, in a rural community. In the current phase we are looking at service providers' perceptions of and suggestions for addressing wife abuse in rural and farm areas.

6. Different team members had knowledge of abused women from rural communities and approached them, explaining the goals of our research team, and invited them to participate in the developmental phase of the research.

of and silencing of abuse. We probed for specific characteristics of rural and farm life they thought were most salient in keeping abuse hidden and made it difficult for women to seek help. We inquired about the specific factors that led to their decisions to leave abusive relationships. And, importantly, we asked for their suggestions about what would be most helpful to other farm and rural women in similar circumstances. We see this as a central component in our "action-oriented" research.

The transcribed interviews as well as the information gained from the focus groups were reviewed many times, looking for common themes, key phrases, concepts and words.[7] Since we believe that knowing the social context in which abuse occurs is critical for an understanding of women's experiences, much of our analysis to date has focused on barriers women face in seeking help and leaving abusive relationships. By focusing on barriers, we are highlighting the ways in which geographical, economic, and socio-cultural factors amplify the controlling tactics abusive men use against their wives. While all abused women face tremendous difficulties in dealing with abusive relationships, women in rural communities encounter certain unique barriers and attitudinal obstacles that are less problematic in urban areas.

Some Findings and Suggestions for Addressing Wife Abuse in Rural and Farm Communities

In this section, we present some key findings in relation to possible actions, solutions and remedies for eradicating or addressing wife abuse in rural areas. We categorized these findings according to the following broad themes, most of which are well understood by policy makers and family violence researchers alike: the economic environment (employment, training, pensions, etc.), rural infrastructure (access to health, housing, justice and various social services and resources), socio-cultural factors, rural lifestyle, and geographic factors. In light of the commonalities of living in small communities with limited access to services, the experiences of rural and farm women were often very similar. Nevertheless, where appropriate we attempt to identify instances where the structure of farm life may pose unique challenges. As we indicate in our conclusion, our findings substantiate those who have conducted similar research in rural communities.

Economic Environment

Given the high rate of unemployment and the preponderance of seasonal work in rural New Brunswick, it is not surprising that our study found that almost all of the rural women we interviewed tended to be financially dependant on their spouse. Financial dependency creates significant barriers for abused rural women. Many of the women we interviewed had never participated in the paid labour force; some were prohibited from doing so by their spouses. As a result, women often spoke of feeling desperate and trapped. As one women explained, "I had no way to support myself and the children and nowhere to go."

The rural women we interviewed commented on the lack of access to jobs, job training and money. Women who work in short duration seasonal jobs, like fish processing, cannot afford to miss time and risk losing their positions. It is not uncommon for rural women experiencing abuse to decide against going to a transition house for safety if they are involved in seasonal work for fear of being fired. Similarly, farm women who are in the midst of calving or harvest time are more likely to overlook their own safety. Although such critical times are

---

7. Co-authors Jennie Hornosty and Deborah Doherty are indebted to the work of the Family Violence on the Farm and in Rural Communities Research Team. However, much of the analysis and the material presented in this paper are the sole responsibility of the authors.

often associated with higher levels of stress and abuse, farm women are reluctant to jeopardize the farm's economic viability. Financial dependency is compounded for farm women who often do not receive a wage for their work and are unable to save any money of their own. Additionally, farm women may have no employment insurance, no pension, and therefore no economic security if they do leave the farm.

Leaving an abusive relationship usually means turning to welfare. Since affordable housing is scarce in rural areas, leaving might involve moving to an urban area to live in low-income housing. This is anathema to many rural women. Since the opportunities to find a job are limited, many rural women chose to stay in an abusive relationship especially while their children are young. Although we have no we data that would suggest a correlation between abuse and the tendency for more women than men to migrate to urban areas after the childbearing years, this may indeed be one factor to consider.

> *Suggested Solutions:*
>
> *Generate income opportunities.* Part of the solution to empowering rural women who wish to leave abusive relationships lies in generating opportunities for jobs, training and income for women in rural areas. Given the higher than average unemployment rates in rural areas, it is important that future employment strategies create income-generating opportunities for rural women while recognizing the particular vulnerability of abused women.
>
> *Establish homemakers' pensions.* Farm women who have stayed in an abusive relationship for the sake of children suggest that access to a homemaker pension may provide an incentive to leave the abuse. Elderly rural women in our study who continued to stay in abusive relationships even after the children were grown did so largely because of the lack of income opportunities. Those who did leave generally saw a significant decline in their standard of living.
>
> *Educate rural employers and promote supportive workplace policies and practices.* Rural employers should be encouraged to bring in specialists or train their own staff to conduct family violence workplace awareness sessions for all employees and to develop policies and practices that recognize and support women who are being abused in their intimate relationships. Given the seasonal nature of rural employment, family violence awareness training, along with the promotion of supportive policies and practices, should be provided to fish processing plants, silviculture operations, agri-food producers and so on.

Rural Infrastructure (Access to Services and Resources)

Like other studies in British Columbia (Jiwani 1998) and Ontario (Epprecht 2001), we found that rural women have limited access to social services including health care, mental health services, justice and law enforcement services, affordable housing, places of shelter, and so on. Nor do they have access to readily available information to help them learn about their options or their rights. Given the scope of this problem, we could easily have focused the entire paper on reviewing needed services; however, we will limit our discussion to a few key services that are inadequately addressing the needs of rural women dealing with abusive relationships.

For example, most of the rural women we interviewed who had called the police spoke of long frightening response times. The fact that so many people in the country have scanners also means that it is likely that somebody will have informed neighbours, in-laws and others of the situation. Victims find this particularly humiliating. Moreover, in one geographic area of our study, we discovered that the women living the greatest distance from town had experienced the most severe injuries, yet most reported that in their dealings with the police they had not been directed to crisis services or helping agencies (Family Violence on the Farm and in Rural Communities Research Team 1997). On the other hand, the women who had been referred to a crisis service or taken to a transition house reported a high level of satisfaction with the police.

Women's experiences dealing with criminal courts, as well as family law matters, particularly legal aid, also elicited considerable frustration. These matters cannot be resolved during a 30-day stay in a transition house and most criminal and family law matters can only be handled from urban centres. Women found that dealing with the criminal justice system or the family law courts was overwhelming and frightening. Those who did, experienced many unexplained delays, unnecessary trips to town because of court adjournments and confusion. Most of the women had expected the criminal justice system to help set things right by ending the abuse. They did not want to see their spouse fined or jailed. As a result, many of the women we spoke with ended up feeling re-victimization in their dealings with the courts.

Several of the woman poignantly described the ways that abuse affected their mental and physical well-being, such as low self-esteem, anger, depression, suicidal thoughts, fantasizing, substance abuse, and unfortunately, even abuse or neglect of their own children. Trauma during pregnancy seemed to be a common theme. Yet in rural areas there are few medical and mental health services available locally. Many of the women who sought treatment spoke of having their symptoms treated but not the underlying cause. Many women felt that their problems were medicated away by doctors or that they were inappropriately referred for marriage counselling after describing abusive situations. As well, women's drug and alcohol addictions were often seen as the problem rather than a response to abuse.

Although some women spoke of attempting to discuss the abuse with a doctor, one woman explained, "I never dreamed of telling my doctor, I could tell he didn't care." The lack of confidence in health care providers is clearly one aspect of the problem that needs to be addressed. However the overall inaccessibility of mental health and family health care in rural areas is disturbing given that victims of abuse are more likely to require health care services than non-victimized women (Barnett, Miller-Perrin, and Perrin 1997, p. 217).

Farm work may also impact on women's health. It can be physically demanding and rural women may be responsible for heavy chores around the farm as well as housework and looking after the needs of children. Many farm women spoke of fatigue and getting very little sleep, which was greatly exacerbated by abuse. As a result, they had little energy and time to socialize with friends and family, or to seek help. Moreover, the nature of farm work may leave abused women too tired to care about themselves and this can make them vulnerable to farm accidents.

Despite the mounting evidence (Schornstein 1997) that health care providers are particularly well positioned to play a key role in wife abuse intervention, access to health related services continues to dwindle in rural areas, whether it be pre- or post-natal visits, family clinics or emergency services. Yet with appropriate training, universal screening, increased sensitivity and enhanced measures to ensure privacy, many of the women we interviewed felt that health care providers could be particularly effective in helping abused rural women.

Lack of services also affects the youngest of victims. Many of the rural women we interviewed stayed in the abusive relationship to provide their children with the security of growing up in the country. However, most eventually came to recognize the harmful effects of the violence on their children, either directly or through witnessing it. Those who sought counselling or mental health services for their children soon found that very little help was available. Moreover, many of the women were terrified of seeking help in urban areas for fear that child protection workers would remove their children from their care.

Suggested Solutions:

Establish outreach services or centres and safe houses that meet the needs of rural women. Rural and farm women spoke of the need to have non-threatening, local places where they could find information, assistance, advice and support. For example, since physical violence often escalates during pregnancy and at the birth of a child, women suggested that well-trained public health nurses could travel to rural out-reach centres for non-threatening activities such as parenting classes and well-baby clinics. At the same time, they could promote the safety and security of abused women and their children. Pre-natal and post-natal home visits to new mothers in rural areas should be considered.

Co-ordinate services and improve communication among existing service providers, including the police. Rural women should not have to make several long trips to the city to apply for particular services, benefits, housing, legal aid, mental health or counselling services, or welfare. The coordination of services for abused women is an essential support for all women. However, coordination takes on an added degree of urgency for rural and farm women. When services cannot be made available locally, the women we interviewed suggested that the community must find ways to provide free transportation for women from rural areas who must travel to a distant transition home or city for help.

Educate and sensitize key service providers about family violence including health care providers, mental health workers, and police. It is often a struggle for rural women to find a service provider with whom they feel safe to disclose the abuse. When she does initiate contact, being rebuffed, referred to marriage counselling, or receiving no information about non-criminal remedies and assistance is unacceptable. There must be extensive and ongoing family violence awareness training for the key serv-ice providers who work or come into contact with victims of abuse. This should include enhanced training for frontline police/RCMP officers, health care providers, and others. It should also include model policies, universal screening questions and guidelines for ensuring confidentiality.

Disseminate information about abuse and the legal rights of abused women. Accurate information about family violence, legal rights, options and available services must be readily available both to abused women and to all service providers. We should not expect rural women to find out about abuse only if they travel to the city and happen to find a pamphlet at a government office. Many rural women do not real-ize they have legal rights, or they may not know what those rights are. Often their husbands or boyfriends have misinformed them about their rights, especially with regard to the issues of child custody and support. It is important that a variety of sources, including police, health care providers and others, be able to share accu-rate information concerning her rights as a mother, a spouse and as a survivor of abuse. All agencies where a woman might turn should be able to explain the reme-dies and services that exist to help her.

Socio-cultural Factors

In focus groups conducted in rural communities and in the interviews with rural women themselves, we discovered that family violence is usually thought to mean extreme physical violence. The hurt that women feel in their personal lives, ranging from emotional abuse to financial control, is seldom "named" even though it may be well known by neighbours and friends. In fact, the entire community may participate in blaming and using minimizing lan-guage and responses. This can act to normalize abusive behaviour and bolster norms about the private nature of family life. If hurtful and harmful behaviours are not labelled as abuse, women do not recognize themselves when they hear about "wife abuse or family violence."

One woman told us, "My friends don't talk about it [abuse]. They just brush it [an abusive experience] away—all women go through that ... my friends don't believe in it [abuse]." Rural men and women who grow up witnessing or experiencing abuse in their own homes come to feel that this is normal since others in the community seem to minimize or condone it.

Like abused women everywhere, rural women may experience years of controlling tactics, such as threats of suicide, remorse, promises and intimidation which keep them believing that they should stay. However, in a rural or farm context these threats and controlling tactics, whether implicit or explicit, take on a particular dimension. For example, they often relate to harming pets or farm animals or even the woman herself. This can be particularly menacing in a rural context since guns are readily available. Most farmers and many rural households own at least one gun for hunting or pest control. This fact, combined with the geographic isolation of farm and rural women, intensifies women's fear of reprisal if they should choose to leave or to tell someone about the abuse.

In a farm context, emotional abuse often takes the form of blaming the woman for everything that goes wrong on the farm—from the machinery breaking, a failed crop, or the animals getting sick. Many women felt that the abuser used these unfortunate occurrences, such as droughts or failed crops, as a justification for other abuses. Others in the community would sympathize with the abuser as well. Another common form of emotional abuse entailed telling the woman that the farm would go bankrupt if she ever left, and that everyone would blame her. Since farm women are dedicated to the survival of their farms and the preservation of the animals, many stay to protect what they cherish.

The familiarity of people in small communities through family, marriage and friendship can lead to a feeling that "everyone knows everyone else's business." However, rural communities tend to interweave a strong ethic of self-sufficiency with a belief that family issues are private matters. This makes it particularly difficult for abused women to ask for help even when they know that others are aware of the abuse. The belief that family matters should remain private also makes it difficult for others to intervene in cases of abuse. We learned that friends, family and neighbours who are aware of abuse in the rural woman's life often do not want to hear about it, nor do they wish to speak out about it.

Many of the women interviewed spoke about the lack of privacy, anonymity and confidentiality, living in a rural community. This is not to be confused with the strong sense of independence and autonomy which country people value and which makes people reluctant to interfere in another's private family matters. Concerns about confidentiality and anonymity focussed more on access to social and medical services. Rural women may not trust service providers or their staff to keep their "secret."

Women in large urban centres may benefit from anonymity. However, abused women living in the country are afraid that as soon as they seek medical care or talk to the police, everybody would know about it and blame them. The rural women we interviewed spoke of fears that an appropriate level of confidentiality would not be maintained if they sought local services such as mental health counselling, medical treatment, marriage counselling and so on. This fear is complicated by the fact that rural service providers and professionals may be friends with the abuser or his family. This can also promote a reluctance to confide for fear the service provider will not take the complaint seriously. This familiarity in turn may deter professionals and others in the community from offering help. This greatly exacerbates the geographic isolation that farm and rural women tend to experience.

Suggested Solutions:

Encourage her to think about personal safety issues. If she is thinking about leaving the abusive relationship, encourage her to think about the ways in which she can provide for her safety and the safety of her children. She needs to know that an abusive man often looks for ways to continue to contact and harass the woman after she leaves. Suggest ways, both practical and legal, that she can address safety issues. In light of the prevalence of guns in farm and rural households, rural women need to be advised of how to take precautions. Does she know where the guns are stored and where he keeps the ammunition and the keys to the gun cabinets? She should be encouraged to plan an escape route that takes into account the location of guns in the home.

Adopt better measures to assure privacy so women feel safe to disclose abuse. Service providers and professionals must address rural women's lack of trust and develop policies and practices to ensure privacy and confidentiality. They can do so in a variety of ways.

- Ask universal screening questions about abuse in private areas out of earshot of others.

- Exclude the woman's partner from the conversation in a non-threatening way.

- Implement "I believe" policies with staff.

- Train staff on how to promote confidentiality in a rural context.

Change the prevailing ethos that "private" matters are not of public concern. The issue of abuse must be discussed openly and publicly. Rural communities must find opportunities to reflect on issues of family violence and show support for victims while holding perpetrators accountable.

Explain effects of witnessing family violence on children. There should be more public education about the adverse effects on children of witnessing abuse and living with family violence. Living in rural areas often means that there are few opportunities for children to access special services or to participate in extracurricular activities that might offer alternate ways to build self-esteem or provide support. Communities must work hard to offer inclusive, inexpensive programming, recreation and other services for children.

Increase public education about the nature of abuse and its impact. All women in abusive relationships need to be told about the various forms that violence and abuse may take and that none are acceptable. However, in naming the negative harmful behaviours, we must include examples that relate to rural and farm life. Women must hear that the abuse is not their fault. This message must be pervasive and reinforced in public awareness campaigns in which local communities are encouraged to take ownership. Family, friends, clergy, neighbours and others in the community should be encouraged to listen to the voices of abused women and let them know that they are believed, supported and understood.

Use a variety of appropriate formats for reaching rural and farm women. Pamphlets distributed in rural areas must be distributed at appropriate times and places. For example, a blitz of information in a farming community should not happen at harvest time and information in certain rural communities might coincide with the exodus of men working in the woods. Family violence information must be put into places throughout rural areas where women will be able to access it safely. Plain language tips could be put into mail-outs with other materials or in circulars in local papers. It could come home in children's backpacks from the school or it could be put in private washrooms in community halls, malls and churches. Information about abuse should also be targetted at men and disseminated in locations frequented by them such as gyms, bars, pool halls, etc. In light of the low literacy levels in many communities, women suggested putting messages about abuse awareness on the radio and as commercials during soap operas.

Rural Lifestyles

Rural communities tend to promote a way of life that many rural people experience collectively, as well as individually. Under normal circumstances, this is highly valued aspect of rural life. Farm and rural women spoke to us of the benefits of living in the country with helpful neighbours, low crime rates and a peaceful existence where close-knit communities tend to have strong shared attitudes and cultural norms. For many rural women, the church also plays a key role in their lives. However, these same shared norms and values, whether community or religious oriented, tend to reflect a patriarchal view that strongly reinforces traditional gender roles and expectations that women are subservient to men.

These norms are reinforced in the division of labour, traditions and attitudes relating to women as wives and homemakers. These expectations are also reinforced by religious beliefs that promote the duty of a wife to maintain harmony in the family and to preserve the family at all costs. Leaving an abusive situation can mean leaving one's family and faith community as well. This is a far greater disruption to one's life than to leave an abusive relationship in an urban area, and the situation is exacerbated on the farm since there is often no separation between home and work. Farming is more than an economic livelihood; it is a total and unique way of life where survival is often dependent on the cooperation and effort of women. To leave may doom the farm to failure and this fact is not lost on abusers who frequently use it in their arsenal of emotional abuse and blaming tactics. Service providers who do not understand and address the unique context of rural life can impede disclosure and inhibit rural women from attending to their personal safety and security.

As one women explained, "Using services, like the transition house, is difficult not only because it is far away, but they don't really understand farm women. The staff are kind and sympathetic, but they don't seem to know what it means to come from a rural home. You almost feel ashamed for placing so much value on it." In other words, not only are the services inaccessible, the failure of service providers to recognize the unique context in which the abuse occurs creates additional barriers. As a result, we found that interaction between abused farm and rural women, and the service providers they meet sometimes results in heightened frustration and re-victimization. Farm women spoke to us of feeling re-victimized by service providers or by urban women who made them feel guilty for not acting on their rights because of their loyalty or attachment to the farm or farm animals and pets.

> *Suggested Solutions:*
>
> *Demonstrate sensitivity.* Work places, social service offices, faith communities, hospitals, doctors' offices and others demonstrate that they understand the unique barriers faced by rural and farm women. We must create supportive and safe environments for rural women before we can expect them to promote disclosure.
>
> *Validate her rural experiences and the nature of her suffering.* Women interviewed spoke of the importance of telling survivors that they are not to blame. It is essential that an abused woman hear the positive message that her suffering is real, and that she did not cause it. We must also validate the victim's attachment to her rural or farming lifestyle, while at the same time validating her suffering. The two are not mutually exclusive. Just as the abuser uses rural situations to create a sense of blame, service providers should use examples from rural life to talk about abusive situations.
>
> *Address concerns about pets and farm animals.* Not only must service providers learn not to minimize attachments to pets and farm animals, communities must find ways to help alleviate women's concerns. This might involve setting up "safe houses" where women seeking shelter can leave their animals for care until they can make permanent arrangements. Other suggestions were to involve the SPCA in rural outreach programs to shelter the pets of victims of abuse.

Work with local women and farm organizations. The women we interviewed emphasized the importance of listening to the voices of rural and farm women, including those who had experienced family violence. In order to be effective, programs that are being designed to help rural and farm women must have the input of rural and farm women, rural women's organizations and agencies and so on. Local women's groups and farm women's organizations must be involved in identifying ways to help abused women.

Geographic Isolation

Rural women experiencing abuse are not only emotionally isolated from family and friends, but physically isolated as well. A number of women told us how isolated and alone they felt. Some did not have phones. The nearest neighbour can be a couple of miles away. Often there is little opportunity to socialize with other women because of the distances between homes and lack of access to transportation. The geographic distance between farms means that abuse on farms is easier to hide. There are no neighbours nearby to see or hear what is going on. In a crisis, it may take the RCMP up to an hour to respond.

The absence of public transportation in rural communities makes it difficult if not impossible for abused women to get help. Many women had no means of transportation since their husbands would either be off with the car or would not give them access. Some women told us they "did not even have a driver's license and lived 15 kilometres from the nearest town." The lack of transportation means, in the words of one woman, "You don't have the freedom to just go."

The small population base spread out over a vast geographic area makes public transportation costly and impractical. However, some public means for women to access help must be put in place to assist abused women in geographically remote areas.

Suggested Solutions:

Address lack of transportation. Lack of adequate transportation is such a pervasive part of rural life that all service providers should consider how to assist abused rural women who must travel to access services. This might include setting up a program that provides free taxi service or volunteer rides.

Establish a toll-free crisis hot line that is widely advertised. Many of the women interviewed told us that they could not phone the nearest transition house for advice because it would show up on their telephone bill as a long distance call. This would create suspicion and perhaps put them in danger. A toll-free number that is widely advertised and known would bridge that gap. This would also assist rural women to seek information and advice while maintaining a sense of anonymity and privacy. It would help to overcome some of the obstacles created by inadequate transportation.

Conclusion

Although more focus is being given to woman abuse in rural and farm communities, research in the area remains limited. Similar to other studies (Biesenthal et al. 2000; Jiwani 1998; Logan, Walker and Leukelfeld 2000; Martz and Sarauer 2000), our research highlights the importance of looking at the social and cultural context of abuse and understanding community values and norms. An important aspect of our research is that we gave primacy to the voices of abused rural and farm women. As researchers, we have gained new insight into the systemic barriers encountered by abused rural and farm women in attempting to disclose their situations or leave the abuse.

Meeting the needs of rural women means that we must look at their lives and options through their eyes. Their experiences and insights must be the starting point of developing new programmes and policies. As we were so frequently reminded, any strategies and solutions for addressing family violence in rural communities must be rooted in the rural and farm cultures of abused women. By providing a vehicle for the voices of rural survivors of abuse, our research makes an important contribution to the understanding of these cultures.

Governments recognize that rural communities face special challenges. As part of the federal government's Canadian Rural Partnership Initiative, a national workshop was held to discuss issues of importance to Canadians living in rural communities (Rural Secretariat 1998). Ten key issues were identified including economic diversification, lack of access to financial resources, opportunities for rural youth, access to rural health care and access to rural education. Participants at the workshop indicated that there was a lack of awareness, understanding and sensitivity to rural issues on the part of governments and that frequently government policies and programmes were not adapted to rural realities (Rural Secretariat 1998, p.19).

Similarly, our research points to the need to recognize rural uniqueness in terms of providing programs and services for abused women in rural and farm communities. The issues identified at the national rural workshop noted above are clearly important. Many of the recommendations made could potentially help abused women. However, we caution that a gender-neutral approach which fails to consider how polices impact differently on woman and men can make interventions ineffective for abused women.

It is also important to recognize how rural families confront many of the challenges to sustaining healthy, vibrant communities. A shared sense of tradition and common values often helps them to deal with such challenges collectively, whether it be in demanding rural services, addressing rural poverty, or improving transportation. However, our findings indicate that many of these same shared characteristics and values can make it more difficult for women to report abuse, seek help or leave abusive relationships. As noted earlier, the lack of anonymity and confidentiality in rural areas, along with the centrality of farm life for farm women, and the norms around privacy in family matters, also tend to mitigate against naming abuse and foster strong patriarchal values and sex-role stereotyping.

Like Epprecht (2001) and Jiwani (1998), we found that there is reluctance in many rural communities to admit that wife abuse is a serious problem. In addition, the individuals we interviewed suggested that there is a high degree of tolerance for abusive behaviours. In her study of Appalachian women, Gagne (1992) concluded that without a cultural acceptance of men's authority over women, violence would not be as effective a means of social control. As a result, we would stress the importance of promoting a strong countervailing ethos against abusive behaviours, both individually and at a societal level. This is a key component to addressing wife abuse in rural communities.

This does not mean that new services or public awareness programs cannot be built on the strengths of rural communities and lifestyles. Indeed, it is important to recognize women's contribution and commitment to the family and the farm. At the same time, we must encourage communities to speak out against abuse and to end the blame and stigma that is so often directed at rural women leaving abusive relationships. Values that dictate women's responsibility for "keeping the family together at all costs" must be counterbalanced by the value of encouraging women to protect themselves and their children from harm.

In this paper, we explored many findings related to the barriers experienced by abused farm and rural women. We discovered that a variety of social and cultural factors impact on abused women's access to services and resources, while economic conditions in rural areas limit options for becoming financially independent. As the women we interviewed noted, the misunderstandings that arise among service providers in relation to farm and rural life, and the lack of access to programmes and services to help abused rural women, can lead to feelings of frustration and revictimization. This paper offers a number of suggested solutions that are based upon the experiences and needs of the women who participated in our study. Solutions ranged from initiating strategies to eliminate poverty and create employment opportunities for women in rural areas, to increasing sensitivity of service providers and employers, to establishing family violence toll-free numbers and places of safety for farm animals. These solutions are not exhaustive; rather, they are intended to act as springboard for addressing the unique and diverse needs of abused rural women, both at the individual level and systemically.

This is clearly a time of uncertainty and transformation in rural communities. During such periods of rapid change, rural communities tend to be particularly vulnerable. Globalization, out-migration of youth, a deteriorating infrastructure, and a decline in resources and services are some factors that create added stress for rural families. During such crises, it is likely that incidences of wife abuse will increase. However, it is also at such times that the opportunities exist for communities and government to respond in a more positive fashion to the needs of abused rural women. For as Korten (1994) noted, "Functioning, caring families and households are the foundation of functioning, caring communities, which in turn are the foundation of functioning, caring societies." Federal and provincial government plans for economic diversification, as well as the delivery of health care, education, justice and other services, must be designed and evaluated with an eye to assessing their impact on abused rural and farm women. Unless family violence is addressed, rural communities will continue to be a very isolating and fearful place for many women.

Ending violence against women in rural and farm communities requires a societal solution. Communities must learn to name unacceptable behaviours and speak out against all forms of abuse. However, systemic changes are also essential to truly address the problem. Governments must play a key role by ensuring that initiatives to promote overall rural development include gender analysis, with particular attention being paid to the special needs of abused rural and farm women.

References

Barnett, O.W., C.L. Miller-Perrin, and R.D. Perrin (eds.). 1997. "Marital Violence: Battered Women." In *Family Violence Across the Lifespan*. Thousand Oaks, CA: Sage Publications.

Biesenthal, L., L. Sproule, M. Nelder, S. Golton, D. Mann, D. Podovinnikoff, I. Roosendaal, S. Warman, and D. Lunn. 2000. *Research Report: The Ontario Rural Woman Abuse Study (ORWAS) Final Report*. Ottawa: Department of Justice.

Canada, Statistics Canada. 1993. "The Violence Against Women Survey." In *The Daily Juristat*. Ottawa: Statistics Canada.

———. 1996. *1996 Census*. Ottawa: Statistics Canada.

———. 1998. *International Adult Literacy Survey: A New Brunswick Snapshot*. Ottawa: Statistics Canada, 1998.

Canadian Farm Women's Network. 1995. "Family Violence in Rural, Farm and Remote Canada." Unpublished Report. Fredericton, 1995.

Chalmers, L. and P. Smith. 1998. "Wife Battering: Psychological, Social and Physical Isolation and Counteracting Strategies." In A.T. McLaren (ed.), *Gender and Society*. Toronto: Copp Clark.

DeKeseredy, W., and R. Hinch. 1991. *Women Abuse: Sociological Perspectives*. Toronto: Thompson Educational Publishing.

Doherty, D. and S. DeVink, S. 1995. "Family Violence on the Farm and in Rural Communities: 1) Historical Overview and Methodology, 2) A Preliminary Analysis of Family Violence on the Farm and in Rural Communities." Paper presented to Gender Studies Week, St. Thomas University, March 1995.

Epprecht, N. 2001. "The Ontario Rural Woman Abuse Study (ORWAS)." Paper presented at the Domestic Violence in Special Populations 1st Session of the 7th International Family Violence Research Conference, July 2001, at University of New Hampshire, Portsmouth, New Hampshire.

Family Violence on the Farm and in Rural Communities Research Team. 1997. "Barriers to the Use of Support Services by Family Violence Victims in Northumberland County." Report submitted to the New Brunswick Department of the Solicitor General. Fredericton.

Gagne, P. 1992. "Appalachian Women: Violence and Social Control." *Journal of Contemporary Ethnography* 20: 387–415.

Hornosty, J. 1995. "Wife Abuse in Rural Regions: Structural Problems in Leaving Abusive Relationships (A Case Study in Canada)." In Frank Vanclay (ed.), *With a Rural Focus*. New South Whales: Wagga Wagga.

Jiwani, Y. 1998. *Rural Women and Violence: A Study of Two Communities in British Columbia*. Unedited Technical Report. Ottawa: Department of Justice.

Korten, D.C. "Sustainable Livelihoods: Redefining the Global Social Crisis [online]." A feature of the People-Centered Development Forum, May 10, 1994 [cited 05 November 2001]. Available from World Wide Web: (http://www.iisd1.iisd.ca/pcdf/1994/suslive.htm).

LeBreton, S. 1999. *Human Resources Profile of New Brunswick*. Ottawa: Human Resources Development Canada, New Brunswick Region, Pan-Canadian Operations.

LeBreton, S., F. L'Italien and L. Grignon. 1999. *Seasonal Workers In New Brunswick in 1977*. Ottawa: Human Resources Development Canada, Applied Research Branch.

Logan, T., R. Walker, and C. Leukelfeld. 2000. "Rural, Urban Influenced, and Urban Differences Among Domestic Violence Arrestees." *Journal of Interpersonal Violence* 16: 266–83.

Martz, D., and D. Sarauer. 2000. "Domestic Violence and the Experiences of Rural Women in East Central Saskatchewan [online]." Muenster: Centre for Rural Studies and Enrichment, 2000 [cited 05 November 2001]. Available from World Wide Web: (http://www.hotpeachpages.org/paths/rural_dv_eastsask.html)

McLeod, L. 1980. *Wife Battering in Canada: The Vicious Circle*. Ottawa: Minister of Supply and Services.

New Brunswick, Department of Agriculture, Fisheries and Aquaculture. 2000. *Agriculture and Rural Development: 1999/2000 Annual Report*. Government of New Brunswick: Fredericton.

Rural Secretariat. 1998. *Rural Solutions to Rural Problems. Final Report on the National Rural Workshop, 2–4 October, 1998*. Ottawa: Government of Canada.

Schornstein, S.L. 1997. "Societal Perspectives on Domestic Violence." In *Domestic Violence Care: What Every Professional Needs To Know*. Thousand Oaks, CA: Sage Publications.

Van Hightower, N., J. Gorton, and C. DeMoss. 2000. "Predictive Models of Domestic Violence and Fear of Intimate Partners among Migrant and Seasonal Farm Worker Women." *Journal of Family Violence* 15: 137–53.

Websdale, N. 1998. *Rural Women and the Justice System: An Ethnography*. Thousand Oaks, CA: Sage Publications.

Websdale, N., and Johnson, E. 1997. "The Policing of Domestic Violence in Rural and Urban Areas: The Voices of Battered Women in Kentucky." *Policing and Society* 6: 297–317.

CHAPTER FIVE

Rural Women, Regional Development, and Electoral Democracy in Atlantic Canada

Louise Carbert

Introduction

In his recent quantitative study of electoral democracy in the Canadian provinces, Donald Blake highlighted the election of women in terms of its broad linkage to all of the cultural, economic, and institutional indicators of electoral democracy included in his analysis (2001, 28). His work contributes solid empirical evidence to earlier theoretical justifications (e.g., RCERPF, Vol. 1, 1991, 113-5; Phillips 1995; Young 1990) for viewing the election of women as a fundamental component of the quality of electoral democracy.

Coincidentally, this revelation comes just as elections in the past few years have brought the realization that the overall proportion of women elected in Canada has stalled after 25 years of increases. To illustrate this pattern, the top-left frame of Figure 1 presents the historical progression in the ratio of women elected to the House of Commons over the past thirty years, as well as the aggregate provincial ratio. The two ratios have risen roughly in tandem, from below 5% in 1970 to somewhere near 20% at present. The overall pattern of increases that emerged most strongly in the 1980s was clearly not sustained in the 1990s, and appears to have disappeared altogether over the past half decade. As well as varying over time, the progression has been far from uniform across Canada. The other three frames of Figure 1 show the separate historical progression in the ratio of women elected to each provincial legislature alone and by region. All the provincial legislatures included fewer than 5% women in 1970, with the exception of British Columbia, where nearly 10% of the seats were held by women. The ratios in recent years cluster roughly geographically. Since the mid-1990s, they have fallen in the 10–20% range for the Atlantic provinces, 15–20% for Ontario, 20–25% for Quebec, and 20–30% for the western provinces (Carbert 2001a).

What causes these distinctions and variations? Richard Matland and Donley Studlar (1998) performed a regression analysis of women's election to provincial legislature over various periods between 1975 and 1994 which considered the impact of a variety of factors. One of the strongest relationships in their model was a "rural effect," in which significantly more women were elected in urban ridings, especially those in large metropolitan centres. The relative dearth of rural women in the provincial legislatures is in keeping with earlier work in Canada and elsewhere (Brodie 1977; Moncrief and Thompson 1991).[1] Matland and Studlar

---

1. It has been suggested, "it may well be easier for a woman to be voted into US Congress than be elected county commissioner of a nonmetropolitan county" (Bourke and Luloff 1997, 19).

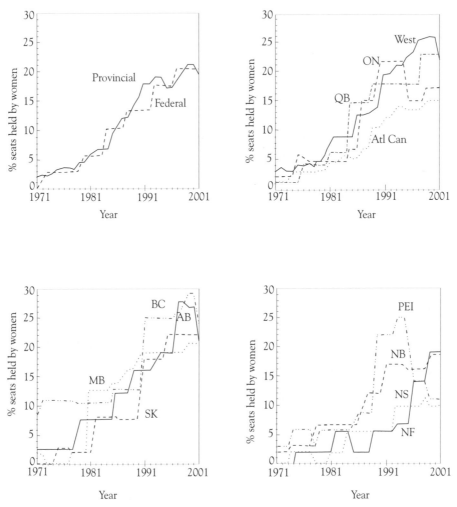

Figure 1. Percentage of seats held by women in various jurisdictions, 1971–2001.

(1998) proposed that the rural effect has effectively depressed overall rates of women's representation in Canadian provincial legislatures, due to rural over-representation. A series of court rulings has upheld the principle of "effective, not necessarily equal representation," and has thus entrenched the practice of over-representation of rural voters.[2] So long as this practise continues, the political dynamics of rural Canada will continue to exercise disproportionate influence over electoral outcomes. Understanding the reasons for this "rural effect" thus becomes central to the study of women's representation in Canada.

There is currently very little to go on, in the way of empirical evidence. For over a century, rural women have honed their leadership skills in voluntary women's organizations, and more recently they have become prominent in high-profile public-sector occupations, small-business groups, and agricultural organizations (Carbert 2001b). There is a pool of qualified, talented rural women, but they are not finding their way to public office in the same proportion as urban women. Why not? The statistical analyses cited above were not designed to

---

2. As further support for their proposition, Matland and Studlar cited higher rates of women's election to the American state assemblies, where electoral districting is based more closely on the principle of one person/one vote.

reveal underlying causal mechanisms. They leave open the crucial question: what are the characteristics of rural life that act as barriers to rural women's election?

Atlantic Canada stands out as a particularly interesting region in which to investigate this question, in that its population is relatively more rural than the other regions of Canada, and relatively fewer women hold elected office there than elsewhere. This paper presents results from a field-based research project that, for the first time, went directly to the women at the centre of action (and inaction). It gathered together and interviewed rural community leaders in Atlantic Canada about their experiences and perceptions of leadership, public life, and running for elected office. These are the qualified and involved women who would form the pool of potential candidates for elected office, but who, for a variety of reasons, are not running and not winning in large numbers. The interviews covered a broad range of topics spanning public and private dimensions, and the interaction among them. This paper focuses on a particular issue whose importance was unanticipated (in terms of the literature), but which kept coming up spontaneously and intensely in one discussion group after another: the dominance of regional development programs in local affairs and its particular consequences for the electoral ambitions of women in leadership positions. As we will see, many of the participants identified deterrents in the way these programs are administered. The discussions on this topic shed new light on important aspects of public life in rural Atlantic Canada, and suggest the possibility of a more general political-economy analysis of what distinguishes the nature of political representation in rural Canada from that in metropolitan centres.

Method

In field work completed in September 2000,[3] the author conducted 14 focus groups involving 126 women in the four Atlantic provinces. Preset exercises and open-ended questions typically led to intense discussions lasting 1.5–2 hours, followed by written questionnaires.[4] Focus groups were arranged and participants recruited in conjunction with major government and non-government organizations; the process is summarized below, roughly in chronological order:

> Courtesy of Executive Director Brigitte Neumann, the Nova Scotia Advisory Council on the Status of Women employed its regional field workers to select interviewees and organize focus groups in Lawrencetown, Amherst, and Truro.

> Stella Lord with the Halifax branch of the Canadian Research Institute for the Advancement for Women put me in touch with the Shelburne County Women's FishNet. This FishNet operates as a resource centre to disseminate information about labour-force retraining opportunities.

> Another meeting was held nearby with the Shelburne Business Women's Association.

> Three focus groups were held with executive members of Federated Women's Institutes of Nova Scotia (Truro), Prince Edward Island (Charlottetown), and Newfoundland (Springdale).

> A focus group in Louisburg, Cape Breton, was arranged by Women's Community-based Economic Development Network. This network promotes women's retraining, home-based business, and integration into community decision-making.

---

3. This project was funded by the Indo-Canadian Shastri Institute / CIDA Partnership Program; the principal investigator was Sara Ahmed, Institute of Rural Management, Anand India.

4. In all, 125 out of 126 focus-group participants completed the written questionnaire; the exception was a mayor who left early to attend another meeting.

The Newfoundland Advisory Council on the Status of Women referred me to the Women and Resource Development Committee, which employed regional field-workers in Clarenville and Stephenville. This Committee works in conjunction with the College of the North Atlantic to promote non-traditional vocational opportunities for women in the new offshore oil and gas industry. The Clarenville fieldworker also arranged the focus group in her capacity as an official with the Progressive Conservative Party of Newfoundland.

An official with the Liberal Party of Newfoundland arranged a focus group in the federal electoral district of Burin-St. George's.

The New Brunswick Advisory Council referred me to one of its rural board members, who arranged a session in an English-speaking enclave on the Acadian Coast.

To balance the Liberal Party strength on the Acadian coast, an official with the Progressive Conservative Party of Canada facilitated a focus group on the traditionally Tory and Loyalist Fundy Coast.

Focus-group participants were chosen for their expertise and experience in local public affairs. Some relevant characteristics were documented in the written questionnaire. Figure 2 displays their wide range of experience in electoral politics. Of 125 women who completed the written questionnaire, 73 had worked on an election campaign; and of that subgroup, 48 had done canvassing, 42 had served as a poll clerk, scrutineer, or other election official, 38 had done campaign administration and office work, including the job of campaign manager, 32 had donated money, and 20 had been a candidate themselves. Two of those candidates had been elected at the provincial level, of whom one had served in cabinet. Figure 3 shows participants' experience in serving on official government boards; 47 of 125 women had been or were appointed to such boards, 20 were appointed to educational boards, 13 to cultural, historical, or tourism boards, 12 to economic development boards, and 6 to recreational boards.

The women interviewed were also exceptionally well educated, with Figure 4 showing that 83% of participants had attended post-secondary institutions, including 38% who held a post-secondary degree as their highest level of education, and a further 22% who held a graduate or professional degree. Data from the 1996 Census (Statistics Canada) helps to put these education levels into perspective. Figure 5 shows the proportion of working-age population listing "university" as their highest level of education in the federal electoral districts where research was conducted; this proportion ranges from a low of 11.6 % in Burin-St. George's to a high of 18.2% in New Brunswick SouthWest. As further context, the figure shows the proportion for the largest urban centre in the region, Halifax (47%), and the overall proportion for Canada (23%). While the Census figures are not directly comparable to the present questionnaire, in terms of educational categories and age distribution, it is eminently clear that the interviewees were highly educated relative to their local populations and Canada in general.

In keeping with their high levels of education, many participants had good jobs. Figure 6 presents a categorization of the occupations. The educational sector employed the largest number of women (28%) interviewed, most often as teachers, but also as college instructors and administrators. The private sector also employed a substantial number of the women, including 9% who owned and operated their own small business. Occupations associated with the economic development field are identified as a separate category because professionals in this field turned out to be particularly astute observers of the local political scene.

The focus-group format used here is particularly suitable for use with sophisticated and engaged respondents speaking directly about their own circumstances (Fern 2001; Krueger

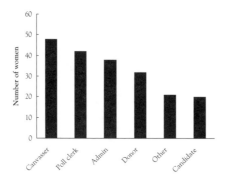

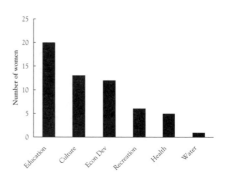

Figure 2. Election campaign activities (73 of 125 participants have done one or more).

Figure 3. Board appointments (47 of 125 participants have served on one or more).

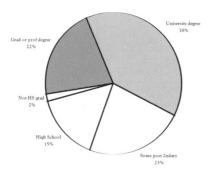

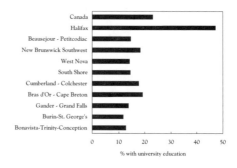

Figure 4. Participants' highest level of education.

Figure 5. Proportion of population (> 15 years) listing "university" as highest level of education (Statistics Canada, 1996 Census).

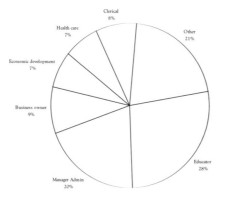

Figure 6. Participants' occupations.

and Casey 2000; Templeton 1994). This method allowed valuable insights to emerge that were not anticipated by the investigator, including those reported here. The interviewees proved to be exceptionally articulate and enthusiastic about the topic. On the whole, they were elite enough to be familiar with the details of local political life, yet most did not occupy such high positions of responsibility that they felt obliged to be reticent or unduly discreet. Over 20 hours of testimony from the focus-group discussions constitutes a rich source of information relating to rural women's leadership in Atlantic Canada. Since the participants are potential candidates themselves, their subjective understanding is directly relevant to what can be referred to as the "supply-side barrier" to women's candidacies; i.e., whether they run or not is to a large degree a personal matter. While it is not possible to determine how "objectively" accurate is their understanding of local political life, these women do speak with considerable authority about the issues discussed. Furthermore, based on their personal familiarity with Halifax, Moncton, Charlottetown, or St. John's, many participants could also speak with some authority about the characteristics of their community that, they thought, were distinctively rural in comparison to those urban centres. They had less personal experience of other parts of Canada, and so spoke with less confidence as to whether these same rural features were unique to Atlantic Canada, or rather apply more generally to all rural areas.

The Job of Being a Rural Politician

As context for how rural women leaders articulate their own electoral ambitions, or lack thereof, it is important to understand what they perceive the job to involve. At the most basic level, focus-group discussions made it clear that the role of a rural politician is far more onerous than that of an urban counterpart. As an example, consider the following discussion led off by a regional economic development officer:

> The realities of [a politician's job] are frightening—the silly phone calls at night, the constant phone calls. This is awful, but [counting on her fingers] I didn't get this cheque, or this bill needs to be paid, or I want this pothole fixed, or a whole series of things—phone calls like that would disrupt my life plenty. And they are still not satisfied with anything in the end.

When I suggested that the constituency office must handle such minor queries, there was much laughter at my naïveté, and the economic development officer continued:

> We feel that we own our politicians. That means own them 24 hours a day. Not me personally, but the public at large, that it gives them the right to call them at whatever time of day or night that they feel appropriate. It also gives them the right to approach you, at whatever time of day or night, in a different light at the grocery store. There is no differentiation between your personal and professional life.

In another focus group, a woman who had recently run unsuccessfully as a candidate in a provincial election voiced a similar understanding:

> It would be nothing to pick up the telephone and call your municipal, provincial or federal representative in this province on your issue. You're calling because the road wasn't sanded properly; you haven't had adequate number of weeks of work, all of those issues.

Astonishingly, this same participant went on to claim that the demands overflow beyond the elected member:

> [John Doe] is the elected member in this area. I ran against [John] in the last provincial election and I get thirty-five, forty calls a week. And it doesn't matter that I'm not the elected representative. [John Doe] is the elected representative.

> Because you ask people, "Why are you calling me?" "Well [they say] I know how it
> works, [your Party's] government is in, and I want this done."[5]

The group then reached a consensus that it is important for politicians to handle constituents' concerns personally, as opposed to delegating them to staff in the constituency
office.

Several straightforward distinctions help to understand why rural politicians might have
more onerous obligations to their constituents than urban politicians. The work of representation is undeniably made more difficult by the fact that rural electoral districts are geographically larger than urban districts, and thus require much more long-distance travelling.
It may also be more difficult as a result of disparities in "system-manipulation skills" between
rural and urban voters. The greater proportion of urban voters with formal education means
that a greater proportion of people can be counted on to have a sense of how government
bureaucracies are organized; they are more likely to phone the relevant government office
themselves than ask their elected member to phone on their behalf. Or in the case of a dispute, urban voters might be more likely to hire their own lawyer rather than depend on local
politicians to defend them. A third major distinction concerns the relative role of the public
sector in the local economy; the resulting effects on the nature of representation will be
explored in some detail in the sections that follow.

Some women cited the time intrusion itself as a barrier to women running for office, in
terms of conflict with traditional gender roles and family responsibilities. For example, the
defeated candidate referred to above explained:

> I'm single so all I have is "me, myself and I." If I had family responsibilities, I'm not
> sure I could take forty calls a week in a job that is not mine. You know the job is
> [John's]. My job is [another job] and then I have my volunteer work, so that makes
> it possible. That is a big issue in this riding is that women don't have the time. But
> that's life in rural [parts of province]. The challenges are there but if you have a
> family plus a full time job, you know, it's not an option that a lot of women would
> have the time to commit to.

Interestingly, this deterrent was usually attributed to other women in general (as above),
but rarely directly to oneself. In fact, one woman who had served as an elected official spoke
eloquently of a positive interaction between her husband's recalcitrance and her political
responsibilities. Because her husband refused to change his life in response to her election,
she returned home to the constituency every weekend, which, in the end, she said, forced
her to stay in touch with her constituents and thus carry out her original mandate to represent rural issues. "On Sunday morning, I would sit down with a cup of tea and a newspaper
and I would say 75% of these Sunday mornings, the phone was ringing or people were walk-
ing in; they'd catch me in my robe with a cup of tea. And your home is an open door." She
further explained that living in the District made her a better politician because she attended the weddings and the anniversaries, and thus moved in a different, more egalitarian, circle of people than she would otherwise, either as a private person or as a member living in
the capital.

The obligations of a rural politician to constituents are no doubt onerous, but is that really a major barrier to qualified women? It is important to keep in mind that all of the participants in this project are highly active and energetic in community affairs, whether or not
their activities are directed toward elected office. These are women who, for the most part,
have gone out of their way to seek additional responsibilities outside the home. It would be

---

5. John Doe is used to refer to any elected official who appears in the transcript by his proper name.

out of character for most of them to claim to be deterred from elected office by the mere existence of time intrusion and responsibilities. As an example, in response to the bathrobe politician above, another woman in the discussion group said that her life too was an "open book," and her house was always open to everyone. Along these lines, several other groups seemed to feature a certain competitiveness regarding willingness and ability to cope with time demands. Overall, the time intrusion, per se, of a rural politician's responsibilities did not emerge as a dominant barrier to running for elected office among the majority of the women interviewed. Delving further into nature of representation in these communities revealed that for many women the dominant deterrent lies more in the substantive nature of the responsibilities and the activities involved in carrying them out.

The Political Fray

One of the strongest common themes to emerge from the Atlantic study was participants' moral disapproval of, and aversion to, political life as they understand it in their local environment. The following comments feature a tone and attitude that was shared in some regard by all of the focus-group discussions:

> Actually, I have been asked to run both provincially and municipally. … My mom always said "Don't become a politician as long as I'm living," and a more staunch [PC] party supporter than my mother, you'd never find. She didn't want me to lead that kind of life. As for getting people to work on my campaign, if I had to do it I would do it. I'd get someone else to go ask for money. I guess a lot of it, you feel, when you look at the people we have running for [municipal and county positions]…

At this point, the economic-development officer in the adjacent chair (who was clearly a close friend) leaned over, touched her arm, and whispered with self-conscious laughter: "Remember the camera." The first speaker then continued:

> I don't know if I would want to be in that group. I really don't know because I think I would get so frustrated. I really feel badly about what's going on, but I don't know why they think they are the be-all-and-end-all, and I don't want to put myself in that position, to have to get in there and fight it. I have better things to do. As [another woman] said, I feel I can do more in the community by working with the organizations that I do. I feel that my work in education and health is far more important than sitting behind that Council desk, listening to others choose sides, wasting my tax dollars. I love these parties they have—these wonderful planning sessions where they go to [a nearby three-star hotel] on my tax dollar.

At this point, the economic-development officer pulled her turtleneck over her mouth, displaying obvious discomfort, and interjected, with a sarcastic tone, in defence of the planning retreats: "They bond." (There appeared to me to be an unspoken understanding between the two that the latter had attended the event in question.) To which her friend replied: "I don't want to put myself in that position of doing what I feel is not right. I'm very comfortable staying at home and doing what I do. I do have family support. My husband says 'Do what you want to do.'"

The tone of the cryptic allegations sounded rather sinister, but was there a valid reason for the economic development officer to squirm uncomfortably? The only substantive allegation in this exchange was that local officials attend a planning retreat. To most urban readers, this activity must seem quite defensible, particularly considering that it was held at a three-star rural hotel in the same province (and not, say, a five-star hotel in the Caribbean). So why did the economic development officer not muster a better defence? Here it is useful to consider the socio-economic disparities in relatively impoverished rural ridings of Atlantic

Canada. Elected members are typically well-educated professionals—most often lawyers—who often enter public life at some personal sacrifice. While their salaries are not competitive with salaries for equivalent positions in the private sector, they are supplemented by generous pensions; and while the overall financial package may not afford a luxurious lifestyle in major urban centres, it certainly affords an affluence that is rare in rural Atlantic Canada. In this environment a weekend at a three-star hotel can appear to some constituents to be an unnecessary extravagance, rather than a minor "perk" to compensate for working on the weekend. A recent national opinion survey on political ethics featured some results that are relevant in this regard. It found that young people and older women preferentially thought that it was unethical for parliamentarians to accept the perks that typically accompany executive-level positions. In contrast, middle-aged employed men tended to see no ethical impropriety because, the authors inferred, they were familiar with, and felt themselves entitled to, such perks based on their own position (Maureen Mancuso et al. 1998, 112, 118).

Many other examples of disapproval emerged in the focus-group discussions, involving varying degrees of impropriety. Few of these involved egregious cases of political corruption.[6] This could indicate either that such activities are rare, or that the subject is too sensitive to have been brought up. On two occasions, women who were very well connected politically took me aside afterwards (once the recorder was turned off), one to relate a case of cronyism at public expense, and the other a case of corrupt election finances. In each case, the allegations had been alluded to in the general discussion, but the informant had waited until after the meeting to substantiate the story, because the politician in question was closely related to another woman at the focus group. Investigating these allegations is beyond the scope of this project, which is concerned primarily with the perceptions of the women interviewed.

At another focus group, women made some rather preposterous allegations about electoral fraud based principally on the fact that the deputy returning officer counted the votes in the same house as (and was married to) the campaign manager for the winning candidate in the most recent provincial election. The discussion had a reckless, blustering tone that gave the impression of a vulnerable group bolstering itself against perceived bullying by local elites. The women making the allegations may have also enjoyed shocking the visiting scholar with how terribly corrupt and oppressive their community is. When I expressed disbelief, they challenged my naïveté and insisted that such things go on all the time. The discussion came back down to earth when a woman who had been an activist in the governing Party a few years earlier said:

> *Speaker 1:* I don't know about that part, in terms of actually fixing the ballots. But in terms of influencing people to vote in a certain way, yes. When you use jobs as the bait, and you use other things, it's just as bad.

> *Speaker 2:* You might as well stuff the ballot boxes. And the bottom line is she's not the only one who is sceptical. Maybe she's the only one who has the balls to say it...

> *Speaker 3:* Watch you don't get shot on the way out of the door.

Soon after, the group resolved that electoral irregularities are bound to occur in rural polls

---

6. When elected members receive financial benefits, over and above their salaries, as a result of holding public office, they are properly said to be "corrupt," and can be charged under the Criminal Code of Canada. To avoid the temptation of corruption, politicians are expected to remove themselves from any situation that has the potential, or even the impression of a potential, for personal enrichment. Elected members are thus required to put their financial assets into a "blind trust" which is administered by a neutral third-party while holding office. In Canada, elected members are not required to put the assets of spouses and dependent children into a blind trust, nor to make family assets a matter of public record.

simply because there are too few people (as scrutineers, poll clerks, and returning officers) involved to avoid conflict-of-interest situations.

One substantive criticism, however, remains in the above exchange: that "using jobs as bait ... is just as bad" as electoral fraud. This comment refers to a practise that was brought up for criticism, in one form or another, by the participants in every single focus group, and more frequently than any other category of disapproved behaviour: political patronage. While this term is sometimes used in a broader sense, it is used here in the restricted sense common in the political science literature: "the giving of employment, grants, contracts and other government perquisites on the basis of partisan affiliation (Stewart 1994a, 92)."

Numerous instances of such practises were cited, mostly in relation to positions on public-works projects such as painting buildings or cutting firewood—jobs for which nearly every able-bodied adult would be qualified. The discussions typically featured harsh moral criticism in terms of nepotism, corruption, and coercion in the electoral process. The following allegations come from a self-described "rabble-rouser on the left":

> Like, for instance, there is a tourist information bureau, and it is run by Joe Bob, so Joe Bob's buddy or his niece or his nephew is going to get the job, so you might not even bother to apply. Cause it's all, you know, regardless of who is on Council, or who is in the political arena, I would have to say from what I have seen thus far, a lot of those jobs that come to the community, they go to families first who are on the council or related to the council or close to them." When pressed further to be more specific, she said: "Okay, we are talking about [this part of the province], and politically speaking, these are the same people who had been there for years, going up on the same Boards and they seemed to be the people reaping the most rewards from outside influences, because they are in office. They hold office and their families are the ones getting the benefits more so than the average Joe's.

Although this woman had been very active in both partisan and non-partisan organizations, she was a "mainlander" who was not well established in the community. In fact, at several points in the discussion, another participant who was professionally employed as an economic development officer corrected the "rabble-rouser" as to who had been hired from which pot of money, and as to who was an appointed official, and who was professional staff. Significantly, though, the insider professional did not defend the politicians and other officials from accusations of nepotism and favouritism; in fact, she went on to substantiate the accusations herself in the following discussion sparked by an account of the last provincial election campaign.

> *Economic development officer:* And there's jobs to get too if you will have the right...
>
> *Speaker 1:* And I know it works for sure, when it comes to political parties cause when I ran projects, I got a call from every politician that was in there looking for a job for one of their constituents or a position for one of their constituents. And all I'd say was there is a[n official] route to go through. We'll choose from whoever has their application in. If it is not in at my table by a certain time, it ain't getting in.
>
> *Economic development officer:* It goes right to a government member's office. In my situation, the Development Association is supposed to be a catalyst and administers the money. My story to [a hypothetical person] when she calls looking for a job is, "We have the authority to put as many people on [a project] as we can. Whoever has less and as many weeks gets to go first." But [John Doe] is behind me, saying "Hire this, this, and this person, and you can't have the money unless this person comes attached to it," because it's patronage, political patronage.
>
> *Rabble rouser:* If you don't give this guy a job, because I'm [John Doe] and I'm in

office right now, then you can kiss your funds for your Economic Development Association out the door. You can kiss it goodbye.

Economic development officer: That's exactly how he would present it.

While a connection between participants' disapproval and their reluctance to run for office was unanticipated, the mere fact that they disapprove is consistent with results of other studies. For example, the above-cited Mancuso et al. survey of Canadian public opinion on political ethics found that the entire country is nearly monolithically opposed to a range of perceived ethical violations. If anything, voters in the most stereotypically traditional regions of Quebec and the Atlantic provinces were less tolerant of patronage and minor ethical infractions than elsewhere. The authors concluded that the "more critical altitudes in those regions may be due to progressive zeal and a reaction to the deficiencies of the bad old days (1998, 195)." Several other studies have also concluded that routine, large-scale patronage no longer occurs on the same scale that it once did in Atlantic Canada (e.g., Young, 1986; Stewart 1994a, 1994b). One focus-group participant whose personal background makes her opinion particularly credible confirmed this view, in regard to lucrative professional contracts:

> If you talk to people a generation above me, like my parents, they talk about the patronage, and will say, "Are you getting [Party] contracts? Is the government giving you business?" Because they feel that I can go in and flash the ancient [Party] card and cash goes into my hand and that is very much the way, and my parents they are in their early sixties and that is very much the way it worked. It does not work near to that degree now. There are still some contracts that are handed out on a patronage basis but with public tendering act and the public services commission, there is such a strong reaction to the flamboyant abuse of it before.

Thus, while the women interviewed in the present study recognize a significant decline in patronage practises, particularly at the high end, they also made it clear that the issue remains a serious concern, and has had a real and negative impact on their attitudes toward electoral politics.

Ironically, while the remaining level of patronage deters some women, the backlash against the practise may itself deter others, especially business owners. One participant related that her family owns a heavy-equipment firm that is often hired to work on construction projects and roadwork. She feels that because her family is partisan, there is always suspicion that the firm got a public-sector contract as a result of patronage. She resents these suspicions because all governments now operate an open tendering system. In fact, she suspects that the government takes these perceptions of corruption all too seriously. Her family's firm sometimes feels that they have to submit ridiculously low bids to get a contract, because the government wants to avoid even the appearance of patronage by giving a fair contract to a family that is known to be active in the local riding association. The group went on to agree that people are suspicious that any kind of wealth or income is derived from patronage if a person or anyone in their family is involved in partisan politics. In this view, partisan people are, in effect, penalized for their participation because they must work twice as hard and bend over backwards to avoid the appearance of unfairness.

Another small-business owner actually claimed to have turned down the NDP nomination in her riding for virtually the same reason:

> Somebody asked me to run for that area, right. And I said no. Because even if you run for some kind of office, I noticed that people got bad-mouthed... This fella runs for office and he gets a new car and all of a sudden it's because he's ... you know. Even though this guy works hard for a living and has his own career, but because he ran for office, he has this kind of funding coming in or there is a stigma involved as well to running for office. If you gain anything material, even if it's gained by your

own work ethic, it's always in the back of somebody's mind in a rural community that said "Oh, yeah, they got funding from the government for that, so they got to build a new house and put a new addition on because now they are on the town council." Do you know what I'm saying? I'm not saying that it's true. I'm just saying that is the perception.

These examples suggest a disturbing, albeit extreme, possibility. What would happen if local elites withdrew from partisanship and the institutions of electoral democracy?

Overall, the discussions with rural women leaders offer a glimpse into a public forum in flux, in which communities struggle to preserve their partisan electoral system, while purging a set of outdated practises that had always formed part and parcel of that system. One net effect is that at least for the time being, negative perceptions of the political fray in terms of patronage and other distasteful practises are viewed by many qualified women as significant deterrents to running for elected office.

Patrons and Clients

At the same time as disapproving of the way in which public-sector resources are allocated, many of the women interviewed expressed an appreciation for the importance of these resources to the economic well-being and future prospects of their communities, and for the role of the elected officials in attracting and overseeing them. The following exchange is a good example of the interplay of these two frames of reference. It begins with a speaker who is professionally and personally immersed in poverty and labour-force development issues, explaining why she does not want to pursue elected office or move closer to the electoral process:

> *Speaker 1:* A lot of the political things that are of importance are not the soft issues or what they call soft issues, like the economics and stuff like that. So for us it's not what really interests us. Like for me, I wouldn't want to run just to increase the … I think it is very good that people get jobs and stuff like that, but I think the infrastructure has to be in place first, so I would want people to be fed, I would want people to be sheltered, I would want to have happy homes, those would be the things I would want first in my community and I know that, that would come from economics and a good economic base but I don't think you can do one without the other. I think there has to be a balance and I think when we get around the tables all we hear is "Oh, we got to create a job for this one, and a job for that one and that fellow over there who has got the ten businesses going, he needs twelve jobs," and that's why he is sitting at the table and 95 percent of the people around the table are there for their own particular interests, because they have financial interests being met at the table.

> *Economic-development professional:* Wait till October. $200,000 will shit in my lap.

> *Speaker 2:* That's when the funds come in and there is a big clamour for money.

> *Economic development officer:* We keep the list of who needs so many hours [of paid labour to qualify for Employment Insurance benefits], but there's still a bigger list on top of that; these people need to be hired because they helped run a campaign…

> *Speaker 2:* So, political motivation is all it is, okay, so [economic development officer] and her Board might decide that this person in the community has a really viable project but [John Doe] might come in and say, "Listen my cousin Bob, he wants to start a goat farm. So you better give him that $100,000."

> *Economic development officer:* It's not that bad. … [Intervening discussion.] … Family is family, and stuff … But we have been beaten down [here] for the last four generations and the major source of income is social services, which is welfare and

besides that, there are a few jobs that [John's] able to create every year which puts a few people on EI [Employment Insurance benefits]. Two per cent of the population is working steady.

In trying to reconcile these dual strands, it is useful to distinguish the role of a "patron"[7] from the practise of patronage. The activities of a political patron responsible for dependent clients need not be corrupt, nor even partisan. In fact, carrying out this role can be construed as a moral responsibility. Politicians in many parts of rural Atlantic Canada are not only expected to secure collective wealth for the community in terms of attracting investment; they are expected to attend to the subsistence of individual voters as well, such as ensuring that voters received government-support cheques on time, or enrolling voters in labour-force retraining programs. This understanding of a politician's role was evident in several focus groups. In the following example, there were chuckles of appreciation in response to this description of the previous Member:

> *Speaker 1:* [John Doe] and [his wife] probably did more career placement than Canada Employment.

> *Speaker 2:* When you run a campaign in [this county], everybody in this room certainly knows, that even the provincial issues are not what people are voting on, not provincial leaders they're generally voting on, and not [policy] agendas. They are voting on who is going to be at the other end of their telephone. Who is going to get them their 15 weeks work? Who is going to see that they get their six months at the government garage? That is the very, very basic issue.

At a different group, the women participating knew the local member personally (and his father and his grandfather before him); the text below cannot convey the warm good humour in their voices:

> *Speaker 1:* The example I was thinking of, look at how many people end up at [John's] office after the election to look for jobs.

> *Speaker 2:* And [John Jr.] still doles out the jobs too.

> *Speaker 3:* I don't know why they bother with an employment office in [town] because they may as well just rely on [John's] office.

> *Speaker 4:* He sure does find a lot of jobs. A lot for young people.

The warmth of these comments was modified, however, when they proceeded to express disapproval for the specific ways in which the jobs in question were filled.

> *Speaker 5:* But [John Jr.] can have the headaches. That guy's phone never stops ringing. Like he is a very close friend of mine, but it would drive me nuts. He's got no private life. I wouldn't want the headaches. In relation to the employment thing, his comment is that people are at his office door, pounding every Monday or whatever. But I have also heard him say, come in. [Local manufacturer], for an example, is looking for forty employees and there is probably sixty, eighty, a hundred [people] every Monday sitting at his office looking for work, but none of them want that job. Because it doesn't pay enough or whatever. It's full time; they want term. "I've made ten dollars an hour at the last job I was at, you don't actually think that I would quit my EI to work for $6.50, with the idea that I could work full-time as opposed to 10 weeks here. I would have to be crazy cause I would make more

7. The original meaning of this word is a relic from feudal relations between landlords and tenant farmers; patrons were custodians of inherited family estates who were responsible for subsistence of their clients (the tenants). Some of this original meaning is incorporated in the contemporary use of the term "clientelism" to describe politicians in analogous environments as "patrons" (Noel 1976). Of course "patronage" comes from the same root originally, but it has acquired the more specialized connotation described earlier.

money sitting at home on my EI half the year, so now I won't take that job." And it's the same with [another local manufacturer].

Speaker 2: See, I think that's where a woman would just say, "You don't want it, that's it."

Speaker 5: They would have to be very, very assertive.

Speaker 6: But you have to be able to go to bed at night and be able to sleep.

Speaker 4: But if she had that attitude, she would never be voted in again.

Speaker 2: I would never be voted in again.

After building a consensus that they would not perpetuate the perceived practise of rounding out seasonal employment with Employment Insurance benefits, the discussion group proceeded to the following rationale for that position:

Speaker 7: The type of arguments that we have at home, now some of them would say, that the fact that [John Jr.] is being hounded by people on EI looking for more work is his father's fault, because that was an idea that he had [that the way to keep] himself elected was to give people jobs.

Speaker 5: Just long enough to get their EI.

Speaker 7: That's right. And that's the conservative argument being made, because he didn't benefit people, he kept them here, giving them work for ten weeks. If he didn't, a lot of our young people might have gone and furthered their education, what have you.

Speaker 2: That's the kind of argument [in which] he takes that 52-week job and divides it up between five people. Why not give one person a full-time job?

Speaker 8: And you're not dealing with black and white in that situation. The ideal is to have five 52-week jobs with full benefits and four weeks vacation. ... But, you know, it's not going to happen.

Speaker 5: But it's about keeping five votes as opposed to one.

Speaker 2: I'm not thinking of votes though, but long-term economics of the county.

Speaker 4: But if you're a politician you have to think of the votes, like it or not it is always there.

Speaker 2: Just long enough to get the government pension, that's it.

In retrospect, the ease with which these women formulated this neo-liberal critique,[8] and the vociferousness with which they spoke suggests that this critique was commonly held and well tested in day-to-day discussions. It also demonstrates that their aversion to the political fray is closely associated with a considered rational concern about the net effect on the best interests of the overall community. These women concurred with those in other groups that they would not run (or, if they did would not be elected) because they would not collude with a system which they saw as hypocritical, dishonest, and manipulative in terms of putting short-term partisan gain (i.e., votes) ahead of the community's long-term economic prosperity.

In some ways, the responsibilities of being a "patron" in rural Atlantic Canada would seem to be compatible with what has been identified as women's service orientation to politics (Kirkpatrick 1976). Yet aspects of such a relationship with the community have been cited by some focus-group participants as deterrents to participation. One woman spoke of being cast unwillingly as something of a patron in her job as economic development officer, and of feeling particularly overwhelmed by expectations on her at the time of the interview.

---

8. The Atlantic Institute for Market Studies makes just this point claiming that labour shortages are a perverse, unintended consequence of public policy (Fred McMahon 2000, 94–97).

Surrounded by sympathetic supporters, she explained that she saw her experience as an economic development officer as positioning her for a credible run at public office, but also as a potential threat to her electoral ambitions. She spoke of the particular difficulties that people face in her riding. "Let's be honest, about 60% of us are on welfare. I mean people are just hanging on." As a result, people scrutinized the newspaper carefully to see if she [as economic development officer] had secured a particular application for Human Resources Development Canada (HRDC) funding, and further scrutinized exactly whom she hired to work under which HRDC program. The stakes were enormous: being hired for an HRDC program meant several months of steady work, and several more of EI benefits; whereas not being hired meant continuing to subsist on social assistance. She was building a record of solid expertise in economic development and a high profile in the area, but by the time she would be ready to run for office (a time-frame left undefined), she felt she would have made too many enemies, including those whom she hadn't hired over the years, and those who blamed her for grants that she had failed to secure. When public-sector expenditures are so important to people's livelihoods, it is difficult to avoid disappointing people's expectations.

Discussion: Rurality and Regional Economic Development

From a wide variety of partisan perspectives and geographic locations, the rural women leaders interviewed for this Atlantic Canada study described specific characteristics of public life in their community that deter them personally from seeking elected office. Despite the fact that the focus-group discussions were not structured in advance around patronage or patron-client relations, these topics were brought up spontaneously for criticism in one focus group after another. This section outlines some of the structural features of rural Atlantic Canada that contribute to these characteristics, and considers the future prospects for the election of more women in rural ridings, in light of the comments of the women interviewed here.

Rurality is deeply embedded in the political fray as described by the participants in this project. In particular, the dynamics relating to patron-client relations are distinctly rural. These dynamics play out under the rubric of what may be described as the public-sector regional economic development industry, principally funded and administered through the Atlantic Canada Opportunities Agency (ACOA) and Human Resources Development Canada (HRDC) at the federal level, and to a lesser degree by provincial departments of economic development. In recent years, regional development initiatives have become increasingly focussed on rural economies, which have lagged increasingly behind their urban counterparts. To the extent that major urban centres attract concentrations of capitalist investment in tertiary service industries, urban populations are more likely to be employed in the formal labour force, with good-paying secure jobs in the private sector. The economies of rural Canada have historically been, and continue to be, characterized by resource-extraction industries. While some of these industries continue to prosper and represent a substantial share of Canada's economy, technological innovation and declining commodity prices have resulted in sharply reduced employment levels. This long-term trend has contributed to the continuous historical process of urbanization and relative rural depopulation. These industries also produce primarily for export to global markets whose business cycles fluctuate unpredictably. The level of profitability and intensity of production cycles in resource industries fluctuate accordingly. Resource-extraction industries are more vulnerable as well to ecological crises, as witnessed by the collapse of the cod fishery in the early 1990s. As a result, the rural population that remains is more likely to be employed in the secondary or informal labour force on temporary contracts, or to be self-employed in household-based enterprises, operating farms or wood lots. Donald Savoie predicts that "in future the split between the 'haves' and the 'less developed' regions will likely be more between urban and rural areas than between Atlantic Canada and Ontario. That is the nature of the new economy" (1997, 50).

So long as regional or rural-urban cleavages continue to exist, there will be a need for governments to facilitate and moderate the bumpy and often painful transitions. In addition to solid economic reasons for addressing such cleavages, Savoie presents a pragmatic consideration: "Politicians will never buy fully into the neo-conservative agenda. Politicians will wish to intervene and we all have a responsibility to assist them in defining the best possible measures" (1997, 59). Thus it seems inevitable that the economic development industry will continue to play a major role in rural economies and rural public life in the foreseeable future.

Many of the most strongly articulated deterrents to electoral aspirations among the women interviewed concerned the interaction between politics and the economic development industry, in its current form. A broad consensus emerged that they would not make moral concessions to perpetuate what they perceived as an unfair and dysfunctional system. A question thus arises whether that system will evolve into a form that they can feel more comfortable working with. In fact there is ample evidence that rural Atlantic Canada has already progressed a good deal in terms of the historical relationship between patron politicians and client constituents. Some of this change was evident to Jeffrey Simpson in his characterization of a mid-1980s rural-urban clash about the administration of patronage inside the governing Progressive Conservative caucus:

> The most emphatic support [for the old system] came from the smaller provinces where patronage still animated political behaviour and where government decisions affected, in ways unknown in more affluent parts of Canada, the livelihoods of individuals and the well-being of whole communities. The importance of a mini-patron in rural Nova Scotia, outport Newfoundland, or small-town New Brunswick had changed less than the importance of a patron in a wealthy, urban part of Canada. True, the social welfare state and the increased bureaucratization of government had ripped some discretionary powers away from politicians and mini-patrons. Decisions on the awarding of benefits could no longer be entirely dependent on the political loyalty of the supplicants. Improved communications and education had nibbled at the intimate dependency of the patron-client relationship. But no one familiar with politics in Atlantic Canada could deny the still enormously important role of patronage, especially that expensive, largely community-directed, embellishment known as pork-barrelling (1988, 32).

As shown earlier in this paper, the participants in the present study recognize the ongoing diminishment of these and other disliked practises, but evidently feel that it has not yet gone far enough. Is it likely to do so in the near future? David Siegel outlines some obstacles that result from the fragile economic base supporting the structures of governance in sparsely populated areas:

> Small towns are, well, small. Small-town politics and administration are much hands-on processes compared to other jurisdictions. The "hands-on'" nature of decision-making means that small-town politicians are more likely to find themselves in situations where they are called upon to make decisions that transparently affect themselves, their families, or their friends (or enemies). This situation personalizes decisions in small towns. When a municipal council is making decisions, it is frequently very clear which individuals and groups will benefit from a decision (1993, 113–15).[9]

---

9. Siegel cites the example of a part-time mayor who partly owns one of three travel agencies in town to show how difficult it is to avoid conflict-of-interest situations. To prohibit the mayor's travel agency from doing work for the municipality would be too big a sacrifice for the travel agency, and the mayor would sooner resign. Even were more strict regulations to be legislated in Canada, the basic problem still remains that politicians are tempted to make public-policy decisions based on their personal financial interests.

It is difficult to see how politics in a rural setting could ever become as formalized as in large cities. It seems likely that some women will always be deterred by a reluctance to incur accusations of conflict of interest, and other women will avoid the moral ambiguities of administering public resources under such intimate circumstances. But there is, of course, a distribution of attitudes. Perhaps there is room to change enough to suit some qualified women. Would a more tightly regulated and transparent system with a bit more distance between the decision-making process and the affected constituents offer more opportunities for women?

It is possible that there has already been a modest impact in helping a few women to "get their foot in the door." The present discussion series included a number of women professionally employed in the economic development industry. These women have acquired positions of some responsibility that were not available to women until recently. They consistently stood out in the discussion groups as sophisticated and knowledgeable "insiders." As relatively privileged women, economic development professionals are not the designated clientèle for recent initiatives to promote "women's empowerment" as part of a policy shift to the development of a community's "soft" human and social capital (Savoie 2000), but they certainly seem to be empowered by the industry. Their detailed knowledge of local affairs typically exceeded that of party insiders at the table, including women who had run as candidates, or who had been invited to run and declined. The sophistication of these economic - development professionals can be related to their position straddling "the slushy intersection of politics and policy" (Sutherland 2001, 10). One implication is that these women are particularly well qualified to stand as candidates for public office.[10] However at this point, perhaps unfortunately, these women shared much of the same disillusionment with public life as the other women interviewed.

References

Arscott, Jane. 1997. "Between the Rock and a Hard Place: Women Legislators in Newfoundland and Nova Scotia." In Jane Arscott and Linda Trimble (eds.), *In the Presence of Women: Representation in Canadian Governments.* Toronto: Harcourt Brace.

Blake, Donald. 2001. "Electoral Democracy in the Provinces" *Choices* 7, no. 2.

Bourke, Lise and A.E. Luloff. 1997. "Women and Leadership in Rural Areas." *Women & Politics* 17, no. 4: 1–23.

Brodie, Janine. 1977. "The Recruitment of Canadian Women Provincial Legislators, 1950–1975." *Atlantis* 2, no. 2: 6–17.

Carbert, Louise. 2001a. "Historical Influences on Regional Patterns of the Election of Women to Provincial Legislatures." In William Cross (ed.), *Political Parties, Representation, and Electoral Democracy in Canada.* Toronto: Oxford University Press.

———. 2001b. "Building Social Capital: Civic Engagement in Farm Communities." In Joanna Everitt and Brenda O'Neill (eds.), *Political Behaviour: Theory and Practise in a Canadian Context.* Toronto: Oxford University Press.

Fern, Edward. 2001. *Advanced Focus Group Research.* Thousand Oaks, CA: Sage.

George, Glynis. 2000. *The Rock Where We Stand: An Ethnography of Women's Activism in Newfoundland.* Toronto: University of Toronto Press.

Kirkpatrick, Jeane. 1974. *Political Woman.* New York: Basic Books

Krueger, Richard and Mary Anne Casey. 2000. *Focus Groups, A Practical Guide for Applied Research.* Thousand Oaks, CA: Sage.

Mancuso, Maureen, Michael Atkinson, André Blais, Ian Greene, and Neil Nevitte. 1998. *A Question of Ethics: Canadians Speak Out.* Toronto: Oxford University Press.

Matland, Richard and Donley Studlar. 1998. "Gender and the Electoral Opportunity Structure in the Canadian Provinces." *Political Research Quarterly* 5: 117–40.

---

10. In a reputational study of rural Pennsylvania community leaders, "younger, college-educated women who were directors of local and county agencies, usually involving economic development, were recognized as leaders due to their position" (Bourke and Luloff 1997, 15).

McMahon, Fred. 2000. *Retreat from Growth: Atlantic Canada and the Negative-sum Economy*. Halifax: Atlantic Institute for Market Studies.

Moncrief, Gary and Joel Thompson. 1991. "Urban and Rural Ridings and Women in Provincial Politics: A Note on Female MLAs." *Canadian Journal of Political Science* 24: 831–37.

Noel, S.J.N. 1976. "Leadership and Clientelism." In David Bellamy, John Pammett, and Donald Rowan (eds.), *The Provincial Political Systems: Comparative Essays*. Toronto: Methuen.

Phillips, Anne. 1995. *The Politics of Presence*. Oxford; New York: Clarendon Press.

Royal Commission on Electoral Reform and Party Financing. 1991. *Reforming Electoral Democracy*. Volume 1 of the research studies of the Royal Commission on Electoral Reform and Party Financing. Ottawa and Toronto: RCERPF/Dundurn Press.

Savoie, Donald. 1997. *Rethinking Canada's Regional Development Policy: An Atlantic Perspective*. Moncton: Canadian Institute for Research on Regional Development.

——. 2000. *Community Economic Development in Atlantic Canada: False Hope or Panacea?* Moncton: Canadian Institute for Research on Regional Development.

Siegel, David. 1993. "Small-town Canada." In John Langford and Allan Tupper. (eds.), *Corruption, Character, and Conduct: Essays on Canadian Government Ethics*. Toronto: Oxford University Press.

Simpson, Jeffrey. 2000. *Spoils of Power: The Politics of Patronage*. Toronto: Collins.

Stewart, Ian. 1994a. "Despoiling the Public Sector? The Case of Nova Scotia." In Langford and Tupper, *Corruption, Character, and Conduct*. Toronto: Oxford University Press.

——. 1994b. *Roasting Chestnuts: The Mythology of Maritime Political Culture*. Vancouver: University of British Columbia Press.

Sutherland, Sharon. 2001. "Biggest Scandal in Canadian History: HRDC Audit Starts Probity War." *Working Paper* 23, Queen's University School of Policy Studies.

Templeton, Jane Farley. 1994. *The Focus Group: A Strategic Guide to Organizing, Conducting and Analyzing the Focus Group Interview*. Toronto: McGraw-Hill Professional Publishing.

Young, Iris Marion. 1990. *Justice and the Politics of Difference*. Princeton, NJ: Princeton University Press.

Young, R.A. 1986. "Teaching and Research in Maritimes Politics: Old Stereotypes and New Directions." *Journal of Canadian Studies* 21, no. 2: 133–55.

CHAPTER SIX

"Bush Parties and Booze Cruises": A Look at Leisure in a Prairie Small Town

Robert A. Wardhaugh

It's 10:00 pm on a warm July, Saturday evening in Borden, Saskatchewan. The year is 1980. The main street is well lit but quiet. A few cars are parked outside the hotel that faces the service road and highway on the southeast corner of Sheppard Street. The Kosy Korner Café that sits on the adjacent corner is dark, having been shut since supper. Further along the street, the post office, Co-op Store, General Store, and Municipal Office also sit quiet. The steady hum of the street lights is joined only by crickets from the slough to the north of town. Every several minutes the "whir" of an engine can be heard, as a car or truck zips past on Highway #16—the Yellow Head—enroute to either Saskatoon or North Battleford.

Suddenly, the calm is broken by the appearance of vehicle headlights. The roar of the engine of the Dodge Ram half-ton breaches the silence; the sound of gravel beneath the tires seems deafening. The vehicle makes a left turn off the service road and slowly proceeds northward up Sheppard Street. Two blocks away, the lights of the half-ton have not gone unnoticed. Another vehicle, this one a Chevrolet Impala, turns left off the gravel road coming in from "the country" and onto Sheppard Street. It moves toward the pick-up truck, the two vehicles drawn together like magnets.

As the vehicles approach, their speeds decrease. From within, drivers and passengers make quick and thorough, but not too obvious, attempts to discern the other. The scrutiny takes only seconds, for as the vehicles pass, all eyes dart immediately to the rear view mirrors. Seconds pass like hours. Suddenly, the break lights of the Dodge truck light up! The car breaks also, and shifts into reverse. The two vehicles back up until they are side-by-side. The drivers' windows roll down.

"Hey man, where's the party?" the 18-year old male driver of the Dodge asks, his girl-friend snuggling beside him, even though the passenger side is vacant.

"Golf Course," is the response. The car holds four teenage occupants with ample room to spare.

The conversation is brief but obviously effective. With a knowing nod, both vehicles speed off in a cloud of dust. They drive quickly to the eastern exit from town, over the service road and highway, and onto the golf course road heading south toward the river. Several miles down the hilly, windy dirt trail enroute to nowhere, they turn off into a scrub-bush field. A piece of barbed wire fencing has been pulled back to reveal a trail into the bush. Fifty metres or so along the dark trail the vehicles come to an opening. The car pulls off to the side while the truck turns about and backs in slowly towards a shallow pit. Within minutes, a fire has been lit. The windows of the truck are opened and small speakers are placed on the roof. Music spills out, the surrounding bush offering muffled acoustics. The rattling of bottles can be heard, as cases of beer emerge from the various ingenious hiding places of each vehicle. The occupants gravitate toward the fire. On the northern horizon, car lights can be seen bobbing up and down, travelling along the golf course road in a haze of grey dust, toward the party place. People are coming; a bush party has begun.

It's 10:00 pm on a cold January, Saturday evening in Borden, Saskatchewan. The year is 1981. The same Dodge Ram half-ton and Chevrolet Impala are parked alongside one another on the main street, drivers' windows rolled down.

"Hey man, where's the party?" the 19-year old male driver of the Dodge asks, his girl-friend snuggling beside him, even though the passenger side is vacant.

"Don't know," is the response. The car holds four teenage occupants with ample room to spare. A long silence ensues as the various occupants of both vehicles ponder their limited options. "Booze Cruise?" the driver of the Impala suggests.

The conversation is brief but obviously effective. With a knowing nod, both vehicles move off, their tires spinning on the snow-packed streets. They pull into the parking lot of the café. The half-ton is parked and after obtaining the now nicely cooled two dozen beer from one of several ingenious hiding places in the truck, the two occupants pile into the seeming unending space of the Impala. The car takes a left onto Sheppard Street, through the first intersection, and then right onto the eastern road that leads into the country. Once the lights of town are in the distance, the car slows down and begins snaking through the back roads. Occasionally, a window is rolled down and an empty beer bottle is hurled at a lone-standing signpost. A booze cruise has begun.

This paper offers a brief glimpse into some of the leisure activities practised in a prairie small town, in this case Borden, Saskatchewan, from the 1960s through the 1990s. It is hoped that a discussion of two rather bizarre examples of youthful leisure in particular can accomplish several relevant objectives. Historians in Canada, despite the dominance of social history, have paid little attention to leisure.[1] Leisure time and its activities should, Peter Bailey argues, "be acknowledged as a significant element of social experience, whose history is of particular importance in the broader exercise of reconstructing the kind of life lived by the ordinary people of the past." Focus should be on popular as well as elitist recreations in order to "understand them not only in the context of their own culture but in relation to the structure of society as a whole and the wider patterns of social change."[2] An examination of leisure activities, even in one small and seemingly insignificant rural setting, can reveal certain social and economic dynamics that serve to highlight important cultural transformations.

Canadian historians, even in the West, are also paying surprisingly scant attention to the rural past. Previous generations of prairie historians focussed almost exclusively on the history of the pioneering, agricultural West, often to the exclusion of the increasingly predominant urban setting. In recent years, however, focus has shifted, as it should, to the urban context. It is here where scholars can more easily employ the now dominant structures of class, ethnicity, sexuality, and gender. The problem, however, is that this inevitable shift from

---

1. Some of the few exceptions are Donald G. Wetherell with Irene Kmet, *Useful Pleasures: The Shaping of Leisure in Alberta, 1896–1945* (Regina: Canadian Plains Research Center, 1990) and Lynne Marks, *Revivals and Roller Rinks: Religion, Leisure, and Identity in Late-Nineteenth-Century Small-Town Ontario* (Toronto: University of Toronto Press, 1996).

2. Peter Bailey, *Leisure and Class in Victorian England: Rational Recreation and the Contest for Control, 1830–1885* (1978; London: Methuen, 1987), 1.

rural to urban has been complete. While the rural West was previously over-represented in both history and literature,[3] there is now little emphasis on the countryside, particularly in the transformative era after 1945.[4]

Since World War II, the rural West has been drastically reshaped by technological, commercial, and democratic forces. Supporters and detractors of globalization will debate whether the process has helped or hindered the economic situation in rural areas, but there is little doubt that the end result has been rapid and turbulent metamorphosis.[5] The small and traditional are being exploded by the big and innovative. Only local rural histories can depict the degree and detail of this massive change. Joseph Amato makes a convincing argument for the relevance of local history amid this "mutation":

> Everywhere, place is being superseded and reshaped. Home, locale, community, and region—and the landscape they collectively form—have entered a stage of transformation. People everywhere live in an increasingly disembodied world, their landscapes and minds increasingly falling under the persuasion and control of abstract agencies and virtual images. Like the ecologies they modified and supplanted, human places—homes, farms, villages, and towns—have increasingly lost autonomy. Space and time, which once isolated places and assured continuity to experience and intensity to face-to-face interaction, have been penetrated, segmented, and diminished by surrounding forces and worlds. The coordinates of community, place, and time no longer define identities and experience or contour desires and expectations.[6]

Borden was settled in the years between 1902 and 1904 and incorporated as a village in 1905, the same year Saskatchewan became a province of the Dominion of Canada. The village site was selected because it was within "The Elbow," the geographical area on the north side of the North Saskatchewan River where it changes direction from southeasterly to almost due north, a place first used by the Cree bands to herd buffalo. It was a logical site, located between the two growing settlements of Saskatoon and the Battlefords, along the path chosen by the Canadian Northern Railroad. The railway came through in 1905. A ferry service also took traffic across the river until 1937 when the first road bridge was completed. The settlement was named "Borden" by the CNR, in honour of the Minister of Militia in the Laurier Cabinet.

The first settlers to pioneer the area were Doukhobors from Russia. English immigrants soon followed, coming directly from Britain during the first waves of the Western immigration boom after 1896. Ukrainian and Danish settlers followed. The Anglo presence was augmented by further immigration from the British Isles, as well as Ontario, in the years after 1905. After 1917, a substantial Mennonite community took shape. And the surrounding area was just as ethnically diverse. To the north, larger Doukhobor and Ukrainian settlements appeared at Blaine Lake, Hafford, and Leask while to the south and west Hutterite colonies sprang up. To the west German Lutherans also moved in, while further north could be found the already established Métis community of Duck Lake.

---

3. This can be seen in the work of historians such as W.L. Morton and V.C. Fowke and literary figures such as Ralph Connor, Robert Stead, Frederick Philip Grove, Sinclair Ross, W.O. Mitchell, Martha Ostenso, Margaret Laurence, and Robert Kroetsch.

4. In 1983 a conference was held on "Western Canada Since 1945" and the proceedings were published. Other than this contribution, however, the era has been largely ignored by historians. A.W. Rasporich (ed.), *The Making of Modern West: Western Canada Since 1945* (Calgary: The University of Calgary Press, 1984).

5. Roger Epp and Dave Whitson, *Writing off the Rural West: Globalization, Governments, and the Transformation of Rural Communities* (Edmonton: University of Alberta Press), xix.

6. Joseph A. Amato, *Rethinking Home: A Case for Writing Local History* (Los Angeles: University of California Press, 2002), 2.

As with most rural communities in the Prairie West, the village of Borden became the service centre for the surrounding agricultural community ready to take advantage of the parkland's fertile soil. The list of local businesses was remarkably long: boarding houses, hotel, school, post office, municipal office, trading company, implements dealer, livery barn, shoe and harness shop, real estate office, barber shop, billiard hall, butcher shop, slaughter house, blacksmith, sawmill and lumber company, flour and feed company, bank, hospital, coal sheds, and corrals. As pioneers took up homesteads, the area was divided into 10 districts, each a distinct community with its own rural schoolhouse. Some of these districts were situated as many as fourteen miles away, a distance that citizens of Borden considered "a world away."[7] The construction of the railroad, linking Edmonton with Saskatoon, drew farmers southward to Borden and the village became an important grain terminal. Villages appeared along this stretch of railroad at eight-mile intervals; elevators punctured the skyline to mark each service centre. Borden's importance as a grain-handling nexus was evident by the six elevators standing sentinel over the village; as late as 1980 Borden still boasted five elevators.

Technology rapidly transformed the community. In 1910 Borden obtained electric lights; in 1931 hydro lines were built to supply more regular electric service. The railway station was the communication depot as well as the means of travel to the nearest urban centres. Mail and most supplies came to the railway station and were then passed on to the local post office. In 1914 the rural telephone companies were formed. A wave of mechanization seriously impacted rural communities in the West in the early decades of the century as automobiles and tractors, along with the development of roads and highways, transformed the world of both work and play. But the recession following World War I, the Depression, and then the onset of another world war diminished the attainability of this new technology.

Borden, by all accounts, reached its height by the late 1940s. The immediate postwar era is remembered as the most prosperous in the village's history and the town population hovered around 300 people.[8] Residents claim that there was still a future for the youth in farming and local business, and so the community remained vibrant. This generation, however, would be the last to remain fixed in Borden. According to the community's locally produced history, "by the early fifties the exodus of people from the rural areas, faster vehicles and better roads encouraging shopping in larger centres and the consolidation of dealerships by machine and automobile companies had taken their toll and small communities became smaller. Borden was no exception."[9]

"It is a truism," Gerald Friesen writes, "that prairie society changed rapidly in the four decades after 1940." The most obvious and well-documented shift followed international norms with the movement of rural residents to the cities. Jean Burnet documented this shift as early as 1946 in her study of rural Alberta, *Next Year Country*:

> The decline was partly a result of changes in community organization, bound up largely with developments in technology occurring almost everywhere in Western European society. Automobiles and trucks made obsolete the old patterns in which villages served as centres of areas a "team haul" in radius. Improved transportation enabled farmers to travel distances formerly prohibitive. The farmers came to look to larger centres, where greater variety in goods and services was attainable, for many things previously secured in the villages.[10]

---

7. Interview with Archie Wainwright, 15 September 2001.

8. Interview with Murray Taylor, 27 August 2001.

9. Borden History Book Committee, *Our Treasured Heritage: Borden and District* (Altona: Friesen Printers, 1980), 9.

10. Jean Burnet, *Next Year Country: A Study of Rural Organization in Alberta* (Toronto: University of Toronto Press, 1951), 55.

People, however, did not only leave the country for the city; the culture of the city came to the country. Improvements in technology, most particularly in transportation and communication, transformed life in the prairie small town. According to Friesen, "the Canadian West became increasingly homogeneous and increasingly like the rest of the developed world between 1945 and the early 1980s."[11] Improvements in communication and transportation have long impacted leisure activities.[12] Peter Bailey notes that such improvements helped "break down regional insularities of mind and practice."[13] That said, the transformation would not be complete. "Despite the apparent homogeneity of modern social history," Friesen notes, "the prairie community also witnessed a flowering of distinctive local cultural expressions…"[14] The local history of the community wryly observes that "from first settlement the residents of the Borden area have looked after their own entertainment."[15]

Significant changes occurred in the leisure activities of rural Canadian society as a whole after 1945. According to Donald Wetherell, World War II "marked not only economic change, but also a number of changes in social attitude and in governments' and individuals' expectations about leisure."[16] Transformations in agricultural technology led to an increase in leisure time and activities. The influence of the traditional authorities, such as the churches, the schools, and the village institutions, diminished significantly. The youth increasingly felt that they possessed a certain right to leisure activities. The debates as to the need to legitimize the position of leisure in modern life, that marked the previous 50 years, faded away. The creation of a more liberal-democratic society shaped by the social movements of the 1960s and 1970s further diminished the impact of "the work ethic" as well as the effect of criticisms against leisure activities. Work became less a virtue than a necessary route to making money; the formula to success changed to working less, playing more, and still making "good money."

In a rural community, however, the increased opportunities for leisure were not met by the same provision of an extensive new range of consumer goods, services, and institutions enjoyed in urban settings. All roads led to an increase in leisure, yet, ironically, the space to enjoy, even on the wide open prairie, was not available.[17] In the past, organized events were held in the local church, school, lodge, and then the hall and the rink—the centres for leisure activities in most rural communities.[18] School and community dances would remain important but these events were not held often enough to match the expanding and changing appetite for leisure. Burnet's comment about Oyen, Alberta, in 1946 is revealing: "Meanwhile there are fewer organizations for the youth than for any other section of the population. The young people have parties and sports among themselves, it is true, but much

---

11. Gerald Friesen, "The Prairie West Since 1945: An Historical Survey," in Rasporich, *Making of the Modern West*, 2.

12. Major improvements in communications and transportation led to the expansion of what we view as "modern leisure" in mid-19th century Britain. Bailey, *Popular Culture and Performance in the Victorian City*, 16.

13. Ibid., 16.

14, Friesen, "The Prairie West Since 1945," 1.

15. *Our Treasured Heritage*, 9

16. Wetherell, *Useful Pleasures*, xvii.

17. Wetherell argues that "it is clear that before World War I there was a sharp difference between the leisure opportunities available to urban and rural people." Wetherell, *Useful Pleasures*, 10. While the gap was closing after this time, substantial differences remained even after World War II.

18. Wetherell demonstrates that prior to 1945 provincial governments on the Prairies urged communities to use schools for leisure activities because the teacher and school were viewed as ideal instructors for "wholesome recreation." The school was the main agency for unity, or in other words, anglo-conformity and assimilation of the "foreign elements." Divisive debates began over the use of schools for leisure and communities turned to halls to serve this function. Ibid., 93–94.

of their time is spent in loitering or mischief. This is a problem of which the village is well aware, and one peculiarly significant for community stability."[19]

On weekends, when events were not organized, young people increasingly sought other activities. Wetherell notes that "rural people could move or travel to the city to obtain the services or they could demand similar services for rural and small town areas." But these were privileged options. Rural folk may have wanted to improve their leisure services, to spurn labels of rural backwardness by levelling cultural differences between town and country, to imitate urban life and its standards of leisure. This, however, was easier said than done.[20] There was another choice: rural people could continue to shape their own distinctive activities.

Bush Parties and Booze Cruises emerged within this transition zone of an increasingly modern and urban promise and a still limited and isolated rural reality. These activities became part of leisurely pursuits for young people in Borden by the late 1960s, as community-organized events gave way to less-sanctioned activities that collectively became known as "partying." These activities were part of the larger revolutions in popular culture sweeping North America and indeed much of Western Europe at the time, and disseminated through such mediums as radio, magazines, film, and television. Culturally, they translated into increasingly liberal views of morality and a social acceptance and availability of "sex, drugs, and rock n' roll." On a local level, they coincided with the closing of the rural schools and the consolidation of the youth into the one school in town.

Alcohol has long played an important role in the leisure activities of rural prairie communities but traditionally it was framed within restrictive codes of respectability. While most groups within the Borden community consumed alcohol, the extent and circumstance of its use constructed social attitudes and ultimately social acceptance. Even though the dominant Anglo-Protestant groups drank, the perceived improper indulgence of alcohol was often used by this "respectable" hegemonic community as a justification for casting scorn upon the so-called "ethnics," in this case the Ukrainian minority.[21] But the protest movements of the post-war era expressed resistance to these forms of authority and scrutiny. The ethnic, class, and gender lines that framed leisure activities became blurred. By the late 1960s marijuana, hashish, mushrooms, and LSD were being used by certain fringe elements of Borden's young adult group. These illegal soft drugs, however, remained for the most part in the hands of the "hardest partiers" and associated more with the urban milieu. Booze remained the "respectable" drug of choice and its use was widespread.

"Partying" increased among the youth of Borden. As young adults turned away from traditional leisure activities, inevitably they sought "places to party." The Borden bar was not a desirable option for the young adult population. The legal age was 19 and there was little chance, in a community where "everyone knows everyone," of gaining entry before this age. Regardless, young adults who were of age did not often frequent the bar in the local hotel. It was more the domain of the elder town regulars, mostly men, as well as traffic coming off the main highway. Even if the local bar had been accessible, its hours of operation, and in particular its closing time, were far too restrictive for emerging leisure tastes.

Automobiles played a critical role in shaping the new leisure activities of the prairie small-town. The postwar boom injected affluence into rural communities such as Borden and vehicles became increasingly available. As with most rural areas, the distances to travel

---

19. Burnet, *Next Year Country*, 74.

20. Wetherell, *Useful Pleasures*, 10–14

21. Because ethnicity was more of a divisive barrier than class in the prairie small town, the oft-used terms of "rough" and "respectable" do not work quite as well.

necessitated automobiles and by the 1950s it was common for young adults, both in town and country, to own or at least have access to cars and trucks. Access to this mode of transportation made the youth mobile and able to locate its own leisured sites.

Prior to World War II, the main street of most prairie towns served as the leisure centre of the community. The advent of motor vehicles allowed farmers to take advantage of the town's services for both shopping and leisure. Rural folk would come to town where they would find cafes, movie theatres, poolrooms, and bars.[22] Main street became a social gathering point, a leisure site in itself, particularly for the male population. In the postwar era, the youth of both town and country would still "loiter" on main street, but they would do so in vehicles rather than on foot. In addition, the leisure pursuits had clearly changed. The small town no longer offered the same array of options. Instead, the youth used the main street more as a meeting point to organize their own activities.

The development of a village such as Borden has, through its history, been seriously influenced by the lure and proximity of the metropolis—"the city"—in this case Saskatoon. The city offered a wide array of leisure options. Saskatoon, however, had always seemed "a very long way" from Borden. The first bridge over the North Saskatchewan River was built in 1937. Prior to this time, residents had to cross the river by ferry, and the journey from Borden to Saskatoon would take several days. Even after the bridge was completed, families would make the trip to Saskatoon only two or three times a year. The winding, bumpy trail to the city changed course several times in these decades, as did the actual distance travelled. Automobiles also travelled at considerably slower speeds. A new highway was built in 1947, making the journey considerably more accessible[23] but the city, even in the period from the late 1960s to the early 1990s, was still too distant for regular leisurely pursuits. As a result, with no place to practice their activities, the youth sought alternatives. They found these alternatives in the few things the rural community could offer—bush and back roads. The search for a place to party came to dominate the weekly routine of leisure. When Friday night rolled around, vehicles would head out in search of that elusive "party spot."

The response of the local authorities to leisure activities has always played an important role in mediating the patterns of social relationships within a community. In the village of Borden, by the 1960s, authority resided in the hands of the Anglo and Ukrainian groups that dominated the village institutions.[24] By literally "going outside" the controlled setting of the church social, community dance, and town fair, the youth ushered a challenge to the authority structure of the village. Unlike previous decades when the village authorities earnestly monitored and maintained control of leisure activities, the challenge met little resistance.

Bush Parties and Booze Cruises met similar acquiescence from legal authorities, despite the fact that a myriad of illegal activities occurred in the process of these events, including underage drinking, drinking and driving, possessing open liquor in a public area, littering, open fires, and trespassing. The attitudes of the local RCMP detachment (based out of Radisson, eight miles up the highway) paralleled those of the village authorities. It seems that both levels of authority accepted the nature of these activities as well as the lack of a place to pursue them and thus offered little resistance. This is not to say, however, that the leisure sites remained completely uncontested. The RCMP remained a constant menace, particularly when it came to the Booze Cruise, but never to the point of seriously curtailing the activities. Bush Parties,

---

22. Donald G. Wetherell and Irene Kmet, *Town Life: Main Street and the Evolution of Small Town Alberta, 1880–1947* (Edmonton: University of Alberta Press, 1995), 221–48.

23. Interview with Archie Wainwright, 15 September 2001.

24. These groups controlled the rural municipality office, the school board, the town council, and the recreation board.

because they did not involve quite the same level of drinking and driving (and therefore the same challenge to the legal authorities), were treated with more tolerance.

It has been argued that leisure involves struggles over social relations and is therefore a highly politicised area.[25] Cultural analyses have been employed to deconstruct and reveal the inner dynamics and relationships of leisured spaces, and to determine the role of ethnicity, class, gender, and sexuality play in mediating the social functions of the participants.

Early in its history, white Anglo-Saxon protestant settlers came to dominate the village, and therefore the community, of Borden. The major businesses as well as the main cultural institutions, such as the Masonic Lodge, Eastern Star, Elks, Lions, and Boy Scouts, represented this hegemonic group. The Ukrainian community to the north was relatively isolated, and clearly marked by its cultural distinctiveness. The larger and even more tightly knit Mennonite community of Great Deer, situated to the east of town, stood garrison in its efforts to remain distinct. The division of the school districts reinforced ethnic separation and as a result community old-timers remember few incidents of ethnic cleavage. They also, however, have few memories of interacting with other ethnic groups or, at times, of these other groups even being present in the community![26] While divisions between the Anglo-Celtic groups and the ethnic "others" have been highlighted in descriptions of small-town prairie life through the work of such authors as Margaret Laurence, W.O. Mitchell, and Sinclair Ross, and undoubtedly did exist in Borden, they apply mainly to the pre-1945 cultural milieu. The ethnic stratification of the rural West has changed markedly since this time.[27]

By the 1960s, traditional ethnic lines no longer marked the same level of community division in Borden. The "Slavic" groups in the form of the Ukrainian, Doukhobor, and Mennonite elements did not suffer economic disadvantage.[28] Class is a difficult structure to apply to the rural, agricultural West. Its distinctive dynamics are more easily identified with the urban milieu of the industrial and postindustrial city.[29] Economic differences in the prairie

---

25. Bailey, *Leisure and Class in Victorian England*, 11.

26. Interview with Archie Wainwright, 15 September 2001.

27. One of the best examples of the shifting nature of divisions in the rural West can be found in discussions of ethnicity. Wetherell observes that "the relationship between the dominant group and the rest of the society has become an increasing concern of historical writing on prairie Canada." Wetherell, *Useful Pleasures*, xvii.

28. Jean Burnet makes this same point in her 1951 study of Hanna, Alberta: "The German-Russians apparently adjusted well to east-central Alberta. The drought and the great depression set in soon after the arrival of many, and during the thirties their ministers had to ask for gifts of clothing for them. Their hardships did not last long, however. By the forties their homes were among the most pleasant and prosperous-looking in the district. The cars they drove were new and expensive. Their neighbours thought them successful..." Burnet, *Next Year Country*, 36; Ted Regehr makes the same comment about the Mennonites: "In the decades following the Second World War Canadian Mennonites became a prosperous people." T.D. Regehr, *Mennonites in Canada, 1939–1970: A People Transformed* (Toronto: University of Toronto Press, 1996), 125.

29. C.B. Macpherson's now dated study is one of the few class analyses of Prairie society. He argued that Alberta possessed a "relatively homogeneous class composition" and that the dominance of independent commodity producers meant that class tensions were mitigated and were directed outwards against external agencies and forces such as the national government. John Richards and Larry Pratt disagree, arguing that class tensions have always existed in Prairie society. C.B. Macpherson, *Democracy in Alberta: Social Credit and the Party System* (Toronto: University of Toronto Press, 1962) 21; John Richards and Larry Pratt, *Prairie Capitalism: Power and Influence in the New West* (Toronto: McClelland and Stewart Ltd., 1979), 150–51. According to Gerald Friesen, the "power of the American dream" of land and upward mobility "was an integral part of the prairie creed" and, as a result, "class identity was correspondingly weak." Friesen offers an explanation as to why class has played such a minor role in literary representations of the prairie West: "in fiction devoted to a study of the individual, and to exploration of earlier images of its own tradition, the issue of social class is not likely to arise." Instead, "ethnic and native identity are more important than class identity in prairie society." Gerald Friesen, "Three Generations of Fiction: An Introduction to Prairie Cultural History," in *The Prairie West: Historical Readings* (Edmonton: The University of Alberta Press, 1985) 658; Friesen, *The Canadian Prairies: A History* (Toronto: University of Toronto Press, 1987), 300.

small-town were apparent from family to family, but these were based more on the early processes of homestead and land selection, the productivity of that land, and the changing fortunes of the agricultural industry as a whole. In fact, much of the best land in the area was, and is, held by the Ukrainian and Mennonite farmers in Borden. The initial Anglo pioneers were primarily from urban England and made the mistake of selecting their homesteads along the banks of the river, which ended up being the most sandy and rocky soil in the region. While these Anglo setters established cultural hegemony, they did not establish the same level of economic dominance.

By the 1960s Borden society was largely homogeneous, and becoming increasingly so. Social distinctions, according to Friesen, were always part of rural communities but "because they changed so rapidly they were not perceived to be permanent barriers to self-improvement or significant indicators of family fortunes."[30] This is not to say they did not exist but rather that they were rapidly and constantly shifting. An analysis of Bush Parties and Booze Cruises, then, reflects this homogeneity. Ethnicity and class did not frame participation. While some scholars point to this homogeneity as evidence of multiculturalism or cultural pluralism, others view it as evidence of Anglo-conformity.[31] According to Wetherell, postwar prairie society reflected the culture of the dominant group: "not an accommodation among many immigrant traditions, not a mosaic, but the values of the Anglo-Canadian and, increasingly, American world."[32]

But Borden had its own very real source of division and this breach became nowhere more apparent than when it came to the leisure activities of the young adult population. The division was framed around traditional ethnic lines but by the 1960s was based more upon religion and morality. It reflected what had become the most serious divide in the overall community—that between the Mennonite and "non-Mennonite" populations. It is dangerous to make generalizations about one Canadian ethnic group, and the level of accommodation and assimilation certainly differed among the diversity of Mennonite communities in rural and urban settings, but as Friesen points out, "the Mennonites were even slower to adapt to British-Canadian ways, but in their case adjustment was delayed by their determination to remain separate from the materialism and godlessness that they associated with the larger prairie society."[33] The leisurely pursuits of the majority of young people in the Borden community certainly represented this "godlessness" to a relatively conservative and isolated Mennonite community.

In the Mennonite community the traditional guardians of public morality still stood vigil. The hegemonic forces of the popular culture revolution were sieging the gate; their images were bombarding every household through the mediums of both print and visual popular culture. But while few Mennonite households went so far as banning radio or television, they could still exert restrictions over morally questionable activities emerging in the new modern age. The influence of the American evangelical movement was very apparent on the

30. Friesen, *The Canadian Prairies*, 319–20.

31. This fact supports John Porter's arguments in *Vertical Mosaic* in which he stresses the forces of modernization in obscuring ethnic distinctions. This position, however, has largely been opposed in the Canadian West. It has been argued that Porter's "overriding concern with stratification, and the need for immigrant groups to forget their ethnic identities in favor of gaining better acceptance in the marketplace, is a more subtle form of anglo-conformity... Porter tended to emphasize the overwhelming influence of technology and urbanization as the master trend which sweeps away all forms of ethnic differentiation before it." Leo Driedger, "Multicultural Regionalism: Toward Understanding the Canadian West," in Rasporich, *Making of the Modern West*, 169–70. Regardless, whether through anglo-conformity or cultural pluralism, the society of the Prairie West had become increasingly homogenous.

32. Wetherell, *Useful Pleasures*, xxii, 373.

33. Gerald Friesen, *The Canadian Prairies*, 267.

Mennonite community and its "brethren" church.[34] The youth was instructed not to drink, dance, smoke, or date individuals outside its own particular community. When young Mennonites graduated from high school, they were directed away from mainstream post-secondary institutions and toward bible schools. Other than sporting activities, the two communities went their own way when it came to leisure. The surrounding rural school districts in the area had all merged with the village of Borden by the early 1960s and children were bussed into town; Great Deer, however, maintained its one-room schoolhouse as late as 1975. The composition of Bush Parties and Booze Cruises in Borden was remarkable in the lack of participation from this significant section of the community.

These leisure activities then, to be successful, had to offer an open atmosphere of participation. The simple lack of people meant that not only were they open to a wide-ranging age demographic from within the community; they were also open to those from neighbouring towns as well. Indeed, outside participation was welcomed and even encouraged. Inter-town divisions and rivalries would inevitably appear, and territorial fights would occasionally break out, but not to the exclusion of outsiders. Partying was used as a means of extending the social network, particularly when it came to expanding the pool of the opposite sex. Likewise, the search for "party spots" often took Borden's young people into these same surrounding communities. While the distance travelled varied from town to town, and each generation would have different relationships with the various neighbouring communities, Borden's range included the towns of Radisson, Maymont, and Hafford to a distance of approximately 16 miles.

A study of leisure in small-town prairie life during the postwar era also reveals considerable transformation in gender roles from the previous generation. The exclusively male domains of the beer parlour, poolroom, and fraternal societies were breached. Sports, and hockey in particular, continued to preserve these stratified roles but most other leisurely pursuits now crossed gender lines.[35] Attitudes of respectability toward drinking, particularly when it came to women, were still evident to a degree but the barriers were gone. Because sex played such a direct role in the events, it was necessary and desirable for females to participate with as much frequency as males. The leisure site remained, however, securely within the masculine "rough" culture.

Bush Parties and Booze Cruises relied heavily on automobiles and because vehicles remained part of the male domain, these activities reinforced traditional gender roles. The social movements of the 1960s and 1970s blurred gender lines but cars and booze remained symbols of male power. "Technological change," Wetherell notes, "especially in transportation, reinforced and even expanded male dominance. Largely operated by men, motor vehicles enhanced male authority, especially as they so quickly became crucial in everyday life.... . As they enabled men to expand their leisure activities…they were integrated with the attendant symbols of male authority."[36] The sexual revolution may have gone a long way in liberating women and allowing them to express their sexuality more openly and aggressivly, but the power relationship remained male-dominated. It certainly, however, succeeded in bringing sex increasingly into leisure. Automobiles, at both the Bush Party and Booze Cruise, became the site for sexual activity.

Bush Parties and Booze Cruises were shaped mainly out of the necessity to find a "place

---

34. Royden K. Loewen, *Family, Church, and Market: A Mennonite Community in the Old and the New Worlds, 1850–1930* (Chicago: University of Illinois Press, 1993), 238.

35. Even in the realm of sports, the change in gender roles is apparent. A good example is the proliferation of co-ed slow pitch leagues.

36. Wetherell, *Useful Pleasures*, 380.

to party" but they did represent more than the material practicalities of space. Both activities became symbols of rural identity and as such were proliferated to mark and proclaim that identity. The Bush Party was heralded as a badge of hardiness. In the small town, rural people were closer to nature and partied under the stars, in the great outdoors. The Booze Cruise, likewise, became a badge of identity. It was inextricably attached to the symbol of power in the rural community—the automobile. It offered the freedom of the rural community. Free from the constraints of the city, people in the small town could party wherever they wished. These meanings attached to Bush Parties and Booze Cruises are obvious constructs built around the reality of a lack of leisure alternatives and facilities in a rural setting. Still, they did represent components of a rural identity.

By the mid-1990s, however, Bush Parties and Booze Cruises were occurring much less frequently, and their era was coming to an end in Borden. The same forces of transportation, communication, and urbanization that had been transforming the world of leisure throughout prairie history continued and indeed, increased in pace. As it had in the past, this shift in leisurely pursuits paralleled the overall transformation of the small town.

Bush Parties and Booze Cruises were part of a rural identity for young people but the fact remains that they took shape primarily out of a lack of alternatives. By the mid-1990s, other leisure options were becoming increasingly available. "The city" that had once seemed "a world away," both in distance and in culture, now seemed much nearer and the village of Borden moved increasingly into the orbit of Saskatoon and the resulting identity as a "bedroom community." Highway #16 was "twinned" past Borden in 1998. As it had in the past, transportation improvements made the lure of the city that much more attractive. Improvements in vehicles also continued apace. Saskatoon was now a mere 25–30 minute drive away. Residents increased the amount of trips they made to the city. They went to school, worked, shopped, and played in Saskatoon. The rural-urban divide had been breached. The dominance of Borden's "old families" diminished in the face of new residents, often retired, moving into the community in search of that small-town atmosphere but still desiring the near proximity to the city. The impact on Borden's remaining services was predictable: local stores were used only when convenient; the hospital was transformed into a local health clinic; the rink fell into disrepair as hockey and skating lost out to the myriad of new options; debate rages on about the sustainability of the school; only one elevator now overlooks the town, and it is privately owned.

The communication revolution has further fractured the sense of community and that distinctive small-town identity. In an age of globalization, this is inevitable. By the early 1990s Borden gained access to cable television. Residents became as attuned to news items in Detroit as they were to events in their own community. By 1999 the community was able to access the internet. Not surprisingly, the youth embraced the new and vast array of leisure options. With so many alternatives, young people are now rarely involved in the same activities with each other. Occasionally, a Bush Party or Booze Cruise takes place, but it is more of a novelty than a regular event.

The Bush Party and the Booze Cruise reflect the perhaps bizarre practices of leisure in a prairie small town from 1960 until the mid-1990s. They do, however, offer a window into the changes occurring within a community. According to Wetherell,

> leisure activity is not isolated or discrete; it is integral to daily life and responsive to social, economic and technological factors. This suggests that its operation in a society is not mechanistic or predetermined, but is in a continual process of change and modification in response to individual, economic and social needs and conditions.[37]

---

37. Ibid., 3.

Within these events, we can discern transformations in rural identity; we can see a rural community responding to the increasing importance placed on leisure, and in particular, mass popular culture; ultimately, we can recognize the continuing decline of the prairie small-town community in the face of changes in transportation, communication, and urbanization in the postindustrial world.

CHAPTER SEVEN

Including Immigration in the Rural First Aid Kit

Manju Varma

From an international perspective, Canada is viewed as a multicultural country. This reputation is equally purported by our own national imaginations; it is what makes us feel unique.[1] This need to express our multicultural characteristic has been so intense that it is legislated in the 1971 policy, *Multiculturalism Within a Bilingual Framework*, a document that recognizes "pluralism as fundamental to Canadian identity, indeed, as the very essence of Canadian identity."[2] While this image is often presented as representative of the entire Canadian landscape, closer inspection reveals a variety of demographic realities and speaks to a more complex presentation of pluralism.

One such reality represents the popular pluralistic perception of our country, the diverse cities that bring images of Toronto, Montreal and Vancouver to mind. Along with becoming immigrant destinations, these urban areas are home to large ethnocultural communities consisting of both foreign and Canadian-born members. However, as Cynthia Baker notes, "Most large ethnocultural communities are found in relatively few metropolitan centers. In Canada, they are established in one or two cities of five provinces: Quebec, Ontario, Manitoba, Alberta and British Columbia."[3] For the moment, highly diverse urban areas dot, rather than cover, the Canadian map. Another demographic reality portrays locations where particular ethnic or cultural groups represent the majority population in a community but still experience minority power status in general Canadian society. These include the mainly rural indigenous Black settlements and First Nation reserves as well as the isolated vast land areas situated in Northern Canada. Like the large diverse urban locations, these communities also do not represent the common Canadian experience.

The prevalent demographic reality within the Canadian multicultural context is, ironically, the predominately White location. Such locations generally experience a low level of immigration and consist of a majority population that is mainly White, English and Christian with a few ethnocultural groups that are small in population. These communities are more apt to associate multiculturalism with part of a national, rather than local, identity. Despite their strong presence, predominately White locations have yet to manifest themselves in the

---

1. This sense of uniqueness often translates to: it is what makes us different from the United States.
2. Helen Harper, "Difference and Diversity in Ontario Schooling," *Canadian Journal of Education* 22, no. 2 (1997): 192–206.
3. Cynthia Baker, Anne Marie Aresenault and G. Gallant, "Resettlement Without the Support of an Ethnocultural Community," *Journal of Advanced Nursing* 20, no. 6 (1994): 1064–72.

multicultural research agenda. Like the general public, multicultural research appears to follow the assumption that multicultural issues are only important in areas with a high number of visible minorities.

This chapter hopes to challenge this supposition by looking at the relationship between ethnic diversity and rural areas. More specifically, the focus is on the issue of immigration and its potential as a viable solution to the increasing disappearance of rural areas. Throughout Canada, predictions warn of future population shortages; however such human resources deficits are already acute in rural areas. Immigration has been identified as one possible solution to the problem[4] but little is understood about how to both attract and retain immigrants in rural areas. There is also the dilemma of maintaining the current diversity in the region. Due to reasons outlined later in this chapter, visible minorities are leaving for other parts of Canada and there is no evidence of the opposite flow.[5] Putting effective strategies in place to counter these challenges is necessary to attract and maintain members of various ethnocultural groups. Changing these ideas to the state of actual strategies involves accumulating data regarding the development of diverse population in rural areas. Such a population would not only help curtail the number of disappearing rural communities but also offer different resources that would help such communities prosper and grow. In this chapter, issues around immigration are extracted out of their familiar visibly diverse venues and onto "a road less taken" for an examination of the challenges and strategies of developing visible diverse populations in rural locations. The setting is the mainly rural and White region of Atlantic Canada but the points made in this chapter are relevant to rural areas across the country.

"What's in a Name?"

In mapping out a discussion on immigration, one is quickly confronted with a landscape of definitions. Some of these terms are straightforward; others are not. For example, the words immigrant and diversity are far from singular in their meaning. Rather their shifting terminology is dependant upon time and place. The next section identifies particular vocabulary terms that hold prominence in this chapter.

Immigrant: The term immigration is an example of the imprecision of definitions. Defined literally, the word immigrant is "someone who leaves one country and settles in another" (Webster's, 1986:89). With such a denotation, time is not of the essence. Such an interpretation therefore implies that immigrant may be a permanent status; an individual arrives as an immigrant and remains the immigrant.

The term is also constructed by the power of memory. Different groups populating Canada for approximately the same amount of time can perceive their immigrant identities differently. For some immigrant groups, the collective memory of their ethnic home is so strong that it overshadows their affiliation with the Canadian identity. There are various reasons for this circumstance. One reason is the clash of values. When an immigrant group experiences a tension between their cultural values and the perceived mainstream Canadian values, the desire to protect their values can result in a reconnection with the immigrant identity. This association is formed by the immigrant group encouraging a remembrance of their valued customs; a process that insists upon maintaining the immigrant identity at the forefront. Ironically, the memory is often a fossil of selective qualities in that the immigrant

---

4. For example, the government of New Brunswick recently developed a statement of understanding with the Department of Citizenship and Immigration Canada to bring in higher number of immigrants to the province. For more information see http://www.gnb.ca/immigration

5. Statistics Canada. Information downloaded April 9, 2003: http://www.statcan.ca/Daily/English/030326/d030326c.htm

groups remember only the positive attributes of their ethnic home identity. When faced with the challenges of settling an unfamiliar world, it is easy to appreciate memory.

Affiliation with an immigrant identity is also encouraged by old country animosities. Immigrant groups from countries divided by ethnic or religious hatreds may retain their feelings in Canada; again this preservation of position insists upon a relationship with one's immigrant identity.

In various scenarios, immigrant groups are apt to maintain their sense of immigration despite possible multigenerational residence in Canada, especially when the identity suggests the preservation of values and customs. Legally, individuals in certain ethnocultural groups may be Canadian citizens but in their hearts, their identity lies elsewhere—with that called the immigrant.

In an opposite scenario, the memory of immigration is imposed upon a group by the beliefs and actions of general society. Even when particular ethnic groups wish to become part of the regular fabric of society, their objectives may be truncated by both overt and covert discriminatory behaviour. Such social attitudes range from explicit racist attacks against particular ethnic groups to more subversive beliefs undermining pluralism as a whole. In these examples, immigrant groups are forced to face their immigrant identity regardless of their history and tenure in this country.[6]

Finally, immigrant is a research and data-gathering term. For example, Statistics Canada's use of immigrant refers to those who self-identify themselves as non-British, non-French, and non-Aboriginal. Considering the differing perceptions of ethnocultural groups, one can see how easily the data obtained through this definition can become distorted.

Diversity: The term diversity is also multifaceted. In the purest sense, diversity applies to any type of variety within a given entity. In Atlantic Canada, two types of diversity emerge as significant. These are language and colour and are both mainly associated with non-immigrant groups. Within these two categories lay a body of other classifications including socio-economics, geography, demographics, religion, gender, sexuality, and culture. Notions of diversity become even more complex when one category is intersected with another, for example, the examination of socio-economic issues in the context of rural vs. urban geographic locations. Therefore, the type of diversity that is addressed in this chapter has to be carefully explained. In the context of this chapter, the region of Atlantic Canada is defined as a location with little *apparent visible* diversity. Most of the discussion surrounding diversity will look at the realities of visible minority groups.

Minority: In this chapter, the term "minority" refers to two different groups: visible and invisible minorities. According to the 1986 *Employment Equity Act,* "visible minorities are persons (other than Aboriginal persons) who are non-Caucasian in race or non-white in colour."[7] Invisible minorities are persons who, although white-skinned, hold a religion, language, and/or culture distinct from mainstream society. For the sake of clarity, unless otherwise specified, use of the word "minority" refers to both groups. Generally, the term identifies individuals and groups regularly marginalized in society because of race, ethnicity, and/or religion.[8]

Aboriginal: Again, I referred to Statistics Canada who define Aboriginal as "those persons

---

6. The current racial profiling occurring at the American/Canadian border is a vivid example of Canadians with certain immigrant roots being forced to adopt an immigrant reality.

7. Treasury Board of Canada. Information downloaded August 8, 2000: http://www.tbs-sct.gc.ca/ee/about-sujet/overview-apercu_e.asp#act

8. R. Berlak, "Teaching and Testimony: Witnessing and Bearing Witness to Racisms in Culturally Diverse Classrooms," *Curriculum Inquiry* 29, no. 1 (1999): 99–127.

who reported identifying with at least one Aboriginal group, i.e., North American Indian, Métis, or Inuit (Eskimo) and/or who reported they were a Treaty Indian or a Registered Indian as defined by the Indian Act of Canada and/or who reported they were members of an Indian Band or First Nation."[9]

White: Atlantic Canada is a predominately White setting. The term "White" has the potential to be problematic, as the possession of white skin can become a point of contention between different racial groups. People of colour often claim that the white skin of invisible minorities, such as the Jewish or French-speaking populations, provides them with the ability to "pass" in mainstream society and thus escape the constant burden of racism.[10] In this chapter, White is defined as persons of Anglo-Saxon decent who are part of the dominant group of society.[11] This group holds the majority of power and enjoys an advantageous role in society's decision-making process.[12] White not only describes a skin colour, but also how institutions are arranged, which values are protected,[13] what knowledge is deemed correct,[14] and what privileges are conferred upon whom.[15]

Minority Voices

In order to lay out the challenges of developing a visible diverse population in Atlantic Canada, a review of the current demographics must be supplied. The next section of this chapter will provide a brief description of the three major minority groups currently living in the area as well as a look at the collective body of visible minorities outside of the three populations. The three major minority groups living in the region are the Acadians, indigenous Blacks, and Aboriginals. Each group has a distinct history and present reality. However, collectively, they provide insight into the treatment of diversity in Atlantic Canada.

The Black Community: Blacks, of different origins, have lived in Canada for nearly 400 years.[16] Their arrival into the Atlantic Canada speaks to different experiences. Many arrived as slaves brought in through port cities such as Halifax, Nova Scotia, while others made their way to the eastern part of the country after escaping to Canada via the Underground Railroad. Blacks also arrived as immigrants, indentured servants, and settlers from other parts of the country. Acadian farms that had been left vacant after the Expulsion were offered to both Black and White settlers. Similarly, Black Loyalists were promised land in New Brunswick cities such as Saint John and Fredericton. However, in the majority of cases, fertile land was awarded to White farmers while smaller less profitable packages were given to Black citizens.[17]

The province of Nova Scotia was the first area to house relatively large Black communities, the most memorable of which was Africville, a settlement in north Halifax.[18] The

---

9. Treasury Board of Canada. Information downloaded April 9, 2003: http://www.tbs-sct.gc.ca/ee/about-sujet/overview-apercu_e.asp#act

10. C. Harris, "Whiteness as Property," *Harvard Law Review* 106, no. 8 (1993): 1707–91.

11. Christine Sleeter, "Teaching Whites about Racism." In R. Martin (ed.), *Practicing What We Teach: Confronting Diversity in Teacher Education* (Albany: SUNY Press, 1995).

12. George J.S. Dei, "Introduction: Anti-racist Education," *Orbit* 25, no. 2 (1994): 1–3.

13. Berlak, "Teaching and Testimony."

14. Dei, "Introduction," 1–3.

15. Peggy McIntosh, "White Privilege: Unpacking the Invisible Knapsack," *Independent School* (Winter 1990): 31–36.

16. Donna Spalding, "The Invisible Minorities: Employment Equity Research Project, Saint John, New Brunswick" (unpublished paper prepared for Pride, Race, Understanding, Dignity Through Education, New Brunswick).

17. Ibid.

18. Lawrence Hill, *Trials and Triumphs: The Story of the African-Canadians* (Toronto: Umbrella Press, 1993).

community began with 54 residents in 1851 but grew to over 400 a century later.[19] By 1960, citizens owned land, ran businesses, held jobs, and achieved success. For example, George Dixon, the first Black boxer to win a world championship, grew up in Africville.[20] Despite the fact that community members paid government taxes, living conditions were extremely poor. Although Africville existed within Halifax city limits, the city refused to provide adequate basic services such as sewage and electricity; residents sometimes had to use old car batteries to keep their homes warm.[21] To add insult to injury, the city located a garbage dump on the outskirts of Africville yet refused to provide the community with garbage service. The community existed for nearly 100 years before it was destroyed. In an act of extreme irony, the Halifax city council decided that the lack of services made the community unfit to live in and demanded its closure. Garbage trucks were sent to collect the people and their property while homes, churches and schools were bulldozed down.[22] Deaf to the community's protest, the city relocated Black citizens to public housing in Halifax where members then faced, and continue to face, high levels of unemployment and underachievement.

Although Blacks in Nova Scotia have experienced centuries of racism, two major events in 1991 brought national attention to the Black community. The first occurred at the high school in Cole Harbour, a small community outside of Halifax. A fight between a Black and a White student led to RCMP charges against 18 youths, 10 of whom were Black.[23] The Black community protested, claiming that the conflict and its results were indicative of larger racial problems in Nova Scotia.[24]

In the same year, Black youths were refused entrance into a downtown Halifax bar. A fight ensued and a Black youth was stabbed. This event precipitated a protest march in which over a thousand people participated. In July 1991, the three levels of government agreed to meet with Black community members and form an advisory group to combat racism in Nova Scotia.[25] Although positive action has come out of both events, they continue to be points of reference for Nova Scotian Blacks' discussions on the continual existence of racism.

Two notable indigenous Black communities exist in New Brunswick, the larger one in Saint John, the other in Fredericton. Collectively, there are approximately three thousand Blacks living in New Brunswick.[26] As it is in Nova Scotia, the legacy of racism for Blacks living in New Brunswick is obvious. While New Brunswick's unemployment rate in 1991 was 12.2%, the unemployment rate for Black citizens was a staggering 25.7%.[27] Research on racism in New Brunswick found that Black youth suffered from extreme racism to the point that many felt fearful of society.[28] Essentially, racism for Blacks is a problem regardless of what part of Atlantic Canada they call home. In Canada, in general, the largest minority group in prisons is Aboriginal people. In Atlantic Canada, the largest incarcerated minority is African Canadian. The number of African Canadians imprisoned increased 62.5% between 1992 and

---

19. Ibid.

20. George Boyd, *Shine Boy* (play, 1989).

21. Ibid.

22. Hill, *Trials and Triumphs*.

23. Frances Henry et al., *The Colour of Democracy: Racism in Canadian Society* (Toronto: Harcourt Brace, 2000).

24. Agnes Calliste, "Anti-racist Educational Initiatives in Nova Scotia," *Orbit* 25, no. 2 (1994): 48–49.

25. Henry et al., *Colour of Democracy*.

26. Spalding, *Invisible Minorities*.

27. Ibid.

28. Cynthia Baker, Manju Varma and Connie Tanaka, "Sticks and Stones: Racism as Experienced by Adolescents in New Brunswick," *Canadian Journal of Nursing Research* 33, no. 3 (2001): 87–106.

1997.[29] Hope for an improvement in this situation is faint as Black communities around the Atlantic Canada continue to experience extreme poverty, unemployment, and high dropout rates.[30]

The Mi'kmaq and Maliseet: The majority of the Aboriginal population living in Atlantic Canada are either Mi'kmaq or Maliseet. There are 38 Indian reserves in the Atlantic region of Canada with a total of 38,000 people.[31] Over half of the reserves are in states of high poverty and social distress.[32] Unlike other minority groups, the majority of Aboriginal people in Atlantic Canada do not live in close contact with the rest of the population, residing instead on reserves. Consequently, the possibility of a non-Aboriginal never encountering an Aboriginal person is high. This lack of contact allows stereotypes and racism to flourish. Even when contact does occur, deeply entrenched stereotypes regarding Aboriginal populations often result in interactions that are tense and potentially violent.[33]

A vivid example of the volatile nature of this relationship is the aftermath of the decision from *Regina v. Marshall*, 1999, in which the Supreme Court of Canada recognized treaties guaranteeing Aboriginal populations' fishing rights. Celebrations among the Aboriginal communities were eclipsed by an instant backlash of anger and hate from the non-Aboriginal population. Reaction against the *Regina v. Marshall* case was especially violent in the rural areas of Atlantic Canada in communities populated by a large percentage of non-Aboriginal fishermen. In recent years, fishermen throughout the region have had to deal with dwindling fish stocks and a capricious economy. However, these conditions are more than a threat to industry. For many fishermen, fishing is part of a long family tradition seeped in folklore, conventions, and proverbial knowledge. Thus the seemingly preferential treatment given to the Aboriginal fishers was perceived by non-Aboriginal fishers as not only a threat to their livelihood but to their personal identity as well.

In an unpublished document prepared for the Department of Canadian Heritage's Atlantic Region Aboriginal Think-Tank, the action following the Supreme Court decision was described as a threat to Canadian social cohesion:

> The latest reaction to the Supreme Court of Canada's Marshall Decision, at its worst, took the form of racism, hate and violence against Aboriginal people and destruction of their property. At best, it was a wake-up call for long overdue action on the concerns of Aboriginal people. Social cohesion was undermined and indications are strong that continuing threats to social cohesion exist as additional confrontations and civil disobedience are forecast for the coming spring of 2000.[34]

Unfortunately, the prediction of future violence proved accurate. After months of deliberations between First Nations reserves and the Department of Fisheries and Oceans, several reserves and their neighbouring communities vacillated between tension and social disintegration.

Tensions between Aboriginal and non-Aboriginal populations hold even greater social

29. R. Safire, "The Cole Harbour Project: Progress and Evaluation Report" (unpublished report for CSC Halifax District, 1998).

30. Henry et al., *Colour of Democracy.*

31. Statistics Canada. Information downloaded April 9, 2003: http://www.statcan.ca/Daily/English/030326/d030326c.htm

32. Government of Canada, Department of Canadian Heritage, "Federal/Provincial Capacity in Aboriginal Issues" (unpublished Atlantic Region Background Paper, 1999).

33. Baker, Varma and Tanaka, "Sticks and Stones."

34. Government of Canada, Department of Canadian Heritage, "Atlantic Region Aboriginal Think-Tank" (unpublished report, 2000).

ramifications when examined in the context of Canada's changing demographics. Although the mainstream population across Canada is exhibiting a declining birth rate, the Aboriginal birth rate is nearly three times greater than the non-Aboriginal population. Furthermore, the majority of the Aboriginal population is quite young with over one-third younger than 15 and over half younger than 25.[35] As the rest of Canadians experience an aging population, the Aboriginal population is just reaching its prime. In Atlantic Canada, discrepancies between the Aboriginal and non-Aboriginal population impact the future workforce. As members of other populations leave, or age, the population bank from which they will have to be replaced will become increasingly Aboriginal in population. Consequently, a decision must be made: will we have a young Aboriginal population that is welcomed in joining the workforce or will racism continue to rob society of its valuable human resource? Choosing the former will require an extensive battle against racism as well as educational policies designed to make schooling a more successful endeavor for Aboriginal students.[36]

The Acadians: While not a visible minority group, a discussion on minorities in Atlantic Canada would not be complete without attention given to the Acadians. The Acadians represent a majority of the French-speaking population living in Atlantic Canada and are the largest minority group in the region.[37] Their presence in Atlantic Canada can be traced back to the early 1600s and represents one of the earliest communities in what would later become Canada.[38] One of the most significant episodes in Acadian history is the Expulsion of 1755 in which, after refusing to swear allegiance to the British government, Acadians were forced to leave their homes and disperse across the globe. In 1763, the Acadians were allowed to return to the area but only on certain conditions. Among these conditions was the restrictive choice of venue, much of it consisting of poor quality land. This constraint forced the concentration of the Acadian population within the rural areas of Atlantic Canada.[39] Although not all Acadian families were involved in the Expulsion, this significant historical occurrence has become a unifying story among the group, tying them together in a collective experience of disempowerment.

Even after the Acadian people returned they continued to experience discrimination on both a personal and institutional basis. For example French secondary schools were often not available in rural areas, forcing parents to either school their children in English or send them away to French schools in larger cities.[40] Even today, many Acadian parents continue to fight for the availability of French schools in their area.

Despite historic racism, the Acadian population has empowered itself in ways not dreamed possible two decades ago. Various members of the population have helped initiate economic and cultural growth throughout Atlantic Canada. Success, however, has not come without a price. The achievements of the Acadian population have produced a backlash of resentment from some members of the English and immigrant population. An example of this is the various sounds of discontent and resentment that filtered through the city of Moncton, New Brunswick as it prepared to host The Francophone Summit. Letters based on misinformation, intolerance, and fear littered the "Letters to the Editor" section of the local papers.

---

35. James Frideres, *Aboriginal Peoples in Canada: Contemporary Conflicts* (Scarborough: Prentice-Hall, 1998).

36. Baker, Varma and Tanaka, "Sticks and Stones."

37. Maurice Basque, Nicole Barrieau and Stephanie Cote, *L'Acadie de l'Atlantique* (Moncton: Université de Moncton Press, 1999).

38. Ibid.

39. Ibid.

40. Paul Axelrod, *The Promise of Schooling: Education in Canada, 1800–1914* (Toronto: University of Toronto Press, 1997).

The letters became so overwhelming that *The Times and Transcript*, Moncton's local paper, published its own letter publicly denouncing positions of intolerance. While the paper explained that various viewpoints regarding the summit would be explored,

> there is one news angle leading into this summit we won't be pursuing. As the summit draws closer, the number of faxes and calls coming into the news desk have increased from people attempting to hide their bigotry behind calls to save what they perceive as Canada's endangered English culture. The tone of a majority of these messages, mostly all anonymous, is the same—why is New Brunswick's largest-circulated English daily newspaper being so anti-English, and so pro-French, by covering the various pre-summit events which have been staged thus far. Our coverage plans have nothing to do with language. If this was a world summit of Spanish-speaking countries, or an international gathering of the clans, our approach to news coverage would be the same.

> *The Times & Transcript* is not going to be drawn into any fear-mongering campaigns involving groups or individuals who are "planning" to do something to disrupt this conference for whatever political or personal motivations they may have. When a group which has nothing but hate as a motive begins making noise about what it might or might not do, it only serves to justify their cause to publish news stories carrying their message.... That's not news gathering; that's providing a platform to those who want to use the media to perpetuate a narrow-minded cause.[41]

Despite letters of support from a variety of sources and a resulting financial windfall for the local communities, the summit closed with the same voices of discontent with which it opened. The experience is symptomatic of a greater problem where the productive contributions of the Acadian culture, language and knowledge continue to be unacknowledged by society. The Acadian experiences of integration, assimilation, and racism carry lessons that cannot be ignored by those attempting to fully understand the intricacies of immigration and integration as well as the influence that this can have on social cohesion and development. Comprehending their struggles and achievement can help develop a rubric to apply for the success of other minority groups.

Visible Minorities and Immigrants: One of the most significant characteristics of the Atlantic Canada setting is its lack of visible ethnic diversity. While the three above-noted groups exist in significant numbers, they still represent a small percentage of the regional population. Numbers regarding immigration are even smaller and the number of non-White immigrants is tiny in comparison to the rest of the population. Compared to the rest of Canada, these four provinces currently have and annually receive the lowest number of immigrants. Among the various ethnocultural communities existing in Atlantic Canada, groups consisting of recent visible and invisible minority group immigrants are small.[42] On the whole, recent immigrants represent between 3–4% of the entire Atlantic Canada population. Of this percentage, approximately 80% are of European descent.[43] Immigrants joining the visible minority community make up less than 1% of the entire population.[44] The reality of the scarcity of these groups is underlined in Table 1. As can be seen from Table 1, much of

---

41. Murray, Guy, "Summit Coverage Won't Be a Platform for Hate," *The Moncton Times and Transcript*, 23 August 1999, A2.

42. Statistics Canada. . Information downloaded April 9, 2003: http://www.statcan.ca/Daily/English/030326/d030326c.htm

43. L. Dyer, "Change is Our New Constant" (paper presented at the World of Difference Conference, April, Fredericton, New Brunswick).

44. Statistics Canada. Information downloaded April 9, 2003: http://www.statcan.ca/Daily/English/030326/d030326c.htm

| | Total | | Non-White | Visible | |
Province	Population	Immigrants	Immigrants	Minorities	Aboriginal
Newfoundland and Labrador	547,155	8,940	2,925	3,815	14,205
Nova Scotia	899,970	41,960	14,735	31,320	12,380
New Brunswick	738,133	24,385	5,470	7,995	10,250
Prince Edward Island	132,855	4,395	1,110	1,525	950

Table 1. Immigrant and Other Populations in Atlantic Canada

Atlantic Canada's general public does not face immigration or apparent diversity on a daily basis. This means that although Canada declares itself a multicultural country, those working in the area of immigration in the eastern part of Canada face the challenge of preparing the mainly Anglo-Saxon population to live and work within a diversity that most have yet to witness.

Part of the challenge lies in the fact that, in the majority of cases, the amount of attention given to immigrant issues has been largely based on demographics. In other words, areas with a high concentration of immigrants have been the recipients of most of the immigration research. While such areas certainly do have a pressing need to ascertain an understanding of the issues, other areas low in immigrant numbers, such as Atlantic Canada, have been left out of the equation. A lack of research leads to a lack of understanding. Consequently, many immigrants either become even more alienated or leave the region for a location with a better support system. Either result is detrimental to the Atlantic region and eventually to Canada as a whole.

Each of above-mentioned groups' histories and realities contribute to a blueprint of understanding upon the diversity in Atlantic Canada. The barriers encountered by each of these groups can help calculate some of the obstacles that newly arrived visible minorities may face. These hindrances include overt and covert racism, limited job opportunities, culturally insensitive school curricula, cultural clashes and a lack of understanding by the mainstream population. Recognizing how such barriers affect the lives of existing ethnocultural communities can help those working in the areas of immigration and multiculturalism to challenge and eventually dissolve such barriers.

Issues for Consideration

As in the rest of Canada, the experiences of immigrants arriving on the Atlantic coast vary both among and within ethnic groups. These variations are dependent upon different characteristics such as country of origin, skin colour, age, gender, and group perception. The demographic character of the Atlantic region poses a number of challenges for immigration, visible minorities, and diversity and suggests a number of important matters to consider.

First, one sentiment that is shared by most newly arrived immigrants is the challenge of integrating into an immigrant-scarce location. This is especially true of immigrants who are either visible minorities or not proficient in one of the official languages. Baker's study of twenty recent immigrants arriving in Moncton, New Brunswick, indicated the stress of settlement without the support of one's own ethnocultural group.[45] Many of the immigrants existed within walls of isolation that had the potential to lead to severe psychological problems.

---

45. Baker, Arsenault, and Gallant, "Resettlement."

Furthermore, problems of integration seem to span the spectrum from a sense of social disconnection to clashes within the group. Baker notes that "with little to tie them [new immigrants] into the social fabric of their new society, they lacked adequate social support which has been identified as a contributory factor in precipitating a crisis."[46] These problems often go unnoticed for, as Baker argues, "The very fact of being culturally isolated, however, tends to reduce the visibility of immigrants who lack the support of an ethnocultural community."[47]

The experiences encountered by new immigrants are problematic for Atlantic Canada as a whole. Larger ethnocultural communities existing in other provinces and the United States have created a one-way retreat out of the area. Not only has this departure aggravated an existing declining population problem but also the variances in potential and human resources are curtailed when specific populations withdraw from a specific region.[48] This outward flow of human resource and potential not only limits growth of multiculturalism within the area but also deters new immigrants from entering an area that other immigrants appear to be leaving. The experience of immigration can be fraught with stressful situations. Attempts to mitigate anxieties often include settling in areas where one's own ethnocultural group has experienced economic and cultural success. This burden of proof creates a specific challenge for rural areas as these communities must demonstrate group success with much smaller populations.

Ironically, even when an ethnocultural group enjoys a high level of success, the ramifications can be unsettling. In the face of various obstacles, some groups have managed to become active members of their community, enjoy educational and economic success and balance two cultures. On the surface their success may appear to propel these groups into positions of power. This assumption, however, is problematic. While it is true that some groups enjoy educational and economic success, their general alienation from society as a whole still disempowers the group. In many cases, prosperous immigrants have encountered resentment from the mainstream population who perceive immigrant success as opportunities stolen from non-immigrants. These feelings intensify during trying economic times, a situation with important implications in Atlantic Canada.

The reasons for prosperity are varied; particular characteristics for success may be specific to certain groups or may be present in all of the flourishing ethnocultural communities. The lack of knowledge in this area requires research attention. This requires research on such things such as best practices, success stories, and group integration. Understanding what factors create a positive and successful environment for ethnocultural groups will not only aid new immigrants but may also help struggling groups. Both scenarios are advantageous for society in general.

Next, cultural supports such as ethnic grocery stores, religious centres, and entertainment venues found in larger cities are frequently absent in smaller areas. The lack of such supports force residents to either do without basic needs, such as their indigenous food staples, or take long and expensive trips to larger cities to acquire such goods. While the dearth of items as particular foods or entertainment may appear to be a small price to pay for a safe and productive lifestyle, many of the missing supports speak to deep traditions which help construct

---

46. Ibid., 1,070.

47. Ibid., 1,065.

48. The McCain company is one such example. Unable to fill positions from a local New Brunswick rural community, the company began to hire both Mexican and European workers. The company also quickly realized that a lack of positive settlement experiences for their new workers could have drastic negative effects on their company and the community it largely employed.

an individual and group's sense of personal, cultural and historical self. For example, the absence of a place of worship and the resulting inability to fully celebrate one's religious beliefs can profoundly impact an immigrant's settlement success in a new home. Furthermore, in larger cities locations such as religious and entertainment venues act as a haven for new immigrants providing them with a place to engage in social networking. In Atlantic Canada, where these settings are few, new immigrants face a greater challenge of identifying a social network and therefore run a greater chance of social disconnection, unsatisfactory settlement and eventual departure to a larger location.

Thirdly, immigrant groups must deal with the destructive results of generation gaps. Although every group, whether new or familiar to its surroundings, experiences generation gaps where the youth feel distanced from the older members of the community, this situation is exacerbated for minorities in low-immigration areas such as Atlantic Canada. Again this is mainly because of the size of ethnocultural groups. In more diverse cities, the larger ethnocultural groups act as a collective memory, preserving critical attributes of a culture, such as religious tradition and language. Although erosion of tradition occurs in all cultures, larger groups have the advantage of providing a greater picture of their culture. The existence of cultural supports such as language, religious cites, and entertainment can help maintain in the youth a sense of their own culture. The lack of such resources in areas such as Atlantic Canada not only leaves immigrant youth feeling distant from their non-immigrant peers, but also estranged from their parents and others who make claim to a culture that the youth have yet to enjoy in its fullness. Local research has recorded the antagonism and hatred that many minority youth have had to endure while growing up in Eastern Canada.[49] A disenfranchised youth population, regardless of how big or small it is, is not conducive to a healthy society. Attention to immigrant youth issues is essential if we are to foster youth willing to contribute to the betterment of society.

Of particular importance to the generation gap is the issue of language retention. Language transfer from one generation to the next needs to have particular supports in order to be successful. Such supports include formalised training such as schooling and heritage language classes to those more informal in nature such as the availability of media and music entertainment in the native tongue.[50] These supports are either scarce or non-existent in Atlantic Canada. Immigrants choosing to locate in Atlantic Canada either must take on the responsibility of language transfer themselves or witness the loss of a major component of their culture. Since the primary goal of most immigrants is to integrate themselves as soon as possible, many place their energies towards ensuring that they and their children learn at least one of the official languages; often this occurs at the sacrifice of their mother tongue.

Compounding the challenge of integration is the problem of disempowerment. Since immigrants in Atlantic Canada exist in such small numbers, they often experience very little decision-making power in the most influential social institutions. Such institutions include the government and the justice, health and education systems. A lack of English skills and small social networks only exacerbates an immigrant's sense of powerlessness. All of this increases the sense of alienation experienced by many immigrants. This exclusion makes bringing immigrant concerns to the forefront highly difficult and does not impress on professionals the need for culturally appropriate knowledge to deal with their clientele. For example, New Brunswick educators and researchers Cynthia Baker and Rosemary Clews have

49. Baker, Varma and Tanaka, "Sticks and Stones"; Spalding, *Invisible Minorities*.
50. James Cummins and Marcel Danesi, *Heritage Languages: The Development and Denial of Canada's Linguistic Resources* (Toronto: Garamond Press, 1990).

both underlined the lack of cross-cultural awareness in their respective fields of nursing and social work.

Feelings of alienation and incapability added to the sense of cultural deterioration have been shown to have detrimental effects on the overall being of the immigrant. The possibility of immigrants suffering from health problems appears to increase when the ethnocultural communities are small. For example, Murphy[51] found that hospitalisation rates for mental illness among immigrants to Canada increased as the size of their local cultural group decreased. Making a similar argument, Beiser[52] noted an increase of emotional disorders among Vancouver-settled immigrants whose corresponding ethnocultural groups were small or absent. Researchers went on to suggest that if immigrants' disempowerment and alienation issues were not resolved in a short period after arrival, long-term health problems often ensued. Immigrants living in the many small ethnocultural groups in Atlantic Canada are in a vulnerable position of personal danger. This situation is of economic concern for the entire region in general for, as Baker notes, immigrants suffering from health problems brought on by alienation often fail to contribute to the region's wealth due to the inability to work and may also tax the health care system with long-term use.

Geography

The final consideration reviewed in this chapter is geography. A large proportion of Atlantic Canada is rural in setting. Ethnocultural groups, which are small in number in such cities as Halifax, Charlottetown and Moncton, are tiny, if present at all, in many of the rural areas. Also, because the eastern part of Canada covers a vast amount of physical space, it is difficult for immigrants to make contact with groups outside of their immediate location. The large spaces of separation can also lead immigrants to situate themselves in specific, usually urban, venues. As a result, a few locations benefit from immigrant arrival while others do not.

Ironically, several rural areas in Atlantic Canada are more pluralistic than urban centres. In some cases, rural locations neighbour First Nations reservations thus creating the presence of a visible minority group. In other cases, even small and scattered minority groups can become visible. Because the populations of rural areas are so low, a small numbers of immigrants can increase the percentage of visible diversity so that it exceeds what exists in the larger cities. These areas are thus rich in information in the potential for diversity in small locations.

Understanding Theory and Practice

While the body of research dedicated to immigration issues is growing, very little attention has been given to predominately White and rural locations such as those existing in Atlantic Canada. However, an issue that is receiving attention is the threat to the existence of rural locations. This chapter contends that attention to the theory regarding the former issue could help develop practices to impede the latter problem. In other words, immigration is a viable strategy for supporting the survival and growth of rural areas. Understanding immigration and diversity in a rural context is essential if rural areas, such as those that exist in Atlantic Canada, are to attract, maintain, and disperse immigrants throughout the area. Data highlighting these issues would focus on understanding immigrant integration into rural settings as well as how host populations adjust to growing visible diversity. The lack of research makes it difficult to pinpoint exact areas of concern, which consequently often results in a

---

51. Cited in Baker, Arsenault and Gallant, "Resettlement."
52. Ibid.

deficit of resources given to explore the situation. Also lacking are the human resources to work on the issue of immigration. The number of people able to be employed with the limited funds remains small and multicultural associations are disempowered through the combination of small local expertise as well as a lack of funding for the immigration question. The lack of large ethnocultural groups makes it difficult to locate people who could provide authentic understanding of the issues acquired through the personal immigration experience. When the lack of research and funding is partnered with a lack of the human expertise, a dangerous chasm of understanding can develop which leaves the area unprepared to deal with potential immigration conflicts.

Research on immigration to rural areas must focus on two questions: 1) how to engage the current population in a dialogue on diversity and immigration, and 2) how to attract new immigrants and promote the retention of all diversity. Fortunately, many of the tactics to ensure one also help to procure the other. The challenge lies in identifying venues and partnerships that can successfully create empowering learning opportunities for both immigrants and the home population.

Education, both formal and public, is a primary strategy for promoting such powerful opportunities. Traditionally, the institute of schooling has been a key forum for teaching social reactions to diversity.[53] These reactions have not always been positive or educative. When Canadian society endorsed the suppression of difference, school suppressed difference. The legacy of residential schools is a legacy to this attitude. When Canadian society supported the dilution of diversity, school diluted diversity and became colour-blind in a promotion of meritocracy. Students succeeded because they worked hard and failed if they did not; who they were or what they came from was irrelevant.[54] Today, multicultural and anti-racist educators advocate conversation rather than direct teaching where participants critically discuss the impact of diversity on Canadian society. Across Canada numerous school boards and provincial departments of education are focussing on modifying the current school curriculum to be more inclusive of Canada's multicultural reality.

In Atlantic Canada, educators who appreciate the need for cross-cultural education face various hurdles. Similar to the general body of multicultural research, the literature on multicultural education is chiefly limited to the experiences of highly diverse classrooms of large urban locations. Information that is relevant to the rural concerns and reality is difficult to obtain and based mostly on the personal experiences of individual teachers. This deficit requires direct attention through the attainment of research, the availability of resources and the development of appropriate curriculum.

A common obstacle faced by multicultural educators attempting to bring a multicultural perspective education to predominately White locations is the mindset that a low number of minority and immigrant students renders cross-cultural education into a low- or non-priority issue. For example, in her study on mainly White British schools, Tomlinson noted that "schools with few or no minority pupils make little effort to revise their curriculum, or develop policies, and tend to dismiss multicultural education as … 'a very low priority,' 'not our concern,' and 'likely to be counter-productive'."[55] Although there are differences between schools in Britain and those in eastern Canada, similar accusations have been made by local educators.[56] This projection of diversity as a low priority leads to the further isolation of immigrant

---

53. Axelrod, "Promise of Schooling."

54. Harper, "Difference and Diversity in Ontario Schooling."

55. Sally Tomlinson, *Multicultural Education in White Schools* (London: B.T. Batsford, 1990), 11.

56. P. Kakembo, *BLAC Report on Education: Addressing Inequalities—Empowering Black Learners* (Halifax: BLAC, 1994); Spalding, *Invisible Minorities*.

groups. Feelings of disconnection, disempowerment, and discontentment are a threat to the sense of a community identity. Traditionally such an identity has been an integral part of the rural experience. In order to sustain and enhance a community identity, members of society need to see evidence of their importance. Official recognition of the importance of pluralism to rural areas involves the cooperation of school curriculum.

Along with recognizing the presence of different groups, regardless of their size, schools must also underline the importance of cross-cultural education for all members of society. As the following statement, cooperatively written by various New Brunswick multicultural organisations, attests, the need to educate all people about diversity is limited to neither visible minorities nor highly diverse areas:

> One could say of certain areas in New Brunswick where there are no "other" ethnic groups, why must we adjust our curriculum? It must be realized that our children are not always going to live in a small village, town or city and therefore must be prepared for the larger world outside, be it Montreal, Toronto, Vancouver or the United States. We must instil in them the knowledge and values that will prepare them to work and live effectively and harmoniously in our culturally diverse society.[57]

As the collective statement highlights, the assumption that children living in isolated and rural areas do not require multicultural education is shortsighted and potentially dangerous.

Schools are only one member of the education partnership. Government departments, universities, NGOs, and corporations each represent a potential voice for public education on immigration in rural areas. Research has demonstrated that silence on this issue can result in consequences in the various facets of society. For example, Howard points out the economic ramifications of a mindset void of the recognition of diversity and positions cross-cultural understanding as necessary for economic success. He notes that today's corporate world demand that employees be capable of working in a diverse community. Working within diversity mandates being able to work with others without falling prey to the prejudices that risk destroying our society:

> Ironically, these negative responses to diversity are destructive not only for those who are the targets of hate but also for the perpetrators themselves. Racism is ultimately a self-destructive and counter-evolutionary strategy. As is true for any species in nature, positive adaptation to change requires a rich pool of diversity and potential in the population. In denying access to the full range of human variety and possibility, racism drains the essential vitality from everyone, victimizing our entire society. ...
>
> The future belongs to those who are able to walk and work beside people of many different cultures, lifestyles, and perspectives. The business world is embracing this understanding. We now see top corporate leaders investing millions of dollars annually to provide their employees with skills to function effectively in a highly diverse work force. ... Diversity is a bottom line issue for employers. Productivity is related to our ability to deal with pluralism.[58]

The lack of attention given to issues of immigration and diversity in rural areas allows for the denial of economic growth and supports the financial destruction of rural communities.

Ironically, it is often the locations with the least amount of diversity that have the most problematic confrontation with difference. This point is outlined in Gwynne Dyer's discussion

---

57. New Brunswick Multicultural Council, Multicultural Association of Greater Moncton Area, New Brunswick Intercultural Education Committee, "A Response to the White Paper for a New Education Act" (unpublished document, 1997), 2.

58. Gary Howard, "Whites in Multicultural Education," *Phi Delta Kappan* 75 (1993): 39.

of racism in homogeneous areas. Using Germany and Ireland as examples, Dyer illustrates how some of the most brutal racist attacks have occurred in areas with a small amount of visible diversity and low immigration. The contention is that citizens of such locations fear diversity because they are not used to it. The article concludes with the observation that "more immigration, not less, [is the] answer to racist attacks."[59] In this light, it becomes apparent that the need to understand immigration and diversity in areas low in both is essential.

Most importantly, resources must be provided to empower the bodies that work within the fields of immigration, diversity and social cohesion, and to enhance public education of the greater population. Only by gaining greater leverage through resources and information can such bodies be successful in both retaining immigrants as well enabling the mainstream population to live and prosper within the diversity. Various studies suggest that the larger the supporting ethnic cultural group, the greater the rate of integration.[60] Immigrants and other minority groups who experience small or non-existent ethnocultural communities are more apt to experience social disengagement. An all too common solution to this feeling is the desertion of rural locations for more diverse venues. For areas like Atlantic Canada, this means the loss of valuable human capital. As the baby boomers reach retirement, the scarcity of skilled individuals has both the private and public sectors scrambling to increase their population. For Atlantic Canada, the challenge is intensified by the constant outflow of youth, especially immigrant youth who feel isolated from society.

When one looks at the issue of immigration within the mainly rural location of Atlantic Canada, one point becomes glaringly obvious—things are not as they seem. At first glance, the social climate of the region suggests that issues surrounding immigration and diversity are simple and relatively minimal compared to the rest of Canada. This position is enhanced by the lack of apparent and visible diversity among the region's general population. However, nothing could be further from the truth. Pull back the top layers of the immigration question and one finds a web of issues waiting to be unravelled. The lack of attention to the potential of immigration in rural areas situates Atlantic Canada as a rich resource for multicultural research. With its particular nuances, the region has the ability to provide a new perspective to the immigration and migration conversation that would impact all parts of Canada, especially predominately White locations similar to Atlantic Canada that have been left out of the diversity conversation. When the same voices participate in a dialogue it is sometimes a challenge to develop fresh ideas. A new voice can question old directions and suggest new pathways.

---

59. Dyer, *Change is Our New Constant*, A6.
60. Baker, Arsenault and Gallant, "Resettlement."

CHAPTER EIGHT

Urban and Rural Aboriginals: Bridging the Divide

John Roslinski

The Aboriginal population in Canada is a markedly divided community. Not only are Aboriginal peoples dispersed across the entire country, they are also members of diverse nations, bands and groupings. Additional classifications such as Indian, Inuit, Métis, status, non-status, and Bill C-31 have served to further divide the Aboriginal population. To make the situation even more complex, as the number of Aboriginal peoples in urban centers begins to more closely resemble the number of Aboriginal peoples in rural areas and those based on reserves, a new urban/rural cleavage has been emerging.

This rural/urban divide stems from a variety of factors but, mainly, can be attributed to the neglect of the urban dimension. From government policy to academic research, urban Aboriginal people have been consistently overlooked. This is most evident when viewing self-government initiatives. The majority of self-government proposals have focussed attention upon the more traditional rural land-based reserves. This concentration on the rural component has been attributed to the fact that it is simpler to implement self-government on a rural reserve than it is to introduce it into a situation without a land base.

While it may be the case that self-government is more easily attainable for on-reserve Aboriginals, limiting it to this segment of Aboriginal peoples is, in effect, dividing the Aboriginal population nearly in half. Furthermore, ignoring the urban dimension limits the potential impacts that economic development in the urban area can have on the entire Aboriginal population. Thus, this paper determines that a bridge must be constructed between urban and rural Aboriginal peoples. Through the establishment of a peak Aboriginal organization, it is deemed possible to unite the two sides and provide both segments of the Aboriginal population with an opportunity to participate in self-government.

At this point it may be worthwhile to devote some attention to the nature of the urban Aboriginal population. Recent statistics suggest that the urban dimension of the Aboriginal population has increased to the extent that the urban component now accounts for 49.5% of the total Aboriginal citizenry.[1] If current trends continue, it is reasonable to assume that in the near future urban Aboriginal peoples will constitute the majority of the Aboriginal population. Thus, in a sense, an urban Aboriginal community appears to be emerging. Yet, for anyone who has ventured to develop policy for this segment of Aboriginal society, the term community may not be entirely suitable. Indeed, Alan Cairns may have said it best when he

---

1. Calvin Hanselmann, *Urban Aboriginal Peoples in Western Canada: Realities and Policies* (Calgary: Canada West Foundation, 2001), 1.

stated that "the typical urban Aboriginal population is a statistical aggregate, not a community."[2] This refers to the fact that Aboriginal peoples living in an urban environment are typically less homogenous than Aboriginal peoples situated in rural areas or especially those residing on the reserve.

Although it is important to recognize the extreme diversity of urban Aboriginal people, perhaps there is a degree of cohesion that should not be entirely dismissed. For instance, it is apparent that Aboriginal people are not evenly distributed throughout the entire country. While all of the provinces and territories have Aboriginal populations, there are a disproportionate number of individuals claiming Aboriginal descent in western Canada. In fact, "four of the five cities with the highest proportions of Aboriginal people are in the West."[3] This does not mean that these cities have a unified Aboriginal community, but it should demonstrate that Aboriginal peoples tend to congregate more in certain urban centres. There are just as many Aboriginal people living in the city of Winnipeg as there are Aboriginal people residing in the Northwest Territories and Nunavut.[4] When illustrated in this way, it is difficult to understand why the urban component has not received an equivalent degree of consideration.

Certainly the division of jurisdictions between the federal government and the provinces has had an impact on the attention received by urban Aboriginal people. In section 91 (24) of the Constitution Act 1867, the federal government was given responsibility for "Indians, and lands reserved for the Indians." However, the provincial governments were the ones with the exclusive right to control municipalities. As a result, the federal government has tended to suggest that it is merely responsible for Indians residing on reserves and for the Inuit living in the North, while the Métis population and any Aboriginal people in an urban setting should be a provincial concern. Provincial governments, for the most part, do not agree with this interpretation. These governments have argued that Ottawa has responsibility for the entire aboriginal population and any attempt to claim otherwise is a form of government offloading. Whether the urban Aboriginal population would be better dealt with under one jurisdiction or the other is not necessarily an issue that needs to be addressed here. Instead, it is clear that both the federal and provincial governments have a justified reason for dealing with this population. Also, by bickering back and forth over which government should be providing which service to these people, the average urban Aboriginal has been subject to substantial neglect.

It is apparent that by neglecting the urban Aboriginal population, governments have placed many individual urban Aboriginal citizens at a disadvantage in comparison to their reserve-based counterparts. Urban Aboriginal people generally do not receive several of the services and benefits that Aboriginal people who reside on-reserve are able to obtain from the federal government. Therefore, "many status people who moved to the city believe they are disadvantaged because they are not eligible to receive all the services to which they had access on-reserve."[5] The recognition of this distinct treatment has fuelled a type of resentment that has divided the Canadian Aboriginal population along urban and rural lines. This stems from the fact that the reserve-based population remains the focus of considerable attention through government policy, media coverage and public concentration. Many

---

2. Alan C. Cairns, "Aboriginal Peoples' Two Roads to the Future," *Policy Options* (January–February 2000): 32.

3. Hanselmann, *Urban Aboriginal People*, 1.

4. Royal Commission on Aboriginal Peoples (RCAP), *Final Report of the Royal Commission on Aboriginal Peoples; Vol. 4: Perspectives and Realities* (Ottawa: Minister of Supply and Services Canada, 1996), 519.

5. Ibid., 538.

Canadians have viewed the recent Royal Commission on Aboriginal Peoples (RCAP) as the epitome of this disproportionate focus. Much of the organized criticism of RCAP has been structured along these same lines of not providing adequate reflection to the growing urban dimension of Aboriginal society.[6]

Of course, RCAP is not the only study of the sort to pay scant notice to the changing complexity of Aboriginal society. While discussions surrounding the notion of Aboriginal self-government have been expanding exponentially, the way that urban Aboriginal peoples are to participate in self-determination has been virtually non-existent. This is basically attributed to the fact that self-government initiatives are exceedingly difficult to implement without an easily identifiable population and a recognizable land base. As such, it should not be surprising that most self-government debates ignore the urban component completely and choose to deal with the status-Indian population living on reserves.

Admittedly, self-government should be designed to allow reserve-based Aboriginal peoples to exercise a greater degree of autonomy. There is a discernible need for self-government proposals to provide meaningful opportunities for these Aboriginal communities to determine their own futures. However, by failing to consider how self-government can be structured to incorporate urban Aboriginal people, nearly half of the Aboriginal population gets excluded from an essential rearrangement of power. It also means that the potential benefits of living in a city must be weighed against the tremendous disadvantage of not being able to have increased self-determination.

By emphasizing the general absence of urban self-government proposals, it is not meant to suggest that there are no recommendations for self-determination for urban Aboriginal people. Rather, the intention is to illustrate the extent to which "self-government off a land base requires a different approach than the land-based models most often associated with Aboriginal self-government."[7] Despite the criticisms that RCAP has received for its limited treatment of the urban Aboriginal population, the Commission did contain a brief overview of how self-government could be extended in an urban environment. These urban designs were basically variations of three main positions that Aboriginal people living in these communities might be able to explore.

The first option that RCAP suggests is the "reform of urban governments and public authority."[8] While the Commission admits that this selection would not technically qualify as self-government, it does view this type of reform as both necessary and attainable. Thus, RCAP recommends that urban Aboriginal peoples be guaranteed representation on appointed local bodies, have the opportunity to create Aboriginal affairs committees, and be active participants in the co-management of a variety of urban projects.[9] By expanding Aboriginal participation in this manner, the commission hopes that urban communities will become more receptive to Aboriginal perspectives and more responsive to their realities.

Although collaborating with urban institutions and agencies would likely serve to improve the position that Aboriginal peoples typically occupy in cities across the country, this method clearly falls short of self-determination. The incorporation of a few Aboriginal peoples in select associations would hardly allow for the type of restructuring necessary for urban Aboriginal peoples to enact substantial changes to the municipal governing system. Instead, this process would simply replicate the indigenizing of non-Aboriginal structures that has

---

6. Cairns, "Aboriginal Peoples' Two Roads to the Future," 33.

7, RCAP, *Vol. 4: Perspectives and Realities*, 580.

8. Ibid., 581.

9. Ibid., 582.

become common practice in recent years. As such, it is not even close to offering urban Aboriginal peoples the kind of self-government that Aboriginal peoples on a reserve are beginning to achieve.

The second option that RCAP outlines has much more potential to allow the urban Aboriginal population to move towards self-government. By uniting in an urban community of interest, Aboriginal peoples would be coming together despite their differences so as to establish a collectivity with the authority to make decisions on their behalf.[10] This community of interest could span an entire city with its membership and legitimately perform numerous political and administrative functions that would otherwise be carried out by non-Aboriginal urban bodies. In a sense, it can be regarded as an umbrella structure that would be capable of both overseeing and coordinating urban Aboriginal peoples' political activities.[11]

There is a possibility, however, for the community of interest approach to be a limited model of self-government. This is due, in part, to the unit being overly concerned with service delivery rather than policy formation. It is possible that a community of interest would succumb to the routine of being a service provider and would fail to have an explicit impression on policy outcome. While being able to administer the programs that affect ones' own people is an essential part of self-determination, it is not nearly as fulfilling as program development. It is through the latter that major advancements for the urban Aboriginal population have a real chance of evolving.

The third option that is described by RCAP is known as the "nation-based approach to urban self-government."[12] The nation-based approach stresses the importance of establishing connections between urban Aboriginal peoples and land-based Aboriginal nations. This relationship can take a variety of forms, but presumably would either be structured on the extension of an Aboriginal nation's extraterritorial jurisdiction over its urban members or a host nation could, in a sense, adopt any urban Aboriginal peoples residing in its traditional territory.[13] These methods allow for a degree of cooperation that would realistically be required for self-government to be attainable for the majority of Aboriginal peoples in urban centres.

While the nation-based approach does acknowledge the necessity for Aboriginal governments to unite in a manner more appropriate for their size and resource possession, it is not truly in touch with reality. Even though a number of Aboriginal peoples who have left their reserves to live in a city still have connections to their home community, there is an abundance of Aboriginal citizens who have never had these ties to begin with. These citizens would not be able to utilize the support of an Aboriginal nation's extraterritorial jurisdiction. A host nation may provide the only real opportunity for these urban Aboriginal people to exercise self-government. Yet, this approach may cause the urban Aboriginal population to lose as much as it gains. As the urban Aboriginal peoples become dependent upon a host nation, it is increasingly likely that their local authority will suffer.

Thus, despite all three of these methods being described by RCAP as having the potential to provide increased local control for urban Aboriginal people, the degree at which they are able to operate is limited. Furthermore, the RCAP proposals fail to consider the interdependence of these self-governing units. Although local authority is an important aspect for any segment of Aboriginal society, it does not allow for the necessary interaction to make self-government truly work. Forms of self-determination based solely on the community level

---

10. Ibid., 584.

11. Ibid., 585.

12. Ibid., 588.

13. Ibid., 588–89.

would not only expand the divide between rural and urban Aboriginal peoples; it would presumably cause a rift to emerge among the various self-governing communities. Thus, a peak Aboriginal organization may be necessary to bridge the divide between the urban and the rural Aboriginal peoples. Such a structure would allow for communication and cooperation to take place amongst the Aboriginal governments and ensure that Aboriginal peoples were able to perform many of the tasks associated with self-government. It would also permit meaningful intergovernmental relations to emerge with the federal and provincial governments.

A peak Aboriginal organization is a way to describe an Aboriginal association that would have the authority to act on behalf of Aboriginal people at a national level.[14] In essence, it would be responsible for those areas that smaller community self-governments could not possibly control. In addition, it would be the means by which Aboriginal peoples could participate in the process of intergovernmental relations. In an ideal model, it would likely be a national body with its constituency being made up of those communities that have already achieved some sort of local self-governing authority. While a peak Aboriginal organization would consist of self-governing communities, it would also need to establish and maintain a direct connection to the Aboriginal peoples living in each of these communities regardless of whether they are urban or rural. This type of a relationship would be essential if it is to have a legitimate role in intergovernmental affairs or executive federalism.

A peak Aboriginal organization should not be mistaken as a substitute for Aboriginal self-governing communities. Rather, it will be a tool that Aboriginal peoples can use to help them to become self-determining. It will coexist with the various urban and rural communities in order to make the operation of self-government more effective. The assumption is that the federal government will continue to devolve self-governing powers directly to the individual aboriginal communities. In return, it will eventually become necessary for Aboriginal peoples to impart some of these powers onto a peak Aboriginal organization. For the most part, Aboriginal peoples themselves will have to decide which powers they want to keep at the community level and which ones would be better off transferred to a peak organization.

Attempting to balance self-governing powers between the communities and the peak organization will not necessarily be unproblematic. For a peak Aboriginal organization to be truly effective it will need to have the authority to negotiate on behalf of its membership without requiring subsequent ratification of decisions that it makes. This does not mean that a peak Aboriginal organization would not consult with its constituents beforehand or be held accountable afterwards; rather, it means that some latitude would have to be extended to it. This is not only necessary for intergovernmental bargaining purposes; it is also required if an organization of this sort is to maintain its legitimacy. Simply put, a peak Aboriginal organization cannot be successful if its membership communities are able to opt out of agreements or constantly threaten to withdraw their support from the organization. Thus, a peak Aboriginal organization would likely have two primary responsibilities. One of its functions would be to unite the self-governing communities so that their policies could be better coordinated. "Without coordination between governments, it could lead to a confusing array of different standards and services."[15] Another function would be to provide Aboriginal self-governing communities with a mechanism by which they could access the intergovernmental process of Canada.

---

14. This portion of the paper draws on the author's M.A. thesis. John Roslinski, "A Peak Aboriginal Organization: The Need to Integrate Self-Government within Canada" (MA thesis, University of Calgary, 2000), 1–35.

15. Jill Wherrett and Douglas Brown, "Models for Aboriginal Government in Urban Areas," in Evelyn J. Peters (ed.), *Aboriginal Self-Government in Urban Areas: Proceedings of a Workshop May 25 and 26 1994* (Kingston: Institute of Intergovernmental Relations Queen's University, 1995), 97.

Certainly it is understood that there has been some opposition to other types of pan-Aboriginal associations in the past. A peak Aboriginal organization is different, however, in that it is structured around the concept of federalism. Federalism would allow Aboriginal people the opportunity to have local control while still benefiting from being part of a larger entity. However, it is unlikely that the federal system that is so deeply embedded in Canada would be able to incorporate an extensive number of Aboriginal self-governing communities. The sheer abundance of Aboriginal self-governing units alone would seriously curtail their ability to interact effectively with the federal and provincial governments. Thus, it is apparent that a peak Aboriginal organization would be necessary in order to facilitate communication between the various levels of government. In essence, it would provide Aboriginal peoples with a mechanism for managing their interdependence.

It is significant to acknowledge the fact that a peak Aboriginal organization would not be something foreign to or imposed upon Aboriginal peoples. Aboriginal people have a long history with "multi-level structures of governance."[16] Indeed, a number of Aboriginal nations were traditionally members of federations and confederacies.[17] These pan-Aboriginal associations were established in such a way that individual Aboriginal nations could accommodate their diversity while still benefiting from increased interdependence. This is essentially why many modern Aboriginal political organizations have a pan-Aboriginal dimension to them. It comes from the realization that, although in principle primary authority can rest with the local community government, in practice many of the powers and responsibilities would have to be exercised at higher levels.[18] In most cases these higher levels are governing bodies that represent an entire nation, treaty group, region or province. Consequently, it makes sense to assume that most Aboriginal people in Canada would be at least capable, if not willing, to unite under the cover of a peak organization.

There are numerous other reasons why Aboriginal self-governing units will need to interact with each other and with the federal and provincial governments. To begin with, various sources have predicted anywhere from 60–80 to well over 1,000 self-governing Aboriginal communities eventually being dispersed across the Canadian landscape.[19] Due to the immense number of self-governing bodies, it certainly will not be possible for the federal and provincial governments to deal with all of them directly. The existing institutions of government in this country have not been designed for a sudden influx of so many additional participants. While some modifications to these institutions will have to occur in order to allow for Aboriginal participation, these adaptations will only go so far. For that purpose alone there is a desire to have the individual segments unite.

Second, although Aboriginal peoples, like any other portion of society, are not a homogenous group, they do have at least some common interests. While it is possible that they will be able to advance some of these interests independently, presumably greater success would be achieved if Aboriginal peoples were to consolidate their efforts. Indeed, it is extremely unlikely that urban- or rural-based Aboriginal governments will be able to accomplish many fundamental goals "unless some way of aggregating their positions is developed."[20] A peak Aboriginal organization would not only be capable of formulating collective positions; it

16. Royal Commission on Aboriginal Peoples (RCAP), *Final Report of the Royal Commission on Aboriginal Peoples; Vol. 2: Restructuring the Relationship* (Ottawa: Minister of Supply and Services Canada, 1996), 159.

17. Ibid.

18. Ibid., 158.

19. Ibid., 166. The Commissioners describe that at best 60–80 self-governing nations could be created out of the 1,000 or so Aboriginal bands and communities that exist in Canada today.

20. Alan C. Cairns, *Citizens Plus: Aboriginal Peoples and the Canadian State* (Vancouver: UBC Press, 2000), 138.

would also be an appropriate means by which these interests could be presented to the rest of the country.

Third, Aboriginal self-governing communities will have to unite because of the small size of individual Aboriginal communities and the limited resources that they have at their disposal. It is not a secret that the various urban and rural Aboriginal communities that are dispersed across the country vary significantly in the types and amounts of resources that they each possess. While certain communities have advanced financial capacities, a skilled labour force and technological expertise, others may be lacking the resources to deal with day-to-day concerns. If the majority of these communities are to prosper despite their differences, Aboriginal self-governing units will have to cooperate and share. Although it is not evident how redistribution among Aboriginal communities would work, it is reasonable to assume that any body that was authorized to allocate resources would require the power to enforce its decisions on its membership.[21] Even without a formal redistribution mechanism in place, urban and rural Aboriginal governments will not only have to associate with one another, but will have to establish working arrangements with the federal and provincial governments. This additional communication will be necessary for any large-scale initiatives and is essential for effective management of shared jurisdictions.

Fourth, because Aboriginal peoples do not want self-government to be merely service administration, they will have to unite. This is primarily because individual communities, whether they are urban or rural, cannot hope to exercise many crucial decision-making powers at a local level. For instance, these self-governing units cannot expect that they will all be able to secure a voice at constitutional conferences or be allowed access to an amending formula that currently incorporates only eleven members. Yet, Aboriginal peoples may be able to gain admittance to these structures if they enter via a single organization. If they do not unite, it is likely that these Aboriginal self-governments will become solely service providers lacking any authority to change the policies that affect their people.

Without a peak Aboriginal organization in the country, it is unlikely that Aboriginal people will be able to accomplish what they want from self-government. This is due to the fact that the various Aboriginal communities do not have access to identical resources:

> Resources consist of the physical means of acting—not only financial, economic and natural resources for security and future growth, but information and technology as well as human resources in the form of skilled and healthy people. Resources are necessary to exercise governmental power and to satisfy the needs and expectations of citizens.[22]

Thus, Aboriginal people cannot expect that all of their self-governing communities will be suited to take on alone the additional responsibilities of self-government. However, a peak Aboriginal organization could ensure that resources were dispersed in such a manner as to support those Aboriginal groups that may need additional assistance. In this way, problems such as a lack of experience in a certain sector or a shortage in skilled labour could largely be avoided.[23]

21. Jodi Cockerill and Roger Gibbins, "Reluctant Citizens? First Nations in the Canadian Federal State," in J. Rick Ponting (ed.), *First Nations in Canada: Perspectives on Opportunity, Empowerment, and Self-Determination* (Toronto: McGraw-Hill Ryerson Limited, 1997), 389–90.

22. RCAP, *Vol. 2: Restructuring the Relationship*, 164.

23. J. Rick Ponting and Roger Gibbins, "Thorns in the Bed of Roses: A Socio-political View of the Problems of Indian Government," in Leroy Little Bear, Menno Boldt and J. Anthony Long (eds.), *Pathways to Self-Determination: Canadian Indians and the Canadian State* (Toronto: University of Toronto Press, 1984), 125.

It would be naïve to think that urban and rural Aboriginal people will be able to consolidate their efforts without encountering any obstacles. There will likely be numerous difficulties and disagreements resulting from the fact that Aboriginal people are not a homogeneous group. Still, the Canadian population is just as diverse a society as the Aboriginal community, yet Canada has discovered that there are benefits to being united. Actually, Canada emerged because the individual provinces realized that they shared some common interests and could not attain these goals without each other's assistance. But, while there was a willingness to concede some sovereignty, the provinces were not inclined to relinquish all of their authority to act independently.

Thus, Canadians decided to form a political union whereby a central government would be responsible for common interests and the provincial governments would retain control over regional matters. In other words, federalism was selected as the manner by which the country's diversity could be reconciled with unity. It did not take long for the federal system to become a firmly entrenched institution in the country. It is now a political institution that Aboriginal peoples will be unable to ignore and one in which self-government will continue to exist. However, it is not apparent that federalism will be a constraint on Aboriginal peoples. It appears as though the federal system would be of benefit to the Aboriginal population. Certainly, there are key differences between Aboriginal and non-Aboriginal Canadians, but ultimately, they do share many of the same problems. Several of these issues emanate from the reality that both populations are distributed over an expansive territory. Therefore, we must remember that federalism was selected for Canada as a way to preserve our regional distinctions while allowing for increased interaction. It appears as though it would be appropriate in the Aboriginal situation as well.

Aboriginal peoples must be realistic in their aspirations for self-government. They can do this by recognizing "that self-government does not occur in a political vacuum."[24] Despite their scope, both urban and rural Aboriginal self-governing communities will continue to be part of the Canadian political system. As such, Aboriginal peoples must be willing to appreciate that Canada has an existing political structure that cannot be ignored. This is not to suggest that changes cannot be made to the governmental order of the country; it merely indicates that self-government will be somewhat confined by its environment. Thus, Aboriginal governments will need to fit into the existing structure not only on account of non-Aboriginal peoples being fairly hostile towards the idea of radically altering their system, but also because changing the country's political institutions may not be appropriate. Indeed, one of the advantages of the federal system is the fact that it can be adapted and modified so as to incorporate Aboriginal governments into this complex network of intergovernmental relationships without much difficulty.[25] Currently, jurisdiction is divided between the federal and provincial governments, with some areas of overlap. One can imagine an Aboriginal government being included in some sort of restructuring of the divisions of responsibilities.[26]

Although self-government is primarily an Aboriginal initiative, its success largely depends on what the governments of Canada do. If Aboriginal peoples are to exercise self-governing powers within the country's federal system, then the federal and provincial governments

24. Peter W. Hogg and Mary Ellen Turpel, "Implementing Aboriginal Self-Government: Constitutional and Jurisdictional Issues," in Royal Commission on Aboriginal Peoples, *Aboriginal Self-Government Legal and Constitutional Issues* (Ottawa: Minister of Supply and Services Canada, 1995), 397.

25. Ibid.

26. George Erasmus and Joe Sanders, "Canadian History: An Aboriginal Perspective," in Diane Engelstad and John Bird (eds.), *Nation to Nation: Aboriginal Sovereignty and the Future of Canada* (Toronto: Irwin Publishing, 1992), 11.

must provide space for this to happen.[27] There must be an opportunity and willingness for both Aboriginal and non-Aboriginal governments to make compromises and concessions. There must also be an awareness that we are not talking about "the existence of solitudes, but the necessity of mutual respect and cooperation between Aboriginals and other Canadians."[28] Therefore, Aboriginal self-governing units will ultimately need the help of the provinces and the federal government in order to be able to meet the needs of their citizens.[29] Without that assistance, Aboriginal self-government will not live up to its potential.

Although Aboriginal self-government has the ability to give Aboriginal people the necessary freedom to be truly self-determining, it also "has the capacity to dissolve [the] moral and political ties between Aboriginals."[30] If Aboriginal self-government simply focuses on the differences between the urban and rural populations, there will hardly be any reason for the two groups to seek out a partnership. However, if both groups spend as much attention on areas of shared rule as they do on self-rule, then an intimate relationship will presumably develop. This type of association would tend to encourage the various governments to work together in the pursuit of common goals.[31] Soon after, the urban and rural populations would become accustomed to constructing political arrangements that were mutually advantageous.

Of course, if Aboriginal self-governments are successfully incorporated into Canadian federalism under a peak Aboriginal organization, it will provide Aboriginal people, regardless of where they reside, with an additional level of government. That is another reason why federalism is an attractive option for Aboriginal self-determination. Not only does the political system allow for sufficient local autonomy and increased interdependence, it also permits there to be "overlapping sovereignties."[32] Essentially this means that the federal government, provincial governments, and Aboriginal governments can exercise sovereign powers over the same territory and the same people, but in different jurisdictions. The outcome would be that Aboriginal peoples from urban and rural areas would not feel as though they were as divided from one another.

A peak Aboriginal organization would provide the urban and rural segments of the Aboriginal population with a mechanism to communicate with one another and also allow them to engage in the process of intergovernmental relations. Although rural Aboriginal peoples have somewhat of an advantage in that they have many more options available to them with regards to self-government, they too would profit from being participants in a peak organization. It is the urban Aboriginal population, however, that would benefit the most from such an arrangement. Clearly, urban Aboriginal peoples have few feasible choices in which they can exercise self-determination. If these people decide that "control over service delivery is not enough to meet their aspirations for self-government," then they will have to unite.[33] It is true that self-government would mean increased autonomy for the individual communities, but if self-government is actually going to succeed, the urban and rural components must recognize and appreciate their mutual reliance on one another.

---

27. RCAP, *Vol. 2: Restructuring the Relationship*, 5.

28. Samuel V. LaSelva, *The Moral Foundations of Canadian Federalism: Paradoxes, Achievements, and Tragedies of Nationhood* (Montreal: McGill-Queen's University Press, 1996), 142.

29. Ovide Mercredi and Mary Ellen Turpel, *In the Rapids: Navigating the Future of First Nations* (Toronto: Penguin Books Canada Ltd., 1993), 131.

30. LaSelva, *The Moral Foundations*, 137.

31. Hogg and Turpel, "Implementing Aboriginal Self-Government," 396.

32. Augie Fleras, "The Politics of Jurisdiction: Indigenizing Aboriginal-State Relations," in David Alan Long and Olive Patricia Dickason (eds.), *Visions of the Heart: Canadian Aboriginal Issues* (Toronto: Harcourt Brace Canada, 1996), 166.

33. Thomas Isaac, *Aboriginal Law: Cases, Materials and Commentary* (Saskatoon: Purich Publishing, 1995), 349.

CHAPTER NINE

From Rural Municipality to School District to Community: Transitions in Rural Saskatchewan

June Corman

The young boy playing third base stretched upward making an incredible catch to put out the batter, his 35-year-old aunt. The pitcher, a 45-year-old man, approached the mound. Smiling, he threw a perfect pitch to his neighbour's granddaughter. She hit a high ball to left field. Safe at first base.

People have enjoyed the intergenerational ball game and the other activities of the summer picnic every year from the construction of the Davyroyd country school in 1913 to the present, even though the school closed in 1959. Children run in track events and every child wins candy from the concession booth. The potluck meal in the evening is always delicious and after the baseball game people dance to local talent into the night.

The activities at the picnic have stayed the same from 1913 to 2001 but the organizational impetus and the residency of the participants have changed. During the early years, the teacher assisted the parents to organize the event. Everyone who attended the picnic lived locally either in the Davyroyd school district or adjacent districts. After the school closed, the men's and the women's community clubs organized the picnic. Both clubs are associated with the country school, which now functions as a community centre. The third-base player in 2001 lived on a local farm, but rode a bus to school in the nearby town of Assiniboia. His aunt lived in Moose Jaw, 60 miles away. The pitcher had farmed locally but was now commuting to Moose Jaw to finish grade twelve, with aspirations to become a teacher. The neighbour's granddaughter had flown in from Toronto for a summer holiday. Something about the magic of the picnic and ballgame continues to attract people—people who live locally, people who live in nearby towns and people who live a considerable distance away. Their participation has sustained this event on an annual basis for 42 years after the school was closed.

The persistence of the picnic and baseball game stems from the deep sense of embeddedness that had developed historically in the Davyroyd school district and the adjacent school district of Zenith. This deep sense of embeddedness also continues to perpetuate flows of support and resources among neighbouring farm families. The forms of social relations for people living in Davyroyd, Zenith and other rural municipalities, though, are changing as a consequence of international grain subsidy programs, advances in transportation and communication infrastructures, concentration in farm ownership, rural depopulation, and small family size.

Sociological research on community relations in urban areas is often framed around the concepts of community lost, community saved or community liberated. Researchers, within the paradigm of community saved or lost, look for the extent to which communities exist within residentially bounded urban neighbourhoods. An alternative approach examines the issue of liberated communities; each person's community is synonymous with his personal network of ties. Personal communities are liberated from the necessity of geographic proximity (Wellman, 1999: 94–114).

This paper uses a case study of two adjoining school districts, Davyroyd and Zenith, to examine the historic development of rural communities. It examines the conditions that fostered a strong sense of place among the people living in these two districts and how the potential for locally based support networks has changed in rural Saskatchewan.[1]

The conditions facing the strangers, who came to homestead, were conducive for the formation of overlapping, geographically based personal networks. Over time, the ties of each person became densely intertwined with other adjacent farm families. Everyone was tied to everyone else, in some way or another, and due to minimal opportunities, few people had active ties of any sort extending beyond the locality. As these locally based networks became larger, multi-facetted and overlapping, a strong sense of place developed. The farm families referred to this sense of place as community. The names of the school districts, Davyroyd and Zenith, became designations for farm families similar to names of the nearby villages of Readlyn and Willows.

By 2001, the few remaining residents were still tied to each other in various social, kin and exchange relationships but each woman, man and child also had an extensive personal network extending outside the districts. For them, the localities of Zenith and Davyroyd had merged into one geographically bounded space that continued to resonate with a sense of place, but each person also had a "liberated" personal community consisting of ties scattered across Canada and, in some cases, the world. Various kinds of support and resources flowed both between the people who resided in Davyroyd and Zenith as well as between themselves and the far-flung members of their networks.

The Development of Community Embeddedness in Davyroyd and Zenith

The potential for high crop yield brought an influx of settlers to Rural Municipality No. 72 from 1900 to 1910, after all the aboriginal people had been relocated and just prior to the construction of the local railway line. The six divisions in R.M. 72 were surveyed into 270 sections. Each of the one-square-mile sections was further subdivided into four quarters. The requirement that homesteaders live on their land meant that this grassland was soon populated with small sod and wood frame houses. At least two farmyards were established per section. The governance of R.M. 72 was typical of other rural, geographically based administrative units. Elected representatives, including a reeve, a secretary and councilors, representing farm families in each of the subdivisions, made important decisions such as the construction and maintenance of roads.

The rural municipality and even the divisions, however, were too large to develop a sense of place because, prior to telephones and passable roads, farm families were limited to making connections with people who lived very close to their farm. The boundaries of the soon-to-be-formed school districts, however, were the right scale and provided the basis for the transition from a collection of strangers to a community of interconnected farm families.

---

1. This paper is based on the school district records for Zenith and Davyroyd, Rural Municipality Maps, and interviews with members of farm families. It is also based on personal observations. I lived in this district between 1952 and 1970 and I have maintained close contact with my family and neighbours in the interim.

Most of the people who settled in the part of R.M. 72 that would become the school districts of Zenith and Davyroyd, were from England, Scotland and Ontario. Sharing English as a common language and similar Protestant religious backgrounds fostered ties among neighbouring farm families. Kin relations also formed the basis for locally based support networks. Of the 78 male farm operators, in 1913, 22 were related to at least one other person living in the vicinity.

The similarity in material circumstances and economic imperatives facing the people in this populated area was another unifying factor. Homesteaders were originally granted one quarter-section and could take preemption on a second quarter. By 1913, 30% of the 78 farms were only one quarter-section, 64% of farms were two quarter-sections and 6% of farms were three quarter-sections. All farm operators resided on their land, with the exception of a few men who left for months at a time to supplement their income. Farm families occupied all the houses.

The distance from these farms to nearby villages and towns created an incentive for these farm families to become institutionally self-sufficient and in this way fostered locally based social networks. The settlers in this region built a small Presbyterian church, which later became a United church. This church was eight miles from the closest village and 13 miles from Assiniboia, the closest town. Those who volunteered to build the church and those who attended the services developed strong ties with each other. After the Sunday service, people spilled onto the front yard and stayed to catch up on the latest news. Not all families participated in the church service but the adjoining graveyard became commonly used.

In 1910, a group of farmers toward the north and a neighbouring group of farmers toward the south began to organize two rural schools. The process of establishing these school districts was fraught with dissension with the consequence that the debate provided bonding among the people within the school boundaries and fueled a sense of "us against them" with people who lived outside the boundaries.

Although two sections of school land were set aside out of every 36, the boundaries of school districts were not set prior to settlement. Farm families, living adjacent to each other, had to petition the provincial government to locate the boundaries of each school district prior to the construction of the school. Natural features such as lakes, hills and scrubland provided logical boundaries to the west for the proposed school districts of Davyroyd and Zenith, but the other boundaries had to be drawn between neighbouring farmyards.

This circumstance created antagonism among families in the proposed adjacent districts as members of the two school districts lobbied for different boundaries. In 1910 the four Davy brothers collected a petition and filed for a school district called Davyroyd in R.M. 72. They set the southern border of their district to include the farmyard of one of the Davy brothers and two other adjoining families. The farm families to the south were also planning to register a school district, called Moose Pond (later to be called Zenith), and wanted to include these three farm families within their northern border. Each district argued that they needed these three families to ensure that they had sufficient children to warrant government authorization and a sufficient property tax base to finance the construction and operation of the school. Representatives of both sides wrote numerous letters outlining their positions to the provincial government.[2] This dispute delayed the establishment of both schools for three years. The bitterness of the debate is captured in the correspondence.

---

2. School District Records for the school districts of Davyroyd and Zenith. These archives are available at the Saskatchewan Archives Board, Regina.

Will Craig, a resident of the proposed Moose Pond, wrote to the Department of Education on 27 October 1910:

> I am forwarding to you today a petition ... against the said school district... We consider that the Davy Brothers did a very low piece of work in holding their meeting after the rest of the people had left and in forming their district by cutting off the top row of our sections. Why are the Davy Brothers urging for the formation of their stolen District? It is for their own personal good. The majority of the people in this neighborhood wishes to see "the greatest good to the greatest number." They believe in the majority ruling not a little minority that wishes everything their own way.[3]

When the schools were built in Davyroyd and Zenith, the boundaries of the districts assigned families the status of being in or out. Some of the 39 school-age children went to Davyroyd School and the others were assigned to Zenith School. For those included within a particular district, the operation of the schools created a sense of place by providing a basis for the development of local ties. Residency in these school districts intensified the connections among farm families because all families paid school tax to the local school, their children went to the same school, and people participated together in the governance of the school through sitting on or electing the local school board. Local farmers on the school board made important decisions regarding which teacher to hire and the amount of the salary.

Although administering the schools brought people together it also caused dissension among the families within the district because of the importance of the location of the school. Schools were very rarely located on the section designated as school land. This land was often not central to the majority of the children. Since a two- or three-mile trip by foot or horse both morning and afternoon was onerous and also dangerous during prairie winters, every family had a stake in locating the school as close as possible to their own children. As a consequence, during the first three decades of the twentieth century, it was not uncommon for schools to be moved or rebuilt in new locations to accommodate demographic shifts in the school district or changes in school boundaries. The location of the school became divisive among members of the Davyroyd school district. Robert Stirling and Claude H. Smith petitioned the Minister of Education to relocated the new school on July 18, 1927:

> We are forwarding to you today under separate cover a Petition protesting against the approved site of the proposed new Davyroyd School No. 93... The main objection of the Signers of the Petition, is the distance of the northern sections from the School... As an alternative to the above plan we would suggest that you enforce the new school being placed in the proper centre of the District.[4]

Despite these quarrels, the schools brought new potential for social life into both Davyroyd and Zenith. School-based events, such as Christmas concerts and picnics, brought the families together in one place. The women in both respective school districts formed community clubs, with names such as the "Willing Workers." They organized dances, card parties, potluck suppers and wedding showers. People came together at the schools to vote in provincial and federal elections. Close friendships developed among the neighbouring children, who spent their days together in school. Conversations among the children at school were a source of news at the supper table in the evening. Playing ball games against neighbouring schools and

---

3. Letter from Will Craig, secretary to the proposed Moose Pond, to the Department of Education, Government of Saskatchewan, 27 October 1910. Zenith School District Records, Saskatchewan Archives Board.

4. Letter from Robert Stirling and Claude H. Smith to the Minister of Education, Government of Saskatchewan, 18 July 1927. Davyroyd School District Records, Saskatchewan Archives Board.

yelling the school cheer solidified their allegiance within the district. In these many ways, the rural school provided an institutional basis for shared interactions for the people living within the school districts and fostered neighbourhood-based communities.

Farm families, to varying extents, developed ties and participated in the locally based activities. Over the years, certain families became close friends; others remained disconnected; animosities between neighbours flared up and disappeared; reciprocal labour sharing between specific families became established and then reorganized.

Through participation in these activities, the geographically bounded space defined by the school districts of Davyroyd and Zenith became a crystallized identity for people living within them. Even people living within other parts of Rural Municipality Number 72, and those living within the surrounding villages and towns, came to know the districts of Davyroyd and Zenith.

Throughout the teens and into the 1920s, the number of farm operators decreased. Some decided they preferred living in the city. Others could not afford to continue farming. In some cases, newcomers bought the land and, in other cases, neighbouring farmers expanded their operation. By 1927, 28 families lived in Davyroyd, a drop from 43 families from 1913, but a record high of 35 school-age children attended the school. Attending school together created an intense familiarity and for some of the people, who became farmers, a deep comradeship evolved that lasted their lifetime.

Some of the children, who attended the rural schools in Davyroyd and Zenith, established their own farms in the districts. The regular use of the church during the summer and the operation of the school continued to provide institutional foundations for locally based support networks. The shared telephone line also intensified familiarity because everyone could listen in on all conversations. By the 1940s and 1950s, the people farming in the two districts shared a common history, either as an early settler or as children of settlers.

After the Schools Closed

When farmers retired in the 1950s and 1960s, either a son took over the farm or a neighbouring farmer bought the land. No new families had moved into the district and bought farmland since the 1940s. By 1965, a combined total of only 34 families lived, owned and farmed land in Davyroyd and Zenith, a huge decline from 78 families in 1913.

By 1960, the connections strengthened either by kin or by childhood associations had fostered multifacetted and overlapping networks among most of the farm families. Three early settlers remained. An adult in another five families had lived in the districts for two decades. Four female and 25 male descendents of early settlers lived and farmed in the district. These people had known each other since their birth and had attended the one-room schools together. Many of the other women, who had married farmers, also had deep connections within the school district. Four women had taught at one of the two schools and the other women integrated easily into rural life. Kin ties had become more predominant. Seven sets of brothers and one set of sisters were farming within the two districts and two men had a sister who farmed in the districts. Six young farmers lived in the same farmyard as their parents. Only six of the 34 families did not have a kin tie within the two districts.

Kin ties not only provided ready-made connections between neighbouring families but also the basis by which many men got established on their farms. Twenty-five of the 34 male farm operators had the assistance of their fathers to establish their farms. Their fathers either assisted them to establish a neighbouring farm or to take over the family farm. In many cases, brothers cooperated together by jointly buying equipment and sharing the labour of seeding, cultivating and harvest as well as the labour associated with keeping cattle. After their farms were established, some brothers chose to farm independently but three of the seven sets of brothers continued this practice.

The institutional structure binding farm families shifted when Zenith School closed in 1958 and Davyroyd closed in 1959. Few of the 60 children born after 1945 attended either country school. Instead, about 30 children a year rode the bus to school in Assiniboia. Some had a 20-minute ride, while those who got on the bus first had rides of 60 minutes both morning and evening. These long rides together continued to create deep familiarity among the neighbouring children.

When Zenith School closed in 1958, the schoolhouse, teacherage, barn and land were sold. The school board was disbanded. No physical or institutional reminder indicated that a school had operated for 45 years. This vacuum prompted a different response the following year when Davyroyd School closed. Farm families living in both Davyroyd and Zenith organized a joint community club to buy Davyroyd School and grounds for $120. Keeping the building allowed the families to continue holding the events that they had enjoyed. The men's club had responsibility for upkeep of the yard and schoolhouse and they had to organize the bar at social events. The women's club decorated the school for events and provided the food. The school continued as a gathering place for summer picnics, New Year's parties, card parties, wedding showers, baby showers and other social events. Every one of the 60 children was entitled to a wedding shower at the school, even if they had moved out of the province.

The church continued to be open during the summer months. After the service, adults still gathered in the front yard to swap news while their children ran through the graveyard examining the gravestones of the early settlers. Many of the 60 children were christened in this church. Each year, the young student minister organized a week of church day-camp at the school during the summer for 30 or more children. Teenage girls taught the younger children from a curriculum provided by the United Church. Adults in both districts gathered on Friday afternoon to watch the final concert. These gatherings were reminiscent of the Christmas concerts of the bygone era.

Other new locally based associations formed during the postwar decades and structured opportunities for neighbours to come together. Volunteers continued to maintain and frequent the curling rink that had been built in a farmyard in the 1940s. Women and men from both districts curled two nights a week and often had bonspiels on the weekends. Families in both communities formed the Community Well Association to pool resources to build a well and maintain an electric pump to provide water. One of the farmers donated his land and water for this resource. In Zenith, local farmers had started an association to purchase a snow plough to keep the roads and driveways cleared for the school bus. Each year, a different farmer volunteered to rise at 5:00 a.m., when necessary, to clear the snow from the roads.

The close connections between farm families during the 1960s and 1970s resembled the community-saved scenario. Various institutions continued to provide a structure for locally based ties and there were enough families at various stages of the life cycle to provide support systems within the districts. Adults visited each other in the evenings. Farm men cooperated with various tasks such as branding cattle and they shared the purchase of rarely used equipment, such as stone pickers. Women supported each other by exchanging vegetables, tips for preserving, and childrearing concerns. The children rode the bus to school together and often socialized together.

Gradually, though, the widespread dissemination of electrical power, better roads and the purchase of television sets and cars in the 1950s connected these farm families to the world. Electrical power reduced the physical challenge of agricultural production and domestic work. Most of the women had driver's licenses and access to cars. Shopping trips to nearby towns were made weekly. Women, men and children developed more extensive connections outside the rural area.

Zenith and Davyroyd in 2001

The structural basis for social ties to be embedded exclusively among residents of Zenith and Davyroyd even more radically changed by 2001. Land ownership continued to become more consolidated into fewer farm families; fewer children lived in the districts; more land was rented; and non-resident ownership had become common. By 2001, only thirteen families owned land, farmed the land and lived in the two districts. Nine miles separated the two most distance families.

From near similarity of farm size in 1913, farm size now varied greatly with consequent differences in the material circumstances of neighbouring farm families. Differential responses by farmers to the economic conditions after World War II increased the gap between large-scale productive units and small operations. By 2001, two families owned four quarters or less. Seven families owned five to seven quarters. Three owned 10 or 11 quarters and one family owned 18 quarters.

Twenty-one landowners lived outside the district. Eight non-residents owned land but rented it to others. Thirteen non-residents owned and farmed land. Of these, two people commuted over 300 miles to seed and harvest their crops.

An additional five families occupied houses in the school districts. Of these, one owned land and rented it out; one person had sold her land but continued to live in the family farmhouse. Two others lived in their childhood houses and drove to Assiniboia for employment. The other couple had no familial connections to the district and both had employment in Assiniboia. Consequently, five out of 18 residences were occupied by people who did not actively farm.

Twelve children lived in the two districts and all of them took the bus to school in Assiniboia. Four farm operators had a total of eight children and two other families had two children each. The absence of many children in the district and the vast distances between their farms meant that most of these children formed closer friendships with school chums than with others who lived within the district.

Two of the 13 male farm operators had full-time jobs not related to farming. Another ran a small business fixing equipment and hauling grain. Of the 12 farm women, two were over 65; of the remaining 10 women, only two had not maintained regular waged or salaried employment in the local town. These other forms of employment for women and men further increased the opportunities to form wider social networks.

Nine of the farm men had attended school in Assiniboia and had friendship and support ties that were connected to their school days in Assiniboia with people outside the district. Some of these friends were also farmers and others lived in towns or cities. These extensive connections with people who lived outside the districts were often associated with membership in the Saskatchewan Wheat Pool, commercial transactions, recreation, and extended kin. In contrast to their fathers, almost all of these people had lived away from home and had held jobs that paid a wage or salary before returning to farm. Some continued to work at these jobs as well as work on the farm. These experiences formed the basis of friendships that are much more dispersed than those of the previous generations of farm operators.

With the decrease in population of the district, the institutional supports declined. The church had discontinued operation in the 1980s but the graveyard was still used for both residents and past residents. Volunteers continued to paint the church and maintain the graveyard. The small number of children, though, could not support a summer church camp at the school. Participation in the snowplough club had dwindled because only four families out of 13 had children at home. The curling rink had collapsed but resident farm families and their descendents kept the tradition alive by holding a weekend bonspiel in Assiniboia each year. Trophies in memory of local family members were given as prizes. The local town had largely replaced the rural neighbourhood as the source of institutions used by rural people.

While many circumstances enhanced relations with people outside the two districts, other conditions, such as deep family roots, continued to bind the remaining farm families together. Most of the current farm families can trace their ancestry to someone who farmed in the district. Nine of the remaining 13 farm families had a member who was a descendant of original settlers. Three of the others were born into local farm families, who had moved in during the 1940s. Only one farm operator was new to the area. Eleven of the non-resident owner/operators were direct descendants of original homesteaders and were tied back into the rural area by family and commercial relations.

Active kin ties provided a basis for connections within the district and also attracted previous residents back for social gatherings. Eleven of the 13 farm operators that lived within the district had kin ties with other resident farm families. Five farm operators had commercial farming ties with kin who lived outside the districts. Of the nine farm operators who had begun farming after 1965, only one did not have the assistance of a father, who had farmed in the district. The remaining four farmers, who established their farms prior to 1965, also had had the assistance of their resident fathers. In addition to assistance from his father, one of the younger farmers had active economic relationships with two brothers who farmed land in the districts but lived outside the district. Kin support had continued to provide the basis for entry into farming and remaining in the district.

Despite the dispersed nature of the networks of these farm families, the country school continued to serve as an important focal point. The community club still organized parties to celebrate New Year's, Halloween, weddings, wedding anniversaries, reunions, baby showers, and stag parties. The benefits of association with the Zenith and Davyroyd Community Club had attracted new members: two women who live in the district but do not farm; one woman who is retired from farming; and four women who live and farm outside the district. The community well had become an even more important resource to accommodate the water needs associated with intensified crop spraying. Instead of gathering outside the rural church, discussions about crop conditions were commonplace while farmers pumped water for another day of spraying.

By 2001, individuals living in Davyroyd and Zenith had personal networks consisting of social ties, which were located locally but also included ties with people who were geographical dispersed. The sense of place, developed by their parents, grandparents and great grandparents, however, lingered on. The continued use of the country school as a community centre and the resource of the community well strengthened the geographically based ties. These ties continued to provide both social and economic support.

The personal networks of the 13 farm families can be characterized as liberated in the sense that they have ties that extend beyond the neighbourhood. These networks, however, depart from the typical urban liberated network in that the people are still embedded in a dense network of ties that are locally based in the two school districts. They know their neighbours very well. The men have known each other since birth and over the years, through close association, the women have come to know each other very well.

The 13 remaining farm families have a strong "sense of place." For them, the people who reside in the school districts of Zenith and Davyroyd still constitute a "community. They feel a sense of obligation toward each other and rely on each other for support of various kinds.

The Structural Basis for Community in Rural Saskatchewan

The conditions in Davyroyd and Zenith that fostered the transition from exclusively locally based social networks and the resultant community spirit to far-flung personal networks are commonplace through Saskatchewan. Fewer people live in rural areas. The decline is phenomenal. The number of farm operators steadily declined from 121,054 in 1941 to 76,970 in 1971, and dropped further to 56,995 by 1996. The decline in the rural farm population mirrored the decline in the number of farms. The number of people living on rural farms increased to a high of 564,012 in 1931. At this time, over half a million people lived on farms and comprised 61% of the population of Saskatchewan. By 1991, only 147,935 people were classified as rural-farm and formed only 15% of the population of Saskatchewan (see Table 1).

Table 1. Saskatchewan Population, Rural Farm Population, and Number and Size of Saskatchewan Farms for Select Census Years, 1901–1996

Year	Saskatchewan Population	Rural Farm Population	% Rural Farm	Number of Farmers	Size of Farm (acres)
1921	757,510			114,153	369
1931	921,785	564,821	61	119,835	408
1941	895,992	514,677	57	121,054	432
1951	831,728	398,279	48	111,586	550
1961	925,181	304,672	33	93,924	686
1971	926,242	233,335	25	76,970	845
1981	968,313	180,255	19	67,318	952
1991	988,925	147,935	15	60,840	1,091
1996	990,237			56,995	1,152

Sources: Census of Canada, 1956, Vol. II, and 1971, Vol. IV, cat. 96 -709; Statistics Canada, Cat 95-370, Cat. 93-357, Cat. 95-179.

The economic circumstances of farm families have become increasingly diverse. In 1911, 91% of the farms were fully owned. During the homestead period, farmers shared many of the same problems, work demands and common enemies. Each farmer owned approximately the same amount of land. The size of the homestead (160 acres) was an arbitrary choice and increasingly did not represent a viable productive unit. Farmers entered into debtor/creditor relationships to expand their farms to a viable size. By 1931, owners worked only 66% of the farms; tenants worked 15%; and 18% were worked by part owner/part tenants. After 1940, farmers entered a period characterized by rapid agricultural development. The cost-price squeeze intensified pressure on farm operators to increase production by consolidated land holdings. This trend was accompanied by a shift from ownership to tenant relationships. By 1981, owners operated only 51% of farms, tenants operated 9% of farms and part-owners/part-tenants operated 40% (see Table 2).

The average farm size rose steadily to 845 acres in 1971 and to 1,152 acres by 1996 (see Table 1). Although the average farm size was increasing, not all farm operators were increasing their holdings to the same extent. Over time, the spread in the amount of land held by farm operators increased. In 1931, 64.4% of farm operators had holdings of 101–479 acres. In 1991, 66% of operators had holdings of 240–1599 acres. In 1931, 91% of farm operators had holdings of 101–959 acres. By 1991, 91% of farm operators had holdings of 70–2,239

Table 2. Land Tenure for Saskatchewan, Farms Classified by Tenure of Operator (Owner, Tenant, Part Owner/Part Tenant Manager) for Select Census Years, 1901 –1981

Year	Total Farms	Owner		Tenant		Part Owner/ Part Tenant		Manager	
		#	%	#	%	#	%	#	%
1901	13,445	12,924	96	212	2	309	2	na	
1911	95,013	86,109	91	3,497	4	5,407	6	na	
1921	119,451	91,587	78	12,942	11	13,841	12	1,081	1.0
1931	136,472	90,250	66	21,044	15	24,737	18	441	.3
1941	138,713	72,954	53	34,028	25	31,028	22	638	.5
1951	112,018	61,157	55	16,495	15	33,760	30	606	.4
1961	93,924	48,374	52	9,521	10	35,687	38	342	
1971	76,970	41,499	54	5,374	6	30,097	39	na	
1981	67,318	34,135	51	5,980	9	27,203	40	na	

Sources: Census of Canada, 1951, Vol. IV, Part 2, Table 1; 1966, Vol.5, Table 2; Cat. 96-709, Vol. IV, Part 3 (Bull. 4.3-2), Table 13; Statistics Canada, Cat. 95-371, Table 3; Cat. 96-901, Table 13.

acres. Consequently, the few farm operators left in rural areas had widely divergent material circumstances from those living on neighbouring farms.[5]

The low price for wheat on world markets, supported by subsidizes of the American government and the European Union, continues to pressure farmers to produce more grain. Farmers are responding by adopting a variety of options. Some farmers are intensifying production through continuous cropping and the application of fertilizer, pesticide and so on. Some are increasing production by farming more land and consequently making further investments in equipment to ensure the fields are sown and harvested in the brief window of opportunity. Others are diversifying into specialty crops such as lentils and chickpeas. This decision entails a major investment in new equipment such as air seeders, high clearance sprayers and specialized harvesting equipment. Diversifying into specialty crops is also risky because large multinational grain-purchasing companies are advantageously placed to manipulate the market price to their advantage. There are thousands of producers and only a handful of buyers.

Unless the trade-distorting subsidies that depress grain prices are eliminated, there will be continuing pressure on farmers to increase production by concentrating ownership of farmland. Fewer farm families will be left in the Saskatchewan countryside. Those who remain will continue to have more diverse farm operations than the preceding generation of farmers. The material circumstances that previously bound neighbouring farm families together will gradually erode. There will be a diminished capacity for farm families to find support from neighbours, to exchange non-market services and to organize locally.

Conclusion

On 3 November 2001, the Zenith and Davyroyd Community Club organized a hoedown to celebrate Halloween. Around 20 people gathered at the school to enjoy a meal together and talk into the evening. They compared notes about the variable price of their new specialty crops, such as lentils and chickpeas. Women talked about their jobs in Assiniboia. The conversations often wandered to include updates on their children now scattered across Canada.

During the next few months, some of these people would fly east to visit children, others

5. Census of Canada, 1971, Vol. 4, Cat. 96-709, Table 4 and Statistics Canada, 95–371, Table 1.

would leave to spend the winter in Arizona, and others would fly to watch the International Curling Championship. All of them would make regular trips to Assiniboia, Moose Jaw and Regina to visit friends and family, to shop for groceries and buy farm inputs, and to enjoy themselves with activities such as curling or movies. On New Year's Eve, they would again gather together at the old country school to enjoy the easy comradeship of friends that they have known for decades.

Events on the provincial, national and international level will continue to shape the character of agricultural development and the lives of these people. Farm families will continue to show their flexibility and accommodate to vagaries of the market. If the trend toward consolidation continues, however, the foundations that generated communities within the boundaries of rural school districts will gradually vanish. Fewer farm operators mean fewer families and fewer children in rural areas. In the case of Davyroyd and Zenith, of the 13 people who live, own and farm land in the districts, only five are under 50 years of age. None is under 40 years. Assuming this trend continues there will not be enough farm families living in close enough proximity to provide a basis for rural friendships and locally based activities. The crystallized identities of Zenith and Davyroyd will disappear and the local support networks for the remaining families will evaporate.

To ensure a reasonable standard of living for farm families, and thereby to avoid this scenario, strong, concerted action by all levels of government is necessary. The provincial government must reassess property/education tax paid on agricultural land to equitable levels. The federal government must take action to establish a fair price for all grains through collective marketing agencies and by taking measures to safeguard against trade-distorting subsidies of other countries. With these policies securely in place, young Canadian women and men could make a reasonable living growing food for the world.

CHAPTER TEN

Social Cohesion and the Rural Community

Polo Diaz, Randy Widdis and David Gauthier

The process of globalization and its desired and undesired changes are occurring at an unprecedented rate in many regions of the world. In this context, the quality of life of many social groups has been impacted by the dramatic economic changes of globalization. Governments and civil society organizations have found it difficult to ameliorate the impact of these global forces and, even less, to manage the uncertainties of the process. In many cases these governments and organizations have been the main supporters of the integration of the national economy to the global economy without assuming the social and environmental costs of that decision. In this context, public and private organizations have searched for those key dynamics that could bring quality of life to *globalized societies*.

Concerns about social cohesion, defined as one of the key dynamics in the restoration of quality of life, seem to be at the top of the policy agenda for many countries. Policy makers and researchers often use the concept as part of a package that includes related ideas, such as "civil society" and "social capital." Its history reminds us of the history of a similar concept that was also defined as a promoter of quality of life: *sustainable development*. Social cohesion is, however, an ambiguous concept and its use in policy-making is difficult as a result of its vagueness.

This paper is an exercise in clarifying social cohesion and outlining both its limitations and potential as a concept around which policy can be developed and as a research concept. The paper is part of a multidisciplinary research project that focuses on the issue of social cohesion in the rural communities of Saskatchewan. The main goal of this project is to support and enhance multidisciplinary social science research in the area of regional and rural community social cohesion. It addresses broad policy issues concerning social cohesion in the context of human adaptation to environmental, social and economic changes on the Prairies of Saskatchewan.

The paper is divided into three sections. The first section discusses the development of the concept in the public agenda. After a brief explanation of the historical conditions that gave rise to recent concerns about social cohesion, discussion focuses on problems related to the definition of the concept, its applicability, and the relationship between social cohesion and the neo-liberal strategy of development. The second section deals with the applicability of the concept to the rural community. Finally, the last section of the paper considers social cohesion and policy in the context of rural Saskatchewan.

The Rise of Social Cohesion in the Public Agenda

Historical Considerations

Most experts agree that the current interest in social cohesion is part of a reaction to economic conditions related to the process of globalization. Since the 1970s, the restructuring of the world economy has created social, political and economic turbulence that has brought radical changes to the lives of people. This economic restructuring aimed at macroeconomic stabilization, structural adjustment, and the globalization of production and distribution has followed a strategy of development that is commonly called neoliberal or neoconservative. According to Collins (2000: 100), this strategy is characterized, first, by an increasing focus on economic growth in terms of the organization and direction of the path of development; second, by a predominance of the free market as the main engine of development and in the allocation of resources; third, by an increasing economic globalization achieved by removing barriers to the free flow of commodities in and out of countries and a growing integration to international markets; fourth, by a privatization of economic resources, which has moved functions and assets from government to the private sector; and finally, by a reduction of state activities, restraining its functions to the provision of infrastructure and law enforcement. In this perspective, *economic success* is defined by and limited to the annual rates of economic growth.

Although these policies have been generally successful in terms of specific economic indicators such as growth and reduction of inflation and account imbalances, they have failed to spread the benefits of economic development. Rather, it seems that the implementation of this neoliberal strategy of development has resulted in drastic socioeconomic implications for large sectors of national populations. People in many countries have experienced rates of unemployment above historical national rates; a lack of job stability, salary reductions and loss of benefits as a result of the process of restructuration and rationalization of private and public corporations; and a more restricted access to basic services such as health and education as a result of new fiscal policies. They have also experienced the negative consequences of high rates of inflation; a more unequal distribution of income; and, in some cases, the deterioration of institutional forms of resistance, such as labour organizations (Jeannote, 2000).

The neoliberal strategy of development seems to have repercussions beyond that of the economic wellbeing of individuals. Social dimensions of decay such as the rise of crime, a decline in personal safety, the breakdown of families and communities, the risk of contracting diseases or illness (the mad cow disease is a good example), homelessness, and increasing negative attitudes towards immigrants are prevalent as well. No less relevant is the increasing deterioration of environmental conditions as a result of an overemphasis on economic growth and the consideration of environmental costs as externalities. To a large extent, the process of globalization has taken us into what Beck (1992, 1999) calls the *risk society* (1992), i.e., a society characterized by an increasing distribution of social and ecological *bad* rather than *goods*. In the past, industrial or pre-globalized society centered around the production and distribution of goods such as wealth, income, and formal employment (stable and permanent employment), while the present-day risk or globalized society is organized around the distribution of the costs and risks of socioeconomic development. Current conditions seem to be characterized by uncertainty, pessimism, and a lack of trust in some of the most important institutions in society. In these terms, the protests against the meetings of the World Trade Organization should be understood in that context and not as a reaction of a few anarchists.

The implementation of this neoliberal strategy of development has resulted in an aggravation of inequalities both within and between countries and deterioration in the quality of life of those who cannot profit from the strategy of development. Bessis argues that the globalization of the economy has been accompanied by a globalization of the social crisis, in which "exclusion and poverty have reached such high levels that they cannot be longer considered as simply accidental or residual phenomena" (1995: 11). This crisis could be characterized, in more abstract terms, as a dual process of marginalisation and concentration. Large sectors of the population have been marginalized from the profits generated by the new economic changes and from the certainty of stable occupations. This dual process has resulted in increasing levels of fear and uncertainty, where tolerance and compassion for others have been the losers and social exclusion, isolation and rejection have became predominant.

In these terms, it is not surprising that social cohesion has emerged as a major concern. There is an increasing awareness that development means more than simple economic growth and that the fruits of economic success should be more equally distributed. In this perspective, the issue of quality of life in general, and social cohesion in particular, is a relevant goal for national policy in many countries.

Social cohesion as a social issue has had a long history in the social sciences. A large number of social scientists, concerned with issues related to social order and social stability, have developed an array of explanations of this concept. Emile Durkheim, a classical sociologist, made social cohesion a central element in his explanation of the process of transformation of European societies, arguing that social solidarity is a fundamental issue for social development. Durkheim argued that the problems created by increasing division of labour required an *organic solidarity* based on mutual dependency. He thought that a perfect organic solidarity was difficult to attain since old disparities of wealth and power were incompatible with this organic solidarity, but that with the help of social scientists it was possible to resolve the problems and create the required social order (1964). Since then, the problems of social order and its associated concepts, such as social cohesion, social exclusion, integration and social capital, have been major themes in sociology and other social sciences (Alaluf, 1999). Other social scientists, however, have approached the issue of social order from a different perspective. They have been more interested in explaining how societies characterized by tensions and contradictions remain together. For them social cohesion is an ideological phenomenon that promotes a *social order* that is not always just. Gramsci's concept of *hegemony* and Althusser's discussion of *ideology* are good examples of this type of approach. The co-existence of these two approaches shows how social integration or cohesion could be analyzed from different perspectives that emphasize distinct consequences.

Social cohesion, as a policy issue and as a policy-oriented research concept, has a shorter history than in the social sciences. Jeannote, in her study about the development of the concept in Europe (2000), indicates that social cohesion became prominent in the policy agenda of several European organizations in the late 1980s. In the case of the European Union, concerns about social cohesion emerged as early as 1987 during the elaboration of the *Single European Act*. The Organization for Economic Cooperation and Development indicated its interest in social cohesion issues in 1996 and the Council of Europe integrated the concept into its agenda in the late 1990s. Other European organizations, such as the Commissariat general du Plan of the French government and the Club of Rome, have also expressed significant interest in the issue of social cohesion (Jenson: 1998).

The Problem of Definition

One of life's great ironies is that it is often easier to define or identify what something is not as opposed to what something is. Social cohesion is one such thing. At the simplest level, we can say that social cohesion is the opposite of what has interchangeably been called *social deterioration* or *social disintegration*, i.e., a state of being that readily brings to mind notions such as increasing polarization, political disenchantment, social exclusion and institutional collapse. Persistent levels of unemployment, income inequality and deteriorating public health are just three examples of structural fault lines that exist within society despite the optimistic picture painted by those in favour of economic and political policies aimed at encouraging the globalization of production and distribution. Yet focusing on its antithesis still does not enable us to come up with a working definition of social cohesion. And defining social cohesion as "not deterioration" or "not disintegration" is precarious because it may lead us into a functionalist trap which asserts that integration is cohesive but ignores the possibility of diverse, cohesive cultures. Yet it is fundamental for policy-making to develop a systematic understanding of the concept and of the phenomena that the concept addresses.

The ever-increasing body of literature both illuminates and obfuscates the subject. Thought-provoking ideas are presented but their diversity and complexity serve to remind us that there is no agreement about either the definition of social cohesion or its links to a number of related concepts such as sustainable development. A brief review of the literature bears testament to this diversity. Some see social cohesion as an outcome of shared values, activities and conditions that make *collective action* more effective. Others focus more on social cohesion as *perception*, viewing it as a social process that enables individuals to feel they belong to a group with which they share values that emphasize trust and solidarity. Still others connote social cohesion with *social capital*, a concept viewed interchangeably as a set of collective activities in which groups and individuals engage, the embeddedness of individuals and households in social networks, or as investment in institutions that support neighbourhood and community interaction (Jenson, 1998: 26–27). Cohesiveness, it is argued, increases social capital because it involves collective action. What is common to these different definitions is the idea that social cohesion is a *process* whereby individuals and groups are included or excluded from participation in the wider society.

Durkheim argues that "social solidarity" was a moral phenomenon and, to this extent, open to different interpretations. Following the history of the concept in the social sciences, we could argue that social cohesion has the same characteristic. In her review of the literature, Jenson (1998) identifies several theoretical approaches in the social sciences that deal with social cohesion from perspectives that combine different understandings of society and conflict. She argues that some theoretical approaches identify social cohesion as a system of shared values and commitments taking place through institutional processes; while other theoretical traditions such as neoliberalism have emphasized social order as "an unintended but real benefit of the market and other individual transactions… (Thus) … a well functioning society is generated as a byproduct of private behaviours. Individual behaviour, especially in markets and voluntary associations, drives social order" (ibid., 10). Accordingly, she identifies two broad camps in the literature according to the unit of analysis: one emphasizing a focus at the level of the individuals, and the other concentrating on the whole of society and the roles of structures and institutions. All these approaches tend to emphasize the idea of social order as the consequence of shared values more than group interests, of consensus more than conflict, and of social practices more than political action.

There is also another approach to social cohesion that rests on the argument that conflict is an intrinsic characteristic of society and that there are distinctive definitions of values and justice within its population. In these terms, the important question with regard to social cohesion is who decides what is just and what is fair? In this theoretical stream, social order is a necessity for those in positions of power. To the extent that large sectors of the population accept as legitimate the unequal distribution of power, social cohesion exists. In these terms social order has the potential to be used to promote the goals and values of one group over those of another, legitimating unjust differences and inequalities. In other words, social cohesion exists in order to ensure social exclusion. Gramsci's argument about hegemony is an example of this approach. For Gramsci, a hegemonic class is one that has been able to articulate the interests of other social groups to its own, creating a unitary worldview that allows for a legitimation process (Hoare, 1971; Mouffe, 1979). He points out that a process directed to legitimate subordination and domination is a *"bastard"* form of hegemony based on a passive consensus, while a hegemony which seeks to construct a social order based on a fair distribution of power should be seen as an *"expansive"* hegemony (Mouffe, 1979: 182).

Regina Berger-Schmitt, in her analysis of the concept, concludes that social cohesion as a concept should incorporate a double dimension: first, a concern with the reduction of inequalities and social exclusion, and second, a concern with the strengthening of social relations, interactions and ties (2000: 4). This provides the concept with both a prescriptive and a descriptive or analytical character, being both a goal and a concept that could be used in the empirical analysis of social cohesion. However, these two dimensions could be treated as independent from each other. Emulating Gramsci, we could argue that social cohesion could be used either in its bastard or expansive forms, emphasizing that only the latter brings these two concerns together.

Further complicating the issue is the fact that any definition must take into account the problems of its applicability, i.e., special consideration must be given to the object upon which it is intended to apply the concept. Only a good and systematic understanding of the object of the policy or the research provides a solid ground for the application of the policy.

There is an increasing acceptance that society does not exist as a single, autonomous entity, with an overarching logic (see, for example, Touraine, 1998). Rather it is an analytical concept that helps social scientists discuss a set of more or less integrated set of open systems that operate to a large extent within the limits of the nation-state. In these terms, we should think of the educational system or the rural economy as systems that are more or less cohesive, but open to the influences—necessary or contingent—of other institutional systems. If this is the case, any intent to attain social cohesion at the national level requires a profound reflection of the relationships between and among the multiplicity of social groups, institutions, processes and dynamics that exist in a society and operate upon each other fostering or inhibiting social cohesion. The task is difficult since it requires defining how increases and decreases in the level of cohesion in one entity such as the rural community may affect the cohesion of a myriad of other entities. An increment of social cohesion in one group, oil companies for example, could have disastrous consequences for the social cohesion and sustainability of isolated communities. If we are not aware of these dynamics and the way they operate, policies aimed to increase the levels of social cohesion of some entities could have a variety of unintended consequences.

The arguments that societies are characterized by interrelated institutional systems and their complex relationships also have implications for cause-effect arguments about social cohesion. Some believe that social cohesion can contribute to economic growth, or that social cohesion has positive effects upon health and education which in turn produce substantial economic benefits (see Dayton-Johnson: 2001, 67–81). We should be careful, however, to avoid seeing such results as direct effects of social cohesion. Social cohesion affects economic growth, but we could also argue that economic growth affects social cohesion and that the degree of influence that each dimension has on the other depends on specific institutional and political contexts.

Another issue that makes the use of the concept confusing is the relationship between the present strategy of development and social order, trust, social capital, sense of belonging and other dimensions of social cohesion. There is strong agreement that the present is characterized by uncertainty and insecurity that results in a decline of social cohesion and that this is somewhat related to the increasing integration of national economies to the global economy.

The debate begins when we try to define the specific relationship between social cohesion and neoliberalism.

For the OECD the lack of social cohesion "threatens to undermine both the drive towards greater economic flexibility and the policies that encourage strong competition, globalization and technological development" (Jenson, 1998: 6). Dayton-Johnson echoes these concerns by arguing about the need for social cohesion as a way to avoid a situation where "citizens distressed by the erosion of public-provided services will demand measures ... that impede the growth of unfettered capitalism—thus 'shooting themselves in the foot' by impairing their own potential prosperity" (2001: 13). These arguments tend to perceive the lack of social cohesion as an absence of equilibrium between the development of the economy and civil society. The solution requires government *to act upon* society in order to revitalize the levels of social cohesion, so that we are able to balance competitive markets with a strong social fabric.

This view of the relationship between social cohesion and neoliberalism is just one interpretation. It is also possible to reason, as in the case of Beck's arguments about the risk society, that the specific form of the process of economic development—the neoliberal path—is the one that has created the problems that we are trying to resolve with policies and programs oriented to increase social cohesion. If this view is correct, we could argue that any serious intent to increase social cohesion would have negative consequences for the existing path of development.

In the context of policy-making, it is essential to clarify the relationship between neoliberalism and social cohesion. Public agendas have priorities, so policies and programs are organized according to different degrees of importance. Economic growth is clearly a priority for the majority of national governments. There are, of course, different paths to achieve this goal, paths that combine in different ways economic and non-economic objectives. If the second view is correct, i.e., the problem is largely the result of neoliberalism, then the possibilities for social cohesion are minimal and the only alternative for governments would be the *management* of social exclusion.

It is clear that there is a lack of cohesiveness in the debate about social cohesion. Yet there is a need to operate from a working definition in order to structure investigation. In this context, we have adopted a flexible conceptual approach in our research, paying attention to several dimensions of social cohesion: the strength of social relations, the existence of shared communities of interpretation, the existence of feelings of common identity and of a sense of belonging, forms of collective action, and social trust.

It is also obvious to us that social cohesion should be understood as a *process*, where the distinction suggested by Regina Berger-Schmitt (2000) should be preserved. It is important to describe the actual degree of social cohesion in the rural community, but it is no less important to discuss how far or how close this social cohesion is from a state characterized by a significant decline of all kind of inequalities.

Social Cohesion and Its Applicability to the Prairie Rural Community

Cohesion in the Face of Rural Decline

Our fundamental interest is in understanding the processes and dynamics of social cohesion in the rural communities of the Saskatchewan Prairies and its possible effects on the viability or sustainability of these communities. This investigation is framed within the context of decline as outlined in the previous section. The decision to use the rural community affords us a clear advantage: its existence in a clearly defined space and its small population provide us with an empirical and clearly delimited setting where we can analyze the dynamics and processes of social cohesion. Yet because our laboratory is rural Saskatchewan, our inquiry must by necessity deal with questions regarding social cohesion within this particular context. This is difficult because the term *rural*, like cohesion, is not well understood. When we assign the term rural to a geographical area, we not only define that area as rural based on certain accepted criteria, we attempt to understand what it means to be called rural in the face of ongoing and changing conditions. The literature reveals that in terms of definition, three main themes are apparent: 1) rural is synonymous with anything non-urban in character, which by default, suggests that the rural environment has no character or qualities of its own; 2) *rurality*, the distinctive characteristics associated with rural, can be defined in various forms; and 3) user perception of distinctively rural uses (e.g., agriculture, forestry, mining, etc.) is the principle agent of rural definition (Veldman, 1984). An all-embracing definition of rural is difficult to achieve because rural definitions depend on the functions designated to the countryside but these vary over space and time; rural areas are undergoing change due to social, economic and technological developments and thus any definition must be dynamic; and a definition also has to take into account spatial and cultural differences, i.e., what is rural here may not be rural there.

Some believe that we must do away with rural because in today's world it is an irrelevant conception lacking explanatory power. Instead, they argue, we are better off looking at extra-rural structures and processes, notwithstanding that these are moulded by local circumstances (Newby, 1985). Others assert that people make their own sense of the rural reinterpreting dominant images through their own cultural practice. Thus it is necessary for researchers to understand how dominant and local images of rural are reinterpreted through everyday experience. What role this reinterpretation plays in cohesion is worth investigating. However, the literature shows us that there is no strong consensus as to what constitutes rural and so any investigation of social cohesion within a rural context must deal with this lacuna.

If we maintain that social cohesion within the rural context is different from cohesion within the context of society in general, then it is incumbent on us to demonstrate that because rural is distinctive, rural social cohesion is by implication different as well. This is a major task given the fact that there is debate over whether or not rural should be worthy of study in its own right. This is a conceptual problem that cannot be avoided. If rural is connoted with function, then we are subject to the criticism that a definition is better seen as a research tool for the articulation of specific aspects of the rural than as a way of defining the rural. This involves trying to fit a definition to what we already intuitively consider to be rural, in the absence of any other justification as to why these functions should be regarded as representing the rural. In other words, the rural has already been defined by those doing the classifying. Descriptive methods based on functions only describe the rural; they do not define it themselves. Critics will argue that we are ignoring what it is we are trying to define.

Other definitions based on size and scale assume that population density and other spatial attributes affect behaviour and attitudes. Somehow properties of the rural, e.g., low density and small absolute numbers, produce a distinctive rural character. Critics argue that this smacks of determinism. The spatial determinism in this kind of definition stands in direct contrast to the spatial indifference inherent in the descriptive functional definition but both demonstrate a mistaken conceptualization of the relationship between space and society. Spatial determinism holds an absolute conception of space, whereby space itself possesses causal powers. Properties inherent in the rural environment are thought to produce a distinctive rural character. Spatial indifference, on the other hand, relegates space, the environment, to the position of being a mere reflection of society, an unimportant detail. This appears unduly deterministic and restrictive of human agency. Also, spatial indifference fails to appreciate the dynamism of space. While this approach sees space as produced, it leaves the matter there: space is merely the residue of social structures and therefore the study of space itself has little merit.

When we consider rural space, we must not only consider the structures producing that space but also the way in which that space is subsequently used to produce other space and to reproduce the original causal structures themselves (Hoggart and Buller, 1987). If we are to develop a conception of rural space and, by implication, a rural environment where distinctive kinds of cohesion processes occur, that are based on the principles that space and spatial expressions are both conditions of underlying structures (i.e., *space is produced*) and a means of producing further spaces (i.e., *space is a resource*), then we have to satisfy two criteria: there are significant structures operating that are associated with the local/community level; and looking at these structures, these parts of society, enables us to distinguish between a rural environment and the larger urban-dominated society. In short, the designation rural would have to identify locations with distinctive causal forces. If these specifications are met, then genuinely local, distinctively rural causal forces that relate to scale, size and function can be said to exist. From this, we could extend our logic to argue that distinctively rural cohesive processes exist as well.

Yet while recognizing the conceptual difficulties inherent in such an exercise, studying social cohesion in a rural community still has its clear advantages. The characteristics of the community, i.e., "the smallness of its scale, the homogeneity of activities and states of minds of members, a self-sufficiency across a broad range of needs and through time, and a consciousness of distinctiveness" (Rapport and Overing, 2000: 60), provide the potential for an almost *natural* presence of social cohesion.

A number of factors have traditionally promoted social cohesion in rural Saskatchewan. In the past, rural community was defined to a large extent by its existence in a circumscribed space that facilitated face-to-face contact and a similarity of contact among its members. Such interpersonal contacts promoted the creation of networks and links among members, although at the same time it also created conflict and tensions among different groups within the community. Living in the same place allowed for a communion of geographical and social experiences that facilitated people's communications. Indeed, in the pioneer period survival often depended on establishing such links in a context where geographical isolation and limited technology necessitated co-operation among settlers. Over time, accessibility improved and technology reduced the need for such collaboration in activities such as breaking the land and harvesting, but at the same time increased the possibilities for people to interact socially in common geographical spaces such as the curling rink and the community hall.

Moreover, the predominance of certain economic activities such as farming involves an increasing similarity of experience in terms of working practices, organizational methods, access to inputs, "experimentation" of new practices and inputs, etc. Stirling (2001) argues that the rural community has been historically sustainable to the extent that it has had a viable economic base and a network of social relations that could be identified as social cohesion. The community, he argues, has been characterized by the predominance of family farms "in which families own all or most of their productive capital—land, building, machinery, and livestock—and do all or most of the productive work themselves. Typically ... their farms are not large, and there are many of them ... but equally important, family farming must develop a supportive network of social relations, including neighbourly helping patterns and exchanges of advice" (2001: 248). Reimer (1997) also makes a similar argument, indicating that social networks and voluntary associations in rural Canada are the primary base for social cohesion for communities. These networks have positive consequences for the vitality and viability of the communities.

Yet the role of common spaces in ensuring cohesion has diminished in the face of developing transportation and communication technologies that enable rural dwellers to travel greater distances to conduct business and take advantage of basic services. The automobile has served to expand the personal space of rural inhabitants beyond that of local community, and e-commerce through the internet has had a negative impact on local businesses struggling to exist in the face of diminishing population and economic decline. For some, the common space through which they interact with others is not the coffee shop or rink, but rather *cyberspace*, a medium that enables individuals from both within and from outside the community to converse with each other. Whether or not this can increase social and cultural participation within the community or accelerate the breakdown of community is open to debate.

The role of the family in promoting cohesion has changed over time as well. Women have traditionally played a role in maintaining both family and community, especially during times of economic turmoil. They often worked alongside the men in the fields during the pioneer period and later performed vital roles at home and in the community where they were often the key players in the planning and operation of social events. Recently, however, the customary roles of women have changed as both economic forces and changing social conditions have combined to both push and pull women out of the domestic space and away from traditional social institutions that have proved to be so important in preserving a cohesive community. In addition, the role of inter-generational transfer in social cohesion has changed. The transfer of the family farm to the next generation ensured persistence in place but increasingly children are choosing to leave rural Saskatchewan, thereby ending that link which served to tie family to community.

Communities exist and function in a larger context. If communities were a closed system, i.e., self-sufficient and closed to foreign influences, the issue of social cohesion would be irrelevant. We would expect that only those communities with a certain degree of social cohesion, leaving aside the problems of inequalities, would survive in the long term and those without that degree of cohesiveness would disappear. Communities, however, are not alone since their fortunes are significantly impacted by forces at the regional, national and international scales.

In these terms, we need to focus our attention on two fundamental factors that affect social cohesion in the rural community. First, the social cohesion of the community is influenced by two sets of processes that should be analysed separately: internal processes of community, i.e., its unique history and the evolution of networks of cooperation and organization; and external processes, such as policies, markets, and relationships with other communities that are related to the dynamics of the society at large. Second, the internal cohesion of the community and its "cohesiveness" with external entities are not always interconnected. Analyzing the rural community as an open system that exists in contact with other open systems necessitates a focus on both the external and the internal facets of the community.

Context of Rural Decline

The Saskatchewan Case: Since the 1960s prairie agriculture has been characterized by continuous instability as a result of the process of modernization of the Canadian productive structure (Diaz and Gingrich, 1992). The economic basis of the community has been seriously affected. Commodity prices have fluctuated considerably, creating a recurring climate of insecurity among agricultural producers. Relationships between the farmers and the markets have been characterized by a "cost price squeeze" that works against agricultural producers. Financial hardships and farm bankruptcies have become as familiar as the profile of the elevators in the prairies, or as is ironically evidenced these days, the sight of these iconic structures being demolished. Net farm income has declined in the last decades, impeding many rural families from reaching a minimum standard of living. The economic picture is generally dramatic.

A side effect of these economic upheavals has been a process of differentiation of the traditional family farming. The trend seems to have a dual direction, toward both the creation of larger more heavily capitalized farms and the persistence of small farms. Conway and Stirling (1985: 6)) show that in Saskatchewan larger farms (1,120 acres and more) increased by 17% while the number of small farms (less than 240 acres) went up by 7% during the period 1971-81. On the other side, medium size traditional farms declined by 25%. This process, of course, has been accompanied by both a reduction in the number of farms (from 76, 970 in 1971 to 56,995 in 1996) and by an increase in the average farm size (845 acres in 1971 and 1,152 acres in 1996).

The centralization of goods and services and associated infrastructure has also affected the rural community. The process of centralization has brought a reduction in the infrastructure and number of community outlets in rural areas in the face of increasing concentration of these outlets in a few urban localities. As indicated by Mitchell (1975), the process started in the 1960, when private outlets such as lumberyards, machinery distributors, and retail stores began to close their doors in small communities and expand their services in large urban centers. During the 1970s and 1980s public services such as schools, hospitals, and post offices and both grain elevators and railroads followed the same road.

Finally, and no less important, has been the process of depopulation of the rural sector. The exodus of a predominantly young and single population has adversely affected the economic and social structure of rural Saskatchewan. A 1991 study of high school students in rural communities indicated that a large majority did not include living in the community as part of their plans for the future. Only 29%, predominantly male students with a farm family background, indicated their eagerness to return to the community after pursuing educational opportunities in other places. The same study shows that only 9% of the respondents were eager to seek full employment after finishing high school, while 80% expressed a desire to attend either a university or a technical institute. A 1980 survey of the Saskatchewan Education Continuing Program offers an interesting point of comparison. In that year approximately 46% of high school students wished to enter full employment after high school, while 41% preferred to attend a university or a technical institute (Diaz, forthcoming). The differences between the 1980 and 1991 surveys illustrate the negative perception that young people have of the rural labour market and demonstrate their belief in the potential that higher education offers for social and geographical mobility.

Preliminary Research Findings

The process of rural restructuring has been directly affected by the strong "urban bias" (Lipton, 1977) prevalent in development strategies pursued by national and provincial governments since the early 1960s, a bias that has marginalized the "rural" in favour of the "urban." Such policies essentially view rural areas as hinterland appendages to urban centres. Lawrence, Knuttila and Gray (2001) argue that neoliberalism has brought further economic decline to the rural sector, an intensification of the consumer culture, a removal of social capital, and environmental degradation. Epp and Whitson (2001) point out that globalization has brought a more pronounced rural-urban division of labour "as government retreats both from regulatory roles and from redistribution on behalf of disadvantaged regions," and a loss of the capacity of local communities to decide about their fate, which is increasingly assumed by regional governments and large corporations. Harder (2001), based on a small set of interviews to farmers in an Alberta rural community, indicates that most of the respondents believe that a significant reduction of community cohesion has resulted in increasing competition, a greater diversity of interests among farmers, and the improper use of foreclosures by some members of the community.

Data produced by a survey of four Saskatchewan rural communities show that social cohesion was still present in the communities during the late 1980s, although its form seems to have experienced some changes (Diaz and Gingrich, 1991: 44–48) The survey provides data for two traditional indicators of social cohesion: networks of solidarity—systems of exchange for goods and services that are important for the reproduction of the household and the community—and participation in organizations. The data, however, indicate some interesting patterns. Networks for mutual support seem to exist only in kinship, not in friendship, which is at odds with the long-standing belief in strong relations among members of the rural community. Does this pattern mean that friendship is no more relevant in the community? Is this a retreat from the community and into the family?

Participation in community activities was also relevant. Just under 30% of the households surveyed indicated that they actively contributed to community decisions, and another 50% said that while they were active in the community, they did not contribute to community decisions. The variety of organizations active at the local level was significant. Church and church-related organizations, recreational and sporting clubs and boards, and farm-related organizations were frequently mentioned by the respondents. The survey shows an interesting pattern with regard to participation: large farmers, in terms of farm income and farm size, were the most active, while some of the smaller farmers appeared to be left out of community activities. Does this mean that the process of class differentiation is affecting the community?

A positive answer to these questions would make you think that there is a certain degree of dislocation in the everyday life of the community, at least in comparison to historical patterns. It is also relevant to keep in mind that these data were gathered in 1987, a moment that can be arguably viewed as the beginning of the neoliberalization of the Canadian economy.

Is this dislocation a sign of the disappearance of the social cohesion of the rural community? Or is it a sign that a new community is in the process of emerging, with new forms of social cohesion? Let us hope that our research will provide a clear answer to these questions.

Social Cohesion and Policy: Some Considerations

Since the beginning of the twentieth century, federal and provincial governments have played a role in the formulation and implementation of rural/community, economic and regional development policies. Earlier on, federal governments were prominent in developing *top-down* development strategies where policy filtered down shifted to greater provincial control of rural development in Saskatchewan and a change in philosophy where more emphasis was placed on the *bottom-up* approach, i.e., a strategy where development programs are initiated from the local level. This transfer was based on the belief that traditional development policies did not work very well in various rural contexts. Bottom-up strategies attempted to deliver both resources and decision-making power over to the hands of rural communities in the hope that they would be better able to make efficient use of local resources and more effectively mediate external forces that affect rural hinterland areas.

More recently, a convergence of both approaches has taken place where the efforts of the dominant grassroots Regional Economic Development Authorities (REDAs) have been supplemented by various partnership agreements between the provincial and federal governments. This has resulted in the implementation of long-term policies and programs instead of the short-term, selective problem areas development programs that dominated in the recent past. This, in turn, has resulted in a preference for regional co-operation in rural and economic development rather than single community development. This convergence requires that federal and provincial governments set the program contexts and provide the financial tools that must be accessed at the regional level. It also requires people at the individual community level to network horizontally, i.e., to mobilize the community, and to network vertically, i.e., to engage in intergovernmental management, to make development successful (Radin et al., 1996: 207).

Such *regional development* involves multi- and inter-community interaction and has resulted in planning that gives preference to providing rural communities with health centres, schools and shopping centres on a regional basis rather than on an individual community basis. Basically, this strategy is based on the conviction that rural communities cannot develop on their own. This shift from single community development to regional development can be viewed as a response to the barriers and problems (e.g., lack of leadership, relative isolation of small communities, small size of communities, low population density, scarcity of fiscal resources, lack of local entrepreneurial know-how, the inability of individual communities to conduct feasibility studies, and the inability of individual communities to obtain funding and hire economic development experts) perceived to be inherent in the single community development approach.

Regional development policies are designed to provide assistance to larger geographical areas to tackle problems that are too large for single communities. The key to such development is *collaboration* among the participant centres. By such collaboration, it is argued, leadership, tax revenues, political influences, and other factors may be pooled to undertake relatively larger initiatives, both economic and social in nature. Theoretically, the consolidation of services to such areas will provide greater administrative efficiency, achievement of scale economies, improvement of communications, more effective use of limited resources, and development of shared infrastructure.

On the negative side, the regional level approach may create tension between or among individual communities, particularly when it comes to the selection of a centre for the location of a particular social or economic service in question. In many cases, communities in central locations seem to benefit more in the location of services than those in the periphery. As well, those who are critical of the trickle-down effect at the international and national scales may also have doubts about its operation at the smaller regional scale.

What impact this shift to regional development has had on social cohesion and sustaining communities is largely unknown. But it is within this planning and policy context that any assessments have to be made. While the economist may see the regional unit as the appropriate scale for implementation of policy, the geographer would argue that we need to acknowledge that while rural communities may be located in the same geographical region, they do not necessarily have the same needs or experience the exact same problems. Thus, it may be necessary to adopt policies that are both regional in scale and yet sensitive to the unique characteristics and resources of communities. For instance, some communities can best be developed through small business assistance while others in the same region may benefit more from tourism or small-scale manufacturing. Different strategic plans for different rural communities may be provided under a single regional, long-term master plan. It is also imperative for communities within the region to overcome competitive tensions and strive to build partnerships. This will require education and information dissemination, collaboration and coordination within regions and among individual communities.

Such policy considerations within the context of rural Saskatchewan will be guided by questions that relate to the concept of social cohesion as we have defined it in the hope that they stimulate further reflection on the role of social cohesion in the sustainability of rural communities within this region.

References

Alaluf, Mateo. 1999. Final Report to the Seminar, "Demographic Trends and the Role of Social Protection: The Idea of Social Cohesion," Centre de sociologie de travail, de l'emploi et de la formation, Universite libre de Bruxelles.

Beck, Ulrich. 1992. *Risk Society*. London: Sage.

Beck, Ulrich. 1999. *World Risk Society*. Cambridge: Polity Press.

Berger-Smith, Regina. 2000. "Social Cohesion as an Aspect of the Quality of Societies: Concept and Measurement," EuroReporting paper, No. 14, Centre for Survey Research and Methodology, Manheim.

Bessis, Sophie. 1995. "From Social Exclusion to Social Cohesion: Towards a Policy Agenda." Management of Social Transformation—UNESCO, Policy Paper 2.

Conway, John and Robert Stirling. 1985. "Fractions Among Prairie Farmers." Paper presented to the annual meeting of the Canadian Political Science Association, Montreal.

Dayton-Johnson, Jeff. 2001. *Social Cohesion and Economic Prosperity*. Toronto: James Lorimer and Company.

Diaz, Polo (forthcoming). "School, Knowledge and Skills in the Farm Community." In R. Stirling, P. Diaz, and J. Jaffe (eds.), *Farm Communities at the Crossroads: The Challenge and Resistance*. Regina: Canadian Plains Research Center.

Diaz, Polo and Paul Gingrich. 1992. "Crisis and Community in Rural Saskatchewan." In David Hay and Gurcharn Basran (eds.), *Rural Sociology in Canada*. Toronto: Oxford University Press.

Durkheim, Emile. 1964. *The Division of Labor in Society*. New York: The Free Press.

Epp, Roger and Dave Whitson. 2001. "Introduction: Writing off Rural Communities." In Roger Epp and Dave Whitson (eds.), *Writing Off the Rural West*. Edmonton: The University of Alberta Press/Parkland Institute.

Harder, Cameron. 2001. "Overcoming Cultural and Spiritual Obstacles to Rural Revitalization," in Epp and Whitson, *Writing Off the Rural West*.

Hoare, Quintin (ed.). 1971. *Selections from the Prison Notebooks of Antonio Gramsci*. New York: International Publishers.

Jeannotte, Sharon. 2000. "Social Cohesion Around the World: An International Comparison of Definitions and Issues." Strategic Research Analysis, Department of Canadian Heritage, Ottawa.

Jenson, Jane. 1998. *Mapping Social Cohesion. The State of Canadian Research*, CPRN Study, F/03. Ottawa: Canadian Policy Research Network.

Lawrence, Geoffrey, Murray Knuttila and Ian Gray. 2001. "Globalization, Neo-Liberalism and Rural Decline in Australia and Canada." In Epp and Whitson, *Writing Off the Rural West*.

Lipton, Michael. 1977. *Why Poor People Stay Poor: Urban Bias in World Development*. Cambridge: Harvard University Press.

Michell, Don. 1975. *The Politics of Food*. Toronto: James Lorimer.

Mouffe, Chantal (ed.). 1979. *Gramsci and Marxist Theory*. London: Routledge and Kegan.

Newby, Howard. 1985. "Locality and Rurality: The Restructuring of Social Relations." *Regional Studies* 20, no. 3: 209–15.

Rapport, Nigel and Joanna Overing. 2000. *Social and Cultural Anthropology: Key Concepts*. London: Routledge.

Redfield, Robert. 1960. *The Little Society, and Peasant Society and Culture*. University of Chicago Press: Chicago.

Reimer, Bill. 1997. "Informal Social Networks and Voluntary Associations in Non-Metropolitan Canada." In Richard Rounds (ed.), *Changing Rural Institutions: A Canadian Perspective*. Brandon: Canadian Rural Restructuting Foundation.

Robbins, Richard. 1999. *Global Problems and the Culture of Capitalism*. Boston: Allyn and Bacon.

Stirling, Robert. 2001. "Work, Knowledge, and the Direction of Farm Life." In Epp and Whitson, *Writing Off the Rural West*.

Touraine, Alain. 1998. "Society Without Society." *Current Sociology* 46, no. 2: 119–43.

Veldman, J. 1984. "Proposal for a Changing Theoretical Basis for the Human Geography of Rural Areas." In G. Clark, G. Groenendijk and F. Thissen (eds.), *The Changing Countryside*. Norwich: Geobooks.

Wellman, Barry. 1999. "From Little Boxes to Loosely Bounded Networks: The Privatization and Domestication of Community." In Janet L. Abu-Lughod (ed.), *Sociology for the 21st Century: Continuities and Cutting Edges*. Chicago: University of Chicago Press.

CHAPTER ELEVEN

The Rural Face of the New West

Roger Gibbins

Introduction

My objective is to ensure that any discussions of rural Canada provide a seat at the table for urban Canada. Or, in the specific context of my paper, the objective is to ensure that discussions about the rural West take into account the growing demographic dominance of the urban West. Only then is it possible to think through the rural face of the new West in the twenty-first century. The thesis of my paper is straightforward. The rural face of the "old West," the West extending from the turn of the last century to the 1970s, essentially defined the region. Simply put, the agrarian West was the West. However, if we turn to the "new West,"[1] and particularly to western Canada in the early twenty-first century, the rural face is fading quickly. Moreover, the rural face that lingers on may be a costly burden for western Canadians trying to position themselves for success in the new global economy.

I would like to approach this thesis by highlighting some important caveats. First, the focus of this essay will be on the prairie West, and not on rural Canada writ large. The perspective is regional rather than national. In this case, however, the regional frame is not a limitation, for in many ways the prairie West is the heartland of rural Canada. It is the primary battleground for the future of rural Canada. Whether western rural Canada "moves forward" or is "left behind" will be indicative of the more general fate of rural Canada. If rural Canada "falls" here, it will fall everywhere.

Second, my paper focuses largely on the agrarian West. I am less interested in cottage country or in the acreages that surround cities like Calgary. These are best seen as extensions of the urban West. Nor am I interested in resource-based communities, in the small communities of the "provincial norths," or in First Nation communities which have their own unique social and demographic dynamics. To put this point somewhat differently, although there will always be a residual rural population that lives outside the major cities and towns of western Canada, my focus is primarily on the rural community that is tied agriculturally to the land.

Finally, to assess the future of rural Canada we need the benchmark provided by the history of the agrarian West. It is to that history that I will now turn.

The Rural Face of the Old West

There is no question that the agrarian West formed a distinctive regional community in

---

1. The term "new West" is not used with any great precision. It came into vogue in the late 1970s to describe an emerging regional resource base that extended well beyond agricultural production, and to capture a regional society that was increasingly urban rather than rural. See John Richards and Larry Pratt, *Prairie Capitalism: Power and Influence in the New West* (Toronto: McClelland and Stewart, 1979).

the early part of the twentieth century. The prairie wheat economy forged a unique and distinctive set of values and experiences that both brought the regional community together and set it apart from the rest of Canada. Patterns of immigration, homesteading on the vast expanse of the prairies, the economic and social importance of the family farm, common agricultural and climatic challenges, and the collective frustration of dealing with remote metropolitan centres of finance and political power all played a mutually reinforcing role in creating a distinctive regional experience and culture. Moreover, the regional dominance of the grain economy meant that for most practical purposes the agrarian West was the West. Most of those not directly involved in farming were employed to support and service the grain economy. The region moved to common rhythms set by the market conditions for wheat.

The distinctive character of the agrarian West is readily apparent to students of Canadian politics. The agrarian West left a deep imprint on Canadian political life. The United Farmers of Alberta, the United Farmers of Manitoba, the Progressive Party of Canada, agrarian socialism in Saskatchewan, and the long-term success of Social Credit in Alberta all left a mark on provincial and national politics. Indeed, observers from outside the West have often seen, and mistakenly seen,[2] the Reform Party of Canada and even Canadian Alliance as continuations of this populist tradition, which found its roots in the revolt of the agrarian West against Canada's metropolitan heartland. The populist revolt was in large part a cultural revolt, pitting the yeoman farmer against the effete financial interests of central Canada. It was country mouse versus city mouse, and there was little question as to where virtue lay.

The political imprint of the agrarian West was easily matched by economic and cultural images. Think, for a moment, about how lines of combines, silhouetted against the prairie sky, provided a defining image of the Canadian frontier experience. Or think of the image of the grain elevator, or of the dust storms during the 1930s. My point here is that in the past, the agrarian West was fundamentally important to the national economy, to our social and cultural understanding, to our national imagery, and to our political lives. *That, however, was then; this is now.* How does the agrarian West fit into the new West of the twenty-first century? Will the new West have a rural face or, at the very least, will there be a significant rural face among the many potential faces of the new West?

The Urban Face of the New West

To answer these questions, we must begin with the demographic decline of the rural West. Simply put, the decline has been steep and relentless. The new West is emphatically urban. Its landscape is dominated by Calgary and Edmonton, by Winnipeg, Regina and Saskatoon, and by the vibrant smaller cities that dot the landscape. This point is illustrated by three figures. Figure 1 shows the percentage of the population in the three prairie provinces that is characterized as urban.[3] As the figure shows, the urbanization of the West has been extensive

2. In the western Canadian survey discussed below, respondents were asked to identify the political party they had supported in the 2000 federal election, held three months before the survey. Among rural respondents, 36% said they had voted for the Canadian Alliance, compared to 31% of respondents in metropolitan centres who said they had voted for the Canadian Alliance. Among rural respondents, 18% voted Liberal compared to 28% of their urban counterparts who voted Liberal. Thus there was a partisan divide between the rural and urban communities, but the divide was far from deep. See Loleen Berdahl, *Looking West: A Survey of Western Canadians* (Calgary: Canada West Foundation, June 2001).

3. The census definitions of urban have changed over time. From 1981 to present, urban Canadians have been defined as those living in an area having a population concentration of 1,000 or more and a population density of at least 400 persons per square kilometres. Urban, therefore, does not mean metropolitan. In the 1996 census, for example, 77.7% of the Alberta population was urban while 66% of the provincial population lived in either Calgary or Edmonton.

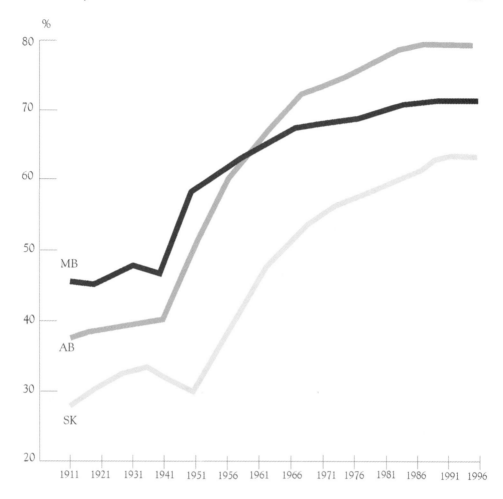

%

Figure 1. Urban population as percentage of total population, 1911–1996 (Source: Statistics Canada).

and progressive. Although there are admittedly significant provincial differences, with Saskatchewan's urban population coming in at 63.3% in the 1996 census compared to 71.8% in Manitoba and 77.7% in Alberta, the trend lines are very similar.

Figure 2 shows the flipside of the same demographic coin; the rural population has been in steady, even relentless decline. In 1996, 36.7% of the Saskatchewan provincial population was deemed rural, compared to 28.2% and 22.3% of the provincial populations in Manitoba and Alberta, respectively. Now it can be argued, of course, that these figures are still significant, representing roughly a quarter to a third of the provincial populations. However, the rural figures include small northern settlements and urban extensions through acreages and bedroom communities. If anything, Figure 2 overstates the size of the truly rural population, one that is in any event shrinking.

Figure 3 zeros in on the farm population rather than on the rural population as a whole, but the story line is essentially the same; the demographic slide has been dramatic. In 1996, the farm population constituted only 14.7% of the total Saskatchewan population, 7.2% of the Manitoba population, and 7.0% of the Alberta population. In Manitoba and particularly

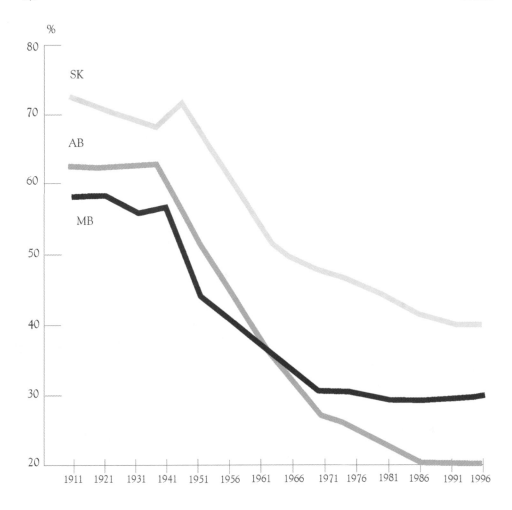

Figure 2. Rural population as percentage of total population, 1911–1996 (Source: Statistics Canada).

Saskatchewan, the growth of the cities has come about through the cannibalization of the rural countryside. Only in Alberta has substantial urban growth been accompanied by real growth, albeit much weaker growth, in the rural population. Even in Alberta, however, the farm population has been in decline.

The rural population is not only shrinking, it is also losing its distinctiveness. This loss shows up in many ways. To provide some quick illustrations, let me turn briefly to a survey conducted by the Canada West Foundation in early 2001. We interviewed just over 3,200 respondents across the four western provinces,[4] and I want to stress the general finding that the attitudinal differences among the residents of large cities, smaller cities and small towns, and rural western Canada were generally very modest. For example:

---

4. The sample contained 812 respondents from British Columbia, 814 from Alberta, 813 from Saskatchewan and 817 from Manitoba. For the sample as a whole, 1864 lived in centres of more than 100,000, 442 lived in smaller cities and towns, and 763 lived in rural areas or communities of less than 10,000 residents. See Berdahl, *Looking West.*

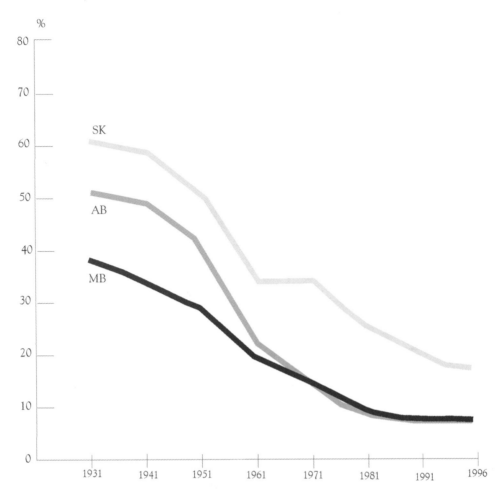

%

Figure 3. Farm population as percentage of total population, 1931–1996 (Source: Statistics Canada).

• Rural residents are more likely to identify first with their province than are urban residents. When presented with an array of local, provincial, regional, national and global identities, 32.6% of the rural respondents first chose a provincial identity, compared to 24.2% of respondents living in the large metropolitan centres. Conversely, 29.5% of the urbanities first chose a Canadian identity, compared to only 22.3% of the rural respondents. If we combine primary and secondary identities, 52.0% of the urban respondents claimed a Canadian identity compared to only 41.4% of the rural respondents. These differences are not huge, but they are statistically significant.

• There were no statistically significant differences between rural and urban respondents when it came to perceptions as to whether Canadian governments have gone too far or not far enough in providing support for Aboriginal peoples. Nor were there any differences when it came to the perception of positive or negative impacts from free trade on the Canadian or provincial economies.

• Rural respondents were modestly less optimistic about their personal futures than were urban or small city respondents.

• Measures of western alienation picked up very small differences based on the size of community. For example, when asked if western Canada would be better off economically if it separated from the rest of Canada, there were no statistically significant differences. Rural western Canadians were fractionally more supportive of Senate reform, electoral reform, and referenda. However, there were no differences in perceptions of provincial power (70.5% of all respondents thought their province had less power than it deserved in Canada).

Overall, the attitudinal differences between the rural and urban Wests were very modest. The modest residency effects that did emerge were overwhelmed by differences attributable to gender, age, education or partisanship. The best conclusion appears to be that the political cultures of the rural and urban Wests are virtually indistinguishable.

This apparent convergence between the political cultures of the rural and urban Wests, and indeed of the cultures more broadly defined, should not come as a surprise, for the two "communities" are converging in other respects. The physical isolation of the rural West has been reduced by much better road access, and any social separation has been reduced by cheaper telephone service and a common media. School systems, health delivery and social services have been increasingly integrated across the rural-urban divide. Consider, furthermore, the impact of new information technologies. The internet is often seen as a means by which people around the world can be brought closer together. If this effect is seen internationally, it will also narrow any remaining gap between urban and rural communities in Canada. In the new, virtual world, we should no longer expect rural residents to have values, beliefs or aspirations that are significantly different from their urban counterparts. In virtual space, country mouse and city mouse become one. If the proposed policies to bring rural Canada "on line" are successful, if the broadband promise is fulfilled, the result will be to shrink even further the remaining space between the urban and rural Wests.[5]

As a consequence of the above, it is increasingly difficult to see the urban and rural Wests as distinct social, economic or political communities. Therefore potential policies to protect a distinctive rural community beg the question as to whether there is much left that is truly distinctive about that community. It may no longer make sense to rhapsodize about rural values, or to seek the protection of rural communities. The internet and associated information technologies will lead to convergence within Canada as they lead to convergence across national communities, and there is little question that it will be rural Canada, and not urban Canada, that will do the converging. If, as Ruben Nelson has observed, bringing high-speed internet access to rural communities is "tantamount to a declaration of war,"[6] there is no question as to who will be the victor. The new information technologies will lead to the urbanization of the countryside.

While the political tensions between the West and the rest remain, they no longer reflect an urban-rural fissure in the Canadian body politic. Western alienation does not reflect the values or aspirations of the rural West alone; its embers burn as brightly in the new West's urban heartland as they do in the countryside; political discourse in Calgary boardrooms differs only at the margins from political discourse in small town coffee shops in Saskatchewan.[7] It is no longer the case that regional discontent reflects the grievances of the rural West against Canada's metropolitan heartland. To cast western discontent as reflecting an urban-

---

5. In the 2001 Canada West survey, 66.6% of respondents in large metropolitan centres were frequent Internet users, compared to 57.9% of the small city respondents and 50.5% of the rural respondents. There is, then, a digital divide which, so long as it persists, may help sustain urban-rural differences.

6. Quoted in *Opinion Canada* 3, no. 28 (August 30, 2001): 2.

7. Federal Liberals elected in the West are much more likely to hold urban rather than rural seats. At the same time, the majority of urban MPs in recent elections have come from the ranks of Reform and Canadian Alliance.

rural division rather than a broad feature of the western Canadian political culture would be a mistake.

The general argument, then, is that rural Canada in general, and the rural West in particular, are becoming increasingly less meaningful or distinct cultural, social, economic or political containers. The rural countryside has been penetrated by the new information technologies, and the consequence will be convergence with urban values, beliefs and aspirations. The cultural and economic footprints of the imperial metropolitan centres are steadily expanding, leaving less and less of the rural West untouched.[8] The rural West that still lies beyond the reach of the cities is shrinking both physically and demographically. The contrast with the prairie West in the early decades of the last century is dramatic, and will become even more so as the urban West advances.

Of course, I may be wrong. The events of 11 September 2001 may lead to a flight from the cities, and the new information technologies may deliver on their promise of allowing individuals to participate in the new economy while living anywhere in the world. Given a laptop and high-speed internet access, it may be as easy to connect to the global economy while living in a small rural community in Saskatchewan as it would be living in Calgary or Winnipeg. To date, however, there is little evidence of either effect. The technologies that in theory make it possible to move from an urban to a rural setting do not appear to be diminishing the attractiveness of an urban lifestyle. If anything, urbanization and the rebirth of city cores may be accelerating in the new technological environment.

What Should Be Done?

If rural Canada is definitely on the skids, it is important to ask whether there should be a public policy response. Should Canadian governments try to arrest the decline of rural Canada by providing public policy supports to rural communities and rural Canadians? Is there a distinctive rural Canada, or rural West, whose protection and preservation should be a public policy priority? Or, conversely, should governments let the demographic decline of the rural West continued unchecked, and direct their resources to the emergent urban West?

Certainly there are things that are being done, and could be done, to support rural Canada. Across the country, for instance, rural voters have disproportionate weight in provincial legislatures, and within the House of Commons. We also find that rural communities are subsidized with respect to the delivery of social services, including schools and health care. Such subsidies could be continued or even increased to ensure that rural residents receive the same level of services for the same tax burden as their urban counterparts. We also have a "rural lens" for federal program initiatives, one through which all new initiatives are to be assessed in terms of their impact on rural Canada. And, we have major federal initiatives to ensure that rural Canadians are fully connected to the internet.

This approach in microcosm reflects Canada's principled commitment to equalization. We currently use federal taxes and the equalization formula to transfer wealth from have to have-not provinces, thereby ensuring that Canadian citizens will not be disadvantaged with respect to public services by their choice of provincial residence. In a variety of ways we try to move jobs to people rather than encouraging people to move to where the jobs might be. It would not be much of a stretch to apply the principle and analogous programs to the divisions between rural and urban Canada. Equalization across the urban-rural divide is not different in principle from equalization across provincial communities.

---

8. The most vigorous defenders of rural values and lifestyles are often those who work in the cities but live on acreages and hobby farms in the adjoining countryside. They bring to the defence of the rural West all the technological, financial and legal resources of the urban centres.

In short, there is much that governments can do to arrest the decline of rural Canada. There is also no question that rural communities are under increasing economic and social stress. But, would it make sense—does it make sense—to do so? To date, rural Canada in general and the rural West in particular have not been overlooked as objects of public policy. I would argue, however, that a continued policy focus on the rural countryside is not sustainable. More emphatically, a strong case can be made that public policies should be directed first and foremost to the vitality of the new West's urban heartland.

The cities are the drivers of the new economy, the sites of the knowledge-based economy. The major cities and not the countryside are the magnets for badly needed immigration; international immigrants are unlikely today to settle in rural Canada, and rural residents in the West are the most wary of immigration.[9] The cities are the sites for the region's research-intensive universities, and they provide the sustaining cores for the regional arts and culture communities. If we starve our cities in order to sustain declining rural communities, the prosperity of the region as a whole will be endangered. Retaining a rural focus could have many adverse effects:

> • it could make it all the more difficult to meet the infrastructure demands created by urban growth. It is difficult when times are tough both to reduce urban congestion and maintain the vast network of public highways and roads found across the rural West.

> • it could increase the tax loads for urban centres, thereby undercutting their global competitiveness.

> • it could help sustain rural images of the West among other Canadians and potential immigrants, thereby reducing the attractiveness of the region. International immigrants are not going to come to the rural West in significant numbers.

All of this is not to suggest that we should abandon the rural West. However, it is to suggest that when push comes to shove, when choices have to be made, then public policies should lean towards the urban face of the new West. As we move towards building a new West, it may not be possible for the cities to continue to carry the weight of the rural countryside. As cities attempt to hook their wagons to the new stars of globalization and the knowledge-based economy, they may have to drop the dead weight of the rural countryside. Certainly the under-representation of urban voters in provincial legislatures should be ended.

Keeping the rural legacy and face of the West alive may ultimately hurt the region. It may perpetuate an image of western Canadians as the bumpkins of Confederation, and it may lead to the casual dismissal of western perspectives supposedly not held by the denizens of the metropolitan heartlands of Toronto, Montreal and Ottawa. It may also hurt the marketing of western Canada to potential investors and immigrants abroad. If the West is seen as a rustic tourist destination, the vanguards of the new economy will go elsewhere.

This conclusion, I realize, sounds harsh and unfeeling. Isn't it the Canadian way to ensure that all citizens enjoy the same level of government services, the same opportunities, regardless of where they choose to live, and therefore should not Canadian governments act to protect and sustain rural Canada? In circumstances where everything is possible, this might make sense. But, in circumstances where choices have to be made, where financial resources are finite, governments in Canada would be well advised to move forward with the urban West even if doing so means that the rural West, and indeed rural Canada, is left behind.

---

9. The 2001 Canada West survey asked respondents if Canada should accept more immigrants, fewer immigrants, or about the same number as we presently accept. Among rural respondents, 38.2% opted for fewer immigrants, which compares to 35.2% for small city respondents and 29.5% for major city respondents. The differences are not huge, but they are statistically significant.

CHAPTER TWELVE

Economics, Equity and Urban-Rural Transfers

Michael Rushton

Introduction

Suppose that changing technology, patterns of trade, and prices have created a situation that, left unchecked by decisive government action, would result in a migration from rural to urban areas. Should the government take an active role to discourage migration, through subsidizing agriculture either through direct payments or through the provision of infrastructure that otherwise would not pass a standard cost-benefit test? Should the government provide such social goods as hospitals and schools to rural areas to a degree unwarranted by the population distribution, again in an effort to stem the flow of migration from rural to urban areas?

A recent example of the kinds of policies I have in mind is provided by the 2001–02 budget of the province of Saskatchewan. In a section on "Saskatchewan's Strategy for Rural Revitalization" (Saskatchewan Finance, 2001: 29–31), the government promises $9.6 million in rural capital projects from the Canada-Saskatchewan Infrastructure Program, enhanced internet services to rural communities and schools, "targeted measures" to attract immigrants to rural Saskatchewan, an increase in small business loans, funding for Regional Economic Development Authorities, and boasts of the fact that Saskatchewan provides more taxpayer support for agriculture, per capita, than any other province and more than three times the support of the federal government, not counting the various provincial tax breaks for the sector. Saskatchewan has also established a Rural Revitalization Office to coordinate efforts across line departments.

This paper seeks to assess such policies from the perspectives of efficiency and equity. The analysis is at a high level of generality; hopefully this will allow for greater clarity as to what are the key conceptual issues from an economist's vantage.

Efficiency

No one can live on the prairies without being aware of the enormous changes that have occurred in agriculture over the past century. Great increases in productivity have contributed to an ongoing decline in the relative price of agricultural products, and subsidy programs, especially in the United States and the European Union, have exacerbated the increases in the supply of products and the resulting decline in prices. A natural consequence is that fewer individuals work in the agricultural sector.

Although the situation is often described in terms of the "fall in income" among farmers, we must be careful to specify exactly what we mean by that. So long as labour is a mobile factor of production, it will migrate to where it can earn the highest income, income being broadly defined. In equilibrium the distribution of population would be such that no one was left with any incentive to relocate. If incomes declined in the rural areas, individuals would migrate to cities. Assuming the usual diminishing returns to factors of production, this should cause the average income in rural areas to rise, and incomes in urban areas to fall, until incomes are equalized between rural and urban areas. If agricultural prices are in a continual, long-term decline, we would expect to observe continual migration. So the inequalities are not permanent, given mobility. As Hendrik Houthakker (1967: 7) put it: "The greater the increase in farm productivity, the greater the imbalance between supply and demand of farm products which has to be corrected by an outflow of labor or by lower farm prices. *Unless the outflow of labor from farming is fast enough*, an increase in farm productivity leads only to lower farm prices and lower farm incomes" (emphasis mine).

Note that in our story so far, migration is a good thing. Migration is efficient in that labour is moving from a lower-valued to a higher-valued activity, so the total income of the population will be rising. This gives rise to the economist's perspective, which some might see as hard-hearted, that inequality in incomes is not altogether a bad thing; inequality is the signal to workers in low-income activities that they might want to try an alternative. For example, Welch (1999) notes that the increasing wage-differentials based on education levels have had the positive role of attracting more investment in education. The role of prices and wages in an economy is not to serve as rewards for what has already been done, but rather to serve as signals for what should be done next.

Rural-urban migration has been going on for a very long time, around the world, in response to shifting economic opportunities. The migration was slower in the twentieth century than in the nineteenth, as urban clusters became less important for manufacturing. The greater use of plastics and nonferrous metals, and transportation networks more flexible than the main rail lines, and innovation in electric power generation and transmission, all played a part, as did the preference of many families for aspects of the rural lifestyle (Easterlin, 1980: 310–11). Still, this was a slowdown in the general pattern, not a reversal (reversals of the migration pattern *have* occurred temporarily, but only in the event of an extreme economic downturn of the magnitude of the 1930s).

But the most challenging task for economists studying rural-urban migration is to explain why it has not occurred faster. Farm incomes are chronically low—labour and capital earn lower returns in farming than in alternative uses on what seems to be a perpetual basis—and so there remains the question of why, in Houthakker's phrase, the outflow of labour from farming is not fast enough. Gardner's (1992: 76) extensive survey of the literature finds

> it doubtful that the present differences between farm and nonfarm wages are a matter of disequilibrium; they are more likely a compensating differential for skill differentials or nonwage aspects of the two employments. While a full explanation of these observations has not been accomplished by research to date, it seems likely that the traditional farm-problem source of trouble—declining demand for farm labor owing to technical progress in agriculture—is not the explanation of relatively low farm wages.[1]

Of course not all rural residents are farmers, and in this analysis we are concerned with

---

1. Prior to the modern economy it was thought that rural labour had superior skills to urban workers, although Gardner's survey suggests those days are past. One eighteenth-century observer of the economy found: "Not only the art of the farmer, the general direction of the operations of husbandry, but many inferior branches of country labour require much more skill and experience than the greater part of mechanic trades. ...The common ploughman ... is less accustomed, indeed, to social intercourse than the mechanic who lives in a town. His voice and language are more uncouth and more difficult to be understood by those who are not used to them. His understanding, however, being accustomed to consider a greater variety of objects, is generally much superior to that of the other, whose whole attention from morning till night is commonly occupied in performing one or two very simple operations" (1776; Smith, 1981: 143–44).

migration from rural areas in general, not just off the farm. But it is still worth stressing that the key economic issue is mobility.

In a simple model of the economy there is no policy problem with rural-urban migration, unless there are artificial barriers to people moving to where their incomes and opportunities are highest. But that leads us to the question of whether our world, in some relevant way, is different from the simple world of supply and demand diagrams. At the foundation of all economic policy analysis is the theoretical result that in the absence of spillover effects, or "externalities," competitive markets will generate an efficient allocation of resources, maximizing our aggregate incomes. Interventionist policy is justified, on efficiency grounds, only when there is evidence that 1) there are externalities or noncompetitive aspects, and at the same time 2) there is a feasible, practicable government policy that could improve matters.

One suggestion commonly made is that the ordinary analysis of efficient migration does not apply because the migration is being driven by policy choices in the United States and the European Union that through the persistent use of large subsidies artificially depress the returns to agriculture in Canada. If there were some indication that these subsidies were temporary there might be a rationale to subsidize agriculture in Canada, on the grounds that we could prevent instability until prices returned to their expected long-run values. As it turns out, there is no indication at all that the US and EU are taking temporary measures. They will continue to subsidize in a substantial way, and this will lower world agricultural commodity prices below what they would otherwise be. But this is *not* a rationale for Canada to stem rural-urban migration through rural-agricultural subsidies. If world commodity prices are low, they are low, and in terms of the efficient allocation of Canada's human and capital resources it doesn't matter how the low prices got that way. We misallocate our factors of production, and lower our total income, if we make policy decisions based on some notion of "true" commodity values that we simply don't, and never will, actually receive through the market. It is an elementary economic point, but worth raising given how often media commentators get it wrong.

In the economics literature on regional economic policy, two types of externalities are raised that could, in principle, lead to a justification of subsidy to rural areas: market failures in labour markets, and the problem of urban congestion (Armstrong and Taylor, 1978). We deal with these in turn. However, what we will find is that neither of these potential externalities are noticeably evident in Canada's current urban-rural mix.

Consider first the seminal work of Harris and Todaro (1970); if there are imperfections in the urban labour market leading to substantial involuntary unemployment, there may be an amount of rural-urban migration that is inefficiently high. People would migrate from rural areas based on the *expected* wage in the urban area, which is the product of the urban wage, perhaps being maintained by policy at artificially high levels, and the probability of actually obtaining a job at that wage. They show that a restriction on migration (about which Harris and Todaro express ethical concerns) could potentially increase national income, although it would harm the rural economy at the expense of the urban and some equalizing transfer might be required. In our full-employment, diversified economy, the problem identified by Harris and Todaro is unlikely to occur, and so their model has not provided us with an efficiency justification in *this* economy for trying to slow migration from rural areas. Bartik (1994) and Courant (1994) also raise the point that involuntary unemployment in a particular region could at least potentially justify government action to spur regional economic development. In their case the labour market failures are where people are leaving, not where they are arriving. But Bartik and Courant are discussing a situation of labour markets simply failing to clear, where there are idle workers who would accept jobs at even less than the going wage rate for their skills if only there were jobs available; a case more applicable to the "rust belt" American urban midwest than rural Canada. Courant (1994: 875) still warns of the fact that "policies designed to shore up such places as old whaling villages and mill towns must fail if they are based on subsidizing increasingly unproductive activities. There may be a high willingness to pay to ensure a way of life in a place of one's choice. Providing effective insurance of this kind, at any price, is something that we simply do not know how to do."

The second type of externality that might arise through rural-to-urban migration results from the congestion of public goods in urban areas. A well-known problem with some public goods such as roads and other public infrastructure is that if it is prohibitively expensive to impose user charges there can result an overuse of such facilities. If public infrastructure in rural areas is relatively underused, there might be a justification for discouraging the typical migration pattern (Bartik, 1994). However, it's not clear that this is a problem that is present in the current Canadian context. Fiscal pressures on Canadian provinces during the past twenty years have generally led to an underinvestment in infrastructure, such that the problem now facing provincial treasuries is not underused capacity, but instead the decision of where replacement infrastructure is most needed. And there is no indication that increased investment in rural infrastructure is justified on the ground that rural Canada is where the marginal value of such investment would be highest.

None of the above should be taken to imply that public policy needs to be directed at boosting the level of economic activity in cities. Following Paul Krugman's (1991) path-breaking essay, the field of economic geography has taken on new life. Economists have long thought that increasing returns to scale might explain many economic phenomena, but only recently have theoretical techniques been developed that allow us to model the implications, and this has led to "new" growth theory, "new" trade theory, and, for our purposes, "new" economic geography. Much of this new work centres on the implications of the increasing importance of "knowledge" as an input in production. If knowledge is prone to substantial positive externalities across economic activities—i.e., "knowledge spillovers"—and these externalities depend on close geographical proximity, then we would be likely to see an increased movement of economic activity from rural to urban areas (Audretsch, 1998). But this research is still at a very early stage, and Krugman (1998) himself is extremely cautious about how we might go about modeling economic policy in such a framework. It is certainly not yet obvious that active policy through subsidy to urban centres is required (Fenge and Meier, 2001). The recent claims by the Canada West Foundation (2001: 17–18)—"The major metropolitan regions are the [Canadian] West's gateways to the new global economy and primary motors of economic growth. The prospects for regional prosperity depend on an explicit and effective urban strategy by all governments active in the region"—are premature.

To summarize this section, changes in technology, relative prices, and trade patterns have led to a situation of migration from rural to urban areas, and as long as this movement is relatively unimpeded, the migration is generally efficient in that it equalizes the marginal value of factors of production across different employments. Rural depopulation does not mean that living standards in rural areas are falling. To the contrary, the migration is the means by which rural incomes remain somewhat level with other incomes. Although we don't live in a perfect economics-textbook world, the major externalities that have been sometimes associated with rural migration are not significant in our time and place, and government intervention in "revitalizing" the rural economy is highly unlikely to be efficient.[2]

---

2. Note that I have not raised the multitude of problems that arise in translating an identified market failure into an effective government policy that actually deals with the economic problem at hand. "Public choice" failures in rural and agricultural policy are legion, and the political economy of massively inefficient government policy towards agriculture fills too many volumes of research to list here.

Equity

Efficiency is not the only thing that matters. As well as the total amount of wealth being created, we are also concerned about its distribution. It is a commonplace assumption in the economics of welfare that as a society we are willing to sacrifice some efficiency if it means creating a more equal distribution of income or opportunity. A progressive income tax is but one example of a case where there is a generally accepted willingness to sacrifice some total wealth in an effort to transfer from the rich to the poor.

But in general the income transfer programs we enjoy are based on personal circumstances of the individual or family independent of where the transfer recipient lives.[3] What we want to ask in this essay is whether we could ever justify subsidization of the rural economy on the basis of the redistributive aspects of the policy, even if at some cost in efficiency terms.

Canada has an extensive welfare state that involves redistribution both in terms of pure income transfers and through the provision of services such as health care and education to all funded through a progressive tax system. Is there an *additional* aspect of the welfare state that needs consideration, beyond all the existing transfers, that would subsidize individuals or families who see a declining economic standard of living where they currently live?

No one would deny that moving is costly in monetary and psychic terms, more so if one has a particular attachment to where he currently lives.[4] Note that the existence of such costs do not invalidate the general result that migration of labour and capital results in an efficient allocation of resources. For example, if a move from country to city would cost Tom $2,000 in monetary and psychic terms, and yield an increased wage which would yield a stream of future income $1,800 more in present discounted value than his current employment, he would choose not to move, even though he is a more productive worker in the city than the country. But it is efficient that he not move, if "income" is defined widely enough to include the emotional and monetary cost of relocation.[5]

How should we treat attachment to place in equity terms? Suppose Maggie and Paul and Sadie do the same job, but Maggie and Paul live and work in the city and Sadie lives and works in the country. Begin in equilibrium, so that they each earn the same annual income. Now suppose two events: the rural economy falters, such that Sadie's income falls, and Paul loses a major customer, so that he also suffers a fall in income of the same magnitude as Sadie's. Sadie could continue to earn the same income as before, but only if she moved to the city to work in Maggie's company. Suppose there is a progressive income tax in place, so that if nobody moves, Maggie's tax bill will rise relative to Sadie's and Paul's. Is it equitable to have an additional transfer program in place that would tax the city residents Maggie and Paul in order to subsidize Sadie's employment so that her income doesn't fall? In other words, does Sadie have a special claim on the basis of where she lives, greater than any claim Paul might have?

---

3. There are exceptions to this rule. For example, the Personal Income Tax contains an allowance for those living in the far north, to compensate them for the very high cost of living.

4. See Bartik, Butler and Liu (1992) for means of econometric estimation of the value of a "sense of place," and Kahneman, Knetsch and Thaler (1991) for general discussion of the "endowment effect." Bliss (1993) notes the problems in trying to make welfare evaluations at all if migration causes a change in the migrant's values and preferences.

5. Bolton (1992) attempts to incorporate the value of a sense of place into economic policy analysis, but still concludes that it is only on the basis of market failure that we would find a rationale for policy intervention to stem the flow of migration.

Traditional economic analysis would say that Sadie doesn't have a special claim—income redistribution should be on the basis of income, dependents, and special needs such as specialized health care, but not to subsidize a preference for living in a particular location. Even when we turn to analysts who have tried to go beyond mere income to estimate the standard of living we find that a desire not to move doesn't enter the calculus. For example, the United Nations Human Development Report (1996) in its "balance sheet of human development" considers, in addition to income and employment, health, education, the status of women, social security (in terms of an income safety net), social fabric (considering such aspects as access to information, crime rates) and environment, but has no mention of the ability to remain in place regardless of economic change. The UN's estimate of the "capability poverty measure," based on the work of Amartya Sen (1987; 1993), considers three basic capabilities: to be well nourished and healthy, to have the opportunity for healthy reproduction, and to be educated and knowledgeable. Again, "sense of place", and the ability to maintain a constant income without ever having to migrate, do not appear. In an extensive critique of the standard methods of economic cost-benefit analysis, Martha Nussbaum (2000: 1021–22) provides a much longer list of what she considers to be the central human capabilities, including various equality rights, political rights and freedoms, rights of association and, interestingly, the freedom *to* move. But the freedom to remain in place regardless of the patterns of economic change does not appear.

The UN and Sen and Nussbaum could hardly be considered narrow minded in their conceptions of what constitutes economic justice. Still, there is a consistent theme in their broadening of the scope of what should be included in measures of the standard of living, and that is that they do *not* include as a factor the preferences, or tastes, of individuals. If sense of place is to have a role in the equity side of policy analysis, it would have to be through this route, that a person living in a rural area places a value on staying there that needs to be taken into account.

Obviously it is difficult to include preferences in the development of redistribution policies. We generally hold that a poor person with champagne tastes is not entitled to a greater transfer through the state than other poor people. One reason is practical: if transfers were based on tastes, people would lie about their tastes—everyone would claim a daily need for expensive items. The other reason is ethical: for the most part we don't feel people with champagne tastes deserve more.

That we shouldn't compensate individuals on the basis of their preferences is one of the central results of the modern liberal theory of John Rawls (1971) and Ronald Dworkin (1981), who begin with the fundamental liberal principle that government should not discriminate between different conceptions of the good life. They are egalitarian, but it takes the form of ensuring that the welfare state provides all individuals with those "primary goods" that anybody would want regardless of their life plans. Primary goods include "rights and liberties, opportunities and powers, income and wealth" (Rawls, 1971: 92), but would not allow for special consideration beyond that.[6]

But perhaps *place* is not a commodity like all the others. Margaret Jane Radin (1986) assesses the standard economic line against residential rent control. If where we live were simply another good, like a television set or a carpet cleaner, then we could easily make the

---

6. See Hausman and McPherson (1996: chapter 10) for general discussion. Arneson (1990) provides a critique, claiming that if we are willing to provide special assistance to those with physical handicaps (as Rawls and Dworkin argue we should) then we cannot escape compensating individuals for having different tastes. See also Levine (1995) and Van Parijs (1991) who analyse the liberal position with respect to individuals who strongly prefer not to work.

case that price controls are a bad idea. But television sets and carpet cleaners are obviously just commodities; if we lose one we can always be compensated with a new one or the cash equivalent. But if location becomes a part of what we are as people, then losing a residence one has rented for a long time, say because of an unaffordable increase in rent, is not easily replaced. Radin's argument, although dealing with urban housing policy, is important in our context because it could be invoked as an argument for rural subsidy—sense of place matters in the determination of equitable policies in a different way than cash income.

There are two large practical flaws in Radin's case. First, sense of place is a preference felt differently by different individuals, and cannot be accurately observed. How could we operationalize attachment to rural living as a criterion for subsidy? It is particularly difficult when for some individuals there will be a negative sense of place—the youth who has been raised in the small town who would strongly prefer living in the city. For subsidizing rural areas means reducing the opportunities in urban areas, and so we benefit one group at the expense of another on the rather arbitrary basis that those who like where they live are privileged over those who do not.

The second flaw is that Radin does not address the creation of the wealth, in her example rental housing stock, that she wants to redistribute. As stated earlier, a growing economy requires flexibility in the allocation of resources and in the prices they command. We cannot take the existing stock of wealth and treat it as if it were simply a gift of nature that can now be redistributed on some just and fair basis.[7]

So it is difficult to justify accounting for the preferences of individuals in redistributive policies, even if we think attachment to a place might be important. There is one last aspect to consider, not found in the academic literature, but that can sometimes appear in popular debates. This is the notion that sense of place in general might not be something appropriate to consider in redistributive policies, but *rural* sense of place is a different case. In popular literature and art there is a strong expression of the idea of nostalgia for rural life, equated with hard work and a stronger sense of morals. It arises from a number of sources, including the frustration many feel from the pressures of modern life, but has a long tradition.[8] Here I will direct my attention to one particularly troubling manifestation of this idea, because it relates directly to the question of economic policy. In the most recent Saskatchewan budget (2001), in its introduction to the discussion of rural revitalization, we are told: "Rural Saskatchewan is an excellent place to live and raise a family. It affords a quality of life second to none, with a clean environment and safe communities. ... Rural residents have the strength, energy and creativity to seize and build upon new economic opportunities" (p. 29). What judgment is being made in this budget document? Should it be the basis of how public infrastructure is allocated across the province?

Conclusion

Is rural Canada moving forward or being left behind? The question is wrong. It is the welfare of *Canadians* that matters, not the level of economic activity in a particular *place*. When we analyze policies affecting the welfare of Canadians, we do so by looking at whether policies are increasing the total wealth of the nation, and at how the total is distributed, with particular attention to those at the bottom of the income scale.

---

7. See Schmidtz (1998) for a powerful critique of those who would entirely separate questions of distribution from how what is being redistributed has come into being.

8. See Hofstadter (1963: 272–82) on the anti-intellectual tradition among American farmers, dating back to the founding of the republic.

When policies are directed at trying to increase economic activity in one place at the expense of another, such as efforts to "revitalize" the rural economy, we lower the total wealth of the nation, and adopt what is an ineffective way to increase the economic opportunities of the worst off. In no way should all this be taken to mean that we should take active government measures to *hasten* rural-urban migration. What it does mean is that so far as possible government current spending, investment, and taxation should be neutral across regions and industry, providing public infrastructure where its economic value is highest, and redistributing income on the basis of individual circumstances, not on whether a family lives on a farm or in a small town.

People currently living in rural areas are only as rich as they are *because* of past out-migration. Our income per person would be tremendously lower if we had the same distribution of population now as 60 years ago. The high standard of living Canadians enjoy is the result of living in a dynamic, not static, economy. We cannot simultaneously say that we want to maintain strong economic growth *and* keep our rural areas looking just the way they always have. Romanticized notions of the goodness of rural life are no escape from the real world of economic growth, and should have no place in government budgetary policy.

References

Armstrong, Harvey and Jim Taylor. 1978. *Regional Economic Policy and Its Analysis*. Oxford: Philip Allan.

Arneson, Richard J. 1990. "Liberalism, Distributive Subjectivism, and Equal Opportunity for Welfare." *Philosophy and Public Affairs* 19, no. 2: 158–94.

Audretsch, David B. 1998. "Agglomeration and the Location of Innovative Activity." *Oxford Review of Economic Policy* 14, no. 2: 18–29.

Bartik, Timothy J. 1994. "Jobs, Productivity, and Local Economic Development: What Implications Does Economic Research Have for the Role of Government?" *National Tax Journal* 47, no. 4: 847–61.

Bartik, Timothy J., J.S. Butler and Jin-Tan Liu. 1992. "Residential Mobility and the Value of a Sense of Place: An Application of Maximum Score Estimation." *Journal of Urban Economics* 32, no. 3: 233–56.

Bliss, Christopher. 1993. "Life-Style and the Standard of Living." In Martha C. Nussbaum and Amartya Sen (eds.), *The Quality of Life*. Oxford: Clarendon.

Bolton, Roger. 1992. "'Place Prosperity vs People Prosperity' Revisited: An Old Issue with a New Angle." *Urban Studies* 29, no. 2: 185–203.

Canada West Foundation. 2001. *Building the New West: A Framework for Regional Economic Prosperity*. Calgary: Canada West Foundation.

Courant, Paul N. 1994. "How Would You Know a Good Economic Development Policy if You Tripped Over One? Hint: Don't Just Count Jobs." *National Tax Journal* 47, no. 4: 863–81.

Dworkin, Ronald. 1981. "What is Equality? Part 1: Equality of Welfare." *Philosophy and Public Affairs* 10, no. 3: 185–246.

Easterlin, Richard A. 1980. "American Population since 1940." In Martin Feldstein (ed.), *The American Economy in Transition*. Chicago: University of Chicago Press for the National Bureau of Economic Research.

Fenge, Robert and Volker Meier. 2001. "Why Cities Should Not Be Subsidized." *CESifo* Working Paper No. 546.

Gardner, Bruce L. 1992. "Changing Economic Perspectives on the Farm Problem." *Journal of Economic Literature* 30, no. 1: 62–101.

Harris, John R. and Michael P. Todaro. 1970. "Migration, Unemployment and Development: A Two-Sector Analysis." *American Economic Review* 60, no. 1: 126–42.

Hausman, Daniel M. and Michael S. McPherson. 1996. *Economic Analysis and Moral Philosophy*. Cambridge UK: Cambridge University Press.

Hofstadter, Richard. 1963. *Anti-Intellectualism in American Life*. New York: Knopf.

Houthakker, Hendrik. 1967. *Economic Policy for the Farm Sector*. Washington DC: American Enterprise Institute.

Kahneman, Daniel, Jack L. Knetsch and Richard H. Thaler. 1991. "The Endowment Effect, Loss Aversion, and Status Quo Bias." *Journal of Economic Perspectives* 5, no. 1: 193–206.

Krugman, Paul. 1991. "Increasing Returns and Economic Geography." *Journal of Political Economy* 99, no. 3: 483–99.

———. 1998. "What's New About the New Economic Geography." *Oxford Review of Economic Policy* 14, no. 2: 7–17.

Levine, Andrew. 1995. "Fairness to Idleness: Is There a Right Not to Work?" *Economics and Philosophy* 11, no. 2: 255–74.

Nussbaum, Martha. 2000. "The Costs of Tragedy: Some Moral Limits of Cost-Benefit Analysis." *Journal of Legal Studies* 29, no. 2, pt. 2: 1005–36.

Radin, Margaret Jane. 1986. "Residential Rent Control." *Philosophy and Public Affairs* 15, no. 4: 350–80.

Rawls, John. 1971. *A Theory of Justice*. Cambridge MA: Harvard University Press.

Saskatchewan Finance. 2001. *Connecting to the Future: 2001–02 Budget*. Regina: Saskatchewan Finance.

Sen, Amartya. 1987. *The Standard of Living*. Cambridge UK: Cambridge University Press.

Sen, Amartya. 1993. "Commentary on 'Life-Style and the Standard of Living.'" In Martha C. Nussbaum and Amartya Sen (eds.), *The Quality of Life*. Oxford: Clarendon.

Schmidtz, David. 1998. "Taking Responsibility." In David Schmidtz and Robert E. Goodin, *Social Welfare and Individual Responsibility*. Cambridge UK: Cambridge University Press.

Smith, Adam. 1981 [1776]. *An Inquiry into the Nature and Causes of the Wealth of Nations*. R.H. Cambell, A.S. Skinner and W.B. Todd (eds). Indianapolis: Liberty Press.

United Nations Development Programme. 1996. *Human Development Report 1996*. Oxford: Oxford University Press.

Van Parijs, Philippe. 1991. "Why Surfers Should be Fed: The Liberal Case for an Unconditional Basic Income." *Philosophy and Public Affairs* 20, no. 2: 101–31.

Welch, Finis. 1999. "In Defense of Inequality." *American Economic Review Papers & Proceedings* 89, no. 2: 1–17.

Rethinking the Relationship Between City and Country: Or Why Urbanites Must Support Rural Revitalization

Bruno Jean

Public authorities, like public opinion, are pondering the future of rurality in modern times. While many socioeconomic indicators point to a rural decline, some researchers watch for the appearance of signs of rural revival. A certain urban discourse, fuelled by politicians, that questions the usefulness of rural communities to our society and to our economy, must be challenged. Our academic and scientific work should consist of bringing to light the symbiotic relationship between this country's rural and urban areas. Were urban populations better aware of these hidden ties, they would surely become the staunchest advocates of policies to support rural revitalization. Japan is a case in point. This essay will examine a number of principles that should serve to justify a new rural development policy based on recognition of the multifunctional nature of rural areas. Moreover, it proposes an "educational" tax on food as a show of national solidarity toward rural communities in order to give back to them, through this rural policy, what market regulation no longer does.

Do non-metropolitan areas, to use the urbanocentric definition of rurality, still serve a purpose for society at large? To answer such a question is another way of asking if we still have something to "learn from rurality." The same question was debated by participants at the recent Université rurale québécoise.[1] While this country's rural areas are places of future promise,[2] they are viewed as poor regions condemned to victimhood. But the real poverty lies in our ignorance of the true nature of the interdependence between urban and rural regions. The outstanding characteristic of rural areas has become impoverishment. Consequently, governments need to find ways to implement a new rural policy that reduces regional disparities while fostering the kind of identification with specific areas that lie at he core of a nation's strength.

Regional Development Policies or Assistance Policies for Regions in Crisis?

Political discourse propagates a distorted and self-serving view of reality in many rural areas by continuing to deal with the rural development issue as a relief operation, or as

---

1. L'Université rurale québécoise est une initiative de formation des acteurs du développement rural qui organise des sessions de formation sur le principe du croisement des savoirs entre les gens d'action sur le terrain, les agents de développement et les chercheurs universitaires qui s'intéressent à la ruralité.

2. Voir: Bruno Jean, *Territoires d'avenir. Pour une sociologie de la ruralité* (Québec, Presses de l'Université du Québec, 1997).

humanitarian aid to threatened regions. Many public policies work that way: tell us you are in bad shape, and we will help. If you show some vital signs, off they go to the next area that can show it is in greater trouble than its neighbour. Such an approach clearly maintains rural regions in a state of unhealthy dependency, despite the fact that François Gendron's white paper, *Le choix des régions*, released more than 20 years ago, defines the State as an authority that must support and encourage local and regional vitality. Twenty years after that fundamental shift in government action, one is forced to wonder if our governments are really committed to the regions.

In the meantime, public opinion quite naturally comes to question the benefit of supporting these regions which, ultimately, cost too much in tax dollars for too little return. After all, villages in the Gaspé, and even an entire mining town, Schefferville, were shut down. Such thinking shows the extent of public unawareness about the deep-rooted interdependence that ties the destiny of urban areas to that of rural regions.

Don't Touch My Town: From Bio-diversity to Socio-diversity

With the rise in ecological concerns has come a new awareness of the need for action to protect endangered species and preserve the richness of ecosystems. Protecting bio-diversity has become a universally held value. Small rural villages, existing in the shadow of cities that have been eclipsing them a bit too much of late, are part of our social, cultural, architectural and scenic heritage. Our governments have negotiated a host of international conventions on heritage protection, but seem unaware of both what they are signing and the local ramifications. Promoting the rich heritage upon which a growing recreational tourism industry flourishes, therefore, should be part of an overall recognition of the need to protect socio-diversity in the human world as one would bio-diversity in the animal and plant world.

Some would have us believe that the urban model is perfectly suitable to the country. Small rural communities have proven their social vitality time and time again, further confirmed by the less frequent occurrence of various social pathologies. Small communities have also shown that they can be economically viable, even in spite of the seasonal nature of their economic activities. Lastly, rural areas are the forum for citizenship, the seat of a civil society capable of managing its collective existence through a fabric of social ties that ensures solid social cohesion.

When a small community opts to merge with a nearby city, the situation may prove to be mutually beneficial. But when urban mainstream thought extols the great advantages of such mergers, why not head out to the Gaspé to see the effects of the more than 30-year-old merger of a number of small surrounding villages? What you would see is that the Air Canada monopoly has made travel to this area more expensive than to its own European destinations. We all know, and those who subscribe to the outdated model of charity are quick to point out, the Gaspé is still in a sorry state.

A Better Understanding of Urban-Rural Interdependence

Here, far-off Japan's experience provides a good example. While known for its many metropolitan areas, it, nonetheless, has adopted an ambitious rural policy rooted in a deep understanding of the symbiosis between urban and rural life. It is easier to understand the need to protect rural areas on that densely populated island. They perform a great many functions that are important to society as a whole: producing food, of course, but also seeing to it that the natural ecosystems on which the cities depend for their water supply are replenished. Therefore, a portion of water tax revenues is put back into rural areas in the form of assistance programs as part of a comprehensive rural policy that compensates those communities for the important ecological services they render to society as a whole. And when Japanese city dwellers head for the country, they find vibrant rural communities. In fact, they are so vibrant that many small schools in declining rural villages are filled with city children whose parents want them in an environment conducive to broad and varied learning. When the citizens of Ste-Paule, near Matane, saved their village school in the same way, they did not need to go all the way to Japan on a fact-finding mission to figure out that the school bus can travel in either direction and can just as easily transport urban children to rural elementary schools.

Japan's rural policy, like that of Europe, is based on the recognition that rural lands are multifunctional in nature. These should serve as a model for our own policy, which might still be a long time coming. The state's role in providing support to rural areas must be upheld by demonstrating that this is not an obstacle to agricultural trade, whatever the civil servants at the World Trade Organization would like to believe.

> *The multifunctional nature of agriculture*
>
> The production function: supplying consumers with safe, quality products whose source and conditions of production are known.
>
> The territorial function: occupying the land, managing the space, preserving the landscape and natural resources.
>
> The social function: contributing to employment and rural community life and producing collective services

Such a policy should also be built on a public awareness campaign that helps society as a whole gain a better understanding of the interdependent relationship between urban areas and even the most remote of rural communities. For example, without the major rivers that flow through these regions, what would have become of our hydroelectric industry, one of the jewels in Quebec's crown and a powerful lever of development for society at large?

Fostering a greater awareness of the interdependence between our country's rural and urban economies is fundamental. Rural areas supply all of society with goods (raw materials), whose prices are on a constant downward trend, and ecological services that are not even remunerated at all (although they will one day have to be through mechanisms yet to be invented). Rural resources (food, energy, rural landscape amenities, etc.) ensure urban dwellers' quality of life. When Canadians pay low prices for these resources (with grocery expenses accounting for only 17% of their disposable income), it is hardly surprising that rural economies fare so poorly. Urban resources, primarily financial in nature, must therefore be brought to bear on a process of rural revitalization. Foundations[3] like the Canadian Rural Revitalization Foundation believe that society as a whole, in a concerted show of solidarity, must support a vigorous rural policy capable of achieving rural revitalization.

Land and Publicly Owned Resources, Private Enterprise and Profits

The richness of rural areas is often measured in ecological (quality of the soil) and economic terms (proximity to markets), while an important social factor is often overlooked: access to land ownership. The old rural farm plots of the Laurentian Valley were developed by small family operations passed down from generation to generation. This heavily capitalized and prosperous form of agriculture is certainly no stranger to the virtues of pride of ownership. Today, there are many who believe that our publicly owned forests would be in much better shape if this collective heritage had been put in the hands of family-based operations using the agricultural model.

---

3. Voir: www.crff.ca

While private property is the driving force behind urban development—in fact, it was urban economic interests that called for the end of the seigniorial system in 1854 to consolidate the private land ownership system—many are unaware that publicly owned land is pervasive in rural areas and often hinders its development. The forestry industry is a good example of this. Though hundreds of rural communities in Quebec are "dependent" upon the forestry sector, they derive little from this resource beyond a few seasonal jobs. Other rural areas house major hydroelectric dams on their territory but see almost none of the economic benefits from making use of these rural resources. What might be considered by some as outright expropriation is seen by the city dwellers, through a providentialist view of natural resources, as a gift of nature.

Soon, the court system will be the only recourse left for rural areas to obtain the right to compensation in exchange for the use of resources on their territory, resources over which they have some ownership rights, or, at least, rights of access, by virtue of their occupation of the land. It has indeed been in this way that some minorities, such as the First Nations, for example, have succeeded in winning certain rights in the Canadian and Quebec political systems.

Learning from the Experience of Others:
Lessons from the European and Japanese Rural Development Experience

We need not repeat the mistakes of others. Europe and Japan have implemented rural policies that can be assessed in terms of their impact on, and potential applicability to, a country like Canada. I recently conducted an in-depth assessment of the matter and have identified several points that should be kept in mind with respect to our rural development strategies.

Lessons from the European and Japanese rural development experience

Development of rural lands requires government assistance, which is easier to justify when there exists a general recognition of the multifunctional nature of farming and rural areas.

The rise in environmental awareness should promote rural development with a new notion of the countryside as a natural heritage in need of protection. In the Canadian context, such a view would be slow to take hold, given that our vast territory is hardly conducive to the development of the kind of collective thinking needed for public authorities to invest in rural areas as a heritage that needs to be preserved.

The demand for safe, quality food is strong in Europe and thus supports the emergence of new, more ecological agricultural models in outlying regions. That demand is still tentative here, and although it has increased appreciably in recent years, it is hard to predict the extent to which it will develop.

Agricultural and agri-food development in restructuring communities will only take place if these communities themselves play an active role in their own development. This requires that an agricultural and agri-food strategy and local and regional agricultural policies be developed in collaboration with local and regional municipalities and the various territorial political bodies.

This policy would have to be part of a broader development plan for the entire region. Farmers are not the only users of the land, and with growing environmental awareness, many social stakeholders want to be consulted on the technical decisions concerning agriculture (as well as on the environmental impact of such decisions). Better dialogue and a clearer understanding of the expectations of rural and urban players would likely result in increased support from urban populations with respect to greater public assistance for rural development.

Food Tax to Support Rural Development

We must find a way to shoulder our responsibility and show solidarity with rural communities, which render important, but often intangible, collective services to society, by transferring needed resources to rural communities so that they can continue serving the common good. In our society, a tool often used for such purposes is taxation. A marginal tax on food should be levied and put into a fund to finance the various development activities laid out in our rural policy.

What are the services that rural people provide free of charge to society as a whole? To use the language of the experts, they can be characterized as rural amenities (landscape, healthy environment, recreational space, local specialty products, leisure, etc.) that are highly valued by urban populations. But given economic conditions, if we want to maintain thriving rural communities, we must provide public support. It would be difficult, if not impossible, for the market system to absorb the huge costs of maintaining rural landscapes. For example, Quebecers know that the 1,200 villages that make up their society's rural fabric are of immeasurable value and constitute an important part of their historical heritage. The current situation requires government action to protect this heritage, and ensure its continued survival. This is the root of the idea of transferring resources back to rural areas.

But there is a much more important reason for doing so. Urban populations have yet to realize that the countrysides that feed them, subjected to the logic of the marketplace, are doing so for a constantly decreasing financial return. Are we aware that 90% of what we pay for groceries is spread out through the agri-food chain and does not reach rural or agricultural producers? On average, the producers only recoup 10% of the price paid by the end consumer. Given the purchasing power of Quebec consumers, that price tends to be very low. At the beginning of the twentieth century, the average Quebec family spent about 40% to 50% of its income on food (as is still the case today in many developing countries). In less than a century, that percentage has dropped to about 17%. Why? Considerable gains have been made in productivity in the sector, compounded by agricultural mechanization and advances in modern agronomy, and it is the consumer who is reaping the rewards today. A certain misinformed press would like us to believe that agricultural producers are inefficient and glutted with government subsidies, and that, in the final analysis, the agricultural sector simply costs us too much. But the truth is—and it is true for all modern countries that provide substantial assistance to their farmers—these subsidies have the effect of lowering food prices, an important cost-of-living factor on which urban workers base their salary demands.

Generous farm subsidies only make a short pit-stop in the agricultural sector on their way to benefiting ultimately urban economies. And lastly, these subsidies, which are also presented as rural development measures, serve to further strengthen urban development while causing an unacceptable level of rural under-development. Achieving the goal of dramatically slashed grocery prices, to where we are now paying more for entertainment than food, necessitated a productivity-oriented agricultural model (also seen in the forestry sector) that raises serious doubts about long-term sustainability as well as the quality of the food on our plates.

In our view, what is needed is a 1% food tax that is symbolic, even educational, that would be entirely earmarked for rural development. It would have to be presented as a compensatory measure, since the market cannot fully compensate rural people for the full value of the work they do which benefits all of society. For many households living under the poverty line, groceries are a major budget item; these families easily could be exempted from the tax.

It goes without saying that such a tax must be accompanied by a public awareness campaign on the rural plight. Properly handled, this exercise in public education could generate a certain sympathy for the government: rather than being seen as an act of political suicide. The government then shows itself as one that dares to govern, and is committed at the same time to both the future of urban and of rural development, in keeping with the grand tradition of distributive justice that is the hallmark of modern states.

Conclusion

Rural populations are not merely producers of goods and services. They also live on and develop the land. In so doing, they carry out a crucial geo-political function by asserting the political sovereignty over this same territory. When presence on the land is threatened by economic conditions, political forces are justified in intervening.

Rural Policy Objectives

Supporting the "capacity building" of communities

Strengthening local governance of local communities

Reducing rural-urban disparities and fostering rural distinctness

Maintaining local services in local communities

Stepping up the promotion of rural amenities and protecting the environment

Promoting the concept of national solidarity with respect to rural communities: adopting assistance programs that shift the focus from dependency to solidarity (solidarity building)

An effective rural development policy must be based on the recognition that rural regions are multifunctional in nature, which demands a difficult yet essential balancing of the economic, ecological and social aspects of any development strategy. In other words, the economic potential of these regions must be brought into line with environmental constraints and the expectations of their populations. This involves strengthening the capacity for action among rural communities. But first and foremost, we must learn from our rurality and take stock of the social, cultural, economic and institutional innovations rural communities have put in place to build their future. They are rich in lessons likely to give us a better understanding of urban-rural relations and to suggest novel solutions for the development of Canadian society as a whole.

INDEX

CONTRIBUTORS

DR. ROBERT ANNIS has a Ph.D. in Psychology from Strathclyde University in Scotland. Prior to becoming the Director of Brandon University's Rural Development Institute (1999 to present), he held appointments as a professor of Native Studies at Brandon University (1983–1988) and a professor of Psychology at Caledonia University in Scotland (1976–1983). From 1988 to 1999, Dr. Annis served as the Executive Director of Brandon University's WESTARC Group Inc.—an applied research training and consulting company. Dr. Annis works with the philosophy that communities have, and can further develop, the capabilities and resources necessary to encourage economic and social development. Dr. Annis has published a large number of reports and foundation documents on rural development.

RAYMOND B. BLAKE is the Director of the Saskatchewan Institute of Public Policy, and he has published essays on several subjects, including the resource industries, social policy, and political history.

LOUISE CARBERT is a political scientist at Dalhousie University. Her current research interests include political participation, women's leadership and holding public office, social capital, rural political economy, and research methods. She has published *Agrarian Feminism: The Politics of Ontario Farm Women* as well as a number of articles in a variety of journals.

JUNE CORMAN is a Professor of Sociology and Chair of the Department of Sociology at Brock University. She received her BA at the University of Regina and her MA and PhD in Sociology from the University of Toronto. She is co-author (with Meg Luxton) of *Getting By in Hard Times: Gendered Labour at Home* and *On the Job* which was runner-up for the John Porter Book Prize in 2002. Her teaching and research interests focus on work, unemployment and community.

HARRY P. DIAZ (Ph.D. York University, 1984) is a professor in the Department of Sociology and Social Studies of the University of Regina. His current research includes a study of the social cohesion of rural communities in Southern Saskatchewan and a study of climate change and water sustainability in the Canadian prairies. His research background is in the areas of rural development, sustainable development, environmental policies, climate change, sciences and society, and immigration and integration. He is a research associate of the Prairie Adaptation Research Collaborative (University of Regina) and a Fellow of the Centre for Research on Latin America and the Caribbean (York University).

Deborah Doherty is a Consultant with the Muriel McQueen Fergusson Center for Family Violence at the University of New Brunswick. For 12 years prior to joining the Center, Dr. Doherty was the executive director of Public Legal Education and Information Service in New Brunswick. She has been a member of the Family Violence on the Farm in Rural Communities Research Team at the Center since 1993.

DR. JOHN EVERITT has a Ph.D. in Human Geography from UCLA, and is currently a Professor in the Department of Geography at Brandon University He has conducted research in both rural and urban contexts since coming to Brandon University in 1973. He specializes in the development and implementation of social science research projects, including regional planning in several parts of southern Manitoba; the historical geography of the Canadian Grain Trade; elderly support services in Manitoba. Dr. Everitt has also directed investigations into the changing status of rural life in the prairies, the changing fortunes of small towns and their inhabitants in Canada, and specifically Manitoba, and tourism development in Manitoba and Mexico. He is currently involved with a major collaborative (Brandon University) SSHRC grant on rural health, and an NHRDP grant (with Mark Rosenberg at Queen's University) on the elderly.

DAVID GAUTHIER is a Professor of Geography and has been serving as the Executive Director of the Canadian Plains Research Center (CPRC), University of Regina since 1995. He founded the Centre for GIS and also helped to found the Prairie Adaptation Research Collaborative (PARC) at the University of Regina. He is currently directing a multi-year, interdisciplinary study of the social cohesion of rural communities on the prairies of Saskatchewan, and is also co-directing an international training program in regional sustainable development with Chile and Costa Rica.

ROGER GIBBINS is one of Canada's best known political scientists. He joined the University of Calgary in 1973, where he served as department head from 1987 to 1996. In 1998, Dr. Gibbins joined the Canada West Foundation as President and CEO. He was elected as a Fellow of the Royal Society of Canada in 1998, and served as President of the Canadian Political Science Association (1999-2000). He has published 20 books and over 100 articles and book chapters, most dealing with western Canadian themes and issues.

JENNIE HORNOSTY is a Professor of Sociology at the University of New Brunswick, and Co-ordinator of the Family Violence on the Farm in Rural Communities Research Team at the Muriel McQueen Fergusson Center for Family Violence. She has written extensively on family violence, equity issues, academic freedom and corporatisation of higher education.

BRUNO JEAN is professor in the Département des sciences humaines de l'Université du Québec à Rimouski and a member of the Groupe de recherche en développement régional de l'Est du Québec. A specialist in rural development, Professor Jean is associated with several research projects, and he has published widely on rural and regional development.

WENDEE KUBIK is a Lecturer in the Womens Studies Programme at the University of Regina. She is presently completing a Ph.D in Canadian Plains Studies, an interdisciplinary degree, through the Canadian Plains Research Centre at the University of Regina. Her study The Changing Roles of Farm Women and the Consequences for their Health, Well-being, and Quality of Life is a follow up to her M.A. study on Farm Stress in Saskatchewan. She is co-author (with Murray Knuttila) of *State Theories, Classical, Global and Feminist Perspectives* and Book Review editor of *Prairie Forum*. Her other current research interests are womens health, violence against women, changing gender roles, and global health issues.

ROBERT J. MOORE is a professor of Psychology at Campion College, The University of Regina, where he teaches courses in Introductory Psychology, Personality Theory, and the History of Psychology. His current research interests are all subsumed in the area of health psychology.

ANDREW NURSE teaches Canadian Studies at Mount Allison University.

DR. DOUG RAMSEY has a Ph.D. in Geography from the University of Guelph. He has been a faculty member of the Department of Rural Development at Brandon University (BU) since July 1999. Since arriving in Brandon, he has pursued a range of research interests including rural health, urban development in the downtown core of Brandon, rural and agritourism, agricultural impact and response to industrialized hog operations, and wildlife habitat preservation. He is currently involved with a major collaborative SSHRC grant (Initiative on the New Economy) that is led by Dr. William Reimer at Concordia University. This project brings together academics from coast to coast who are interested in better understanding how communities respond to the new rural economy.

JOHN ROSLINSKI is a PhD student in Political Science at the University of Calgary. His thesis critically examines the integration of Aboriginal themes in federal commissions of enquiry.

MICHAEL RUSHTON is with the Andrew Young School of Policy Studies at Georgia State University. From 1989 to 2002 he was with the Department of Economics at the University of Regina. During the period 1998 to 2000 he was on leave from the University of Regina to be a Senior Policy Advisor with the Cabinet Planning Unit of the Government of Saskatchewan, and for the 2001–02 academic year was University of Regina Scholar at SIPP.

MANJU VARMA-JOSHI is an assistant professor in the faculty of education at the University of New Brunswick. She teaches in the social studies unit; her areas of research focus on multicultural and anti-racist education, global education and citizenship, especially in predominately-White locations.

ROBERT A. WARDHAUGH, recently been appointed assistant professor in Canadian history at the University of Western Ontario, was a post-doctoral fellow at the Saskatchewan Institute of Public Policy working on a project on productivity. His research and publishing interests include Canadian political, cultural, and regional history, rural issues, national/regional identity, Prairie history and literature. He has published two books, *Mackenzie King and the Prairie West* and *Toward Defining the Prairies*, as well as numerous articles, book chapters, biographies, and book reviews.

RANDY WIDDIS is a Professor of Geography at the University of Regina. His most recent book is *With Scarcely A Ripple: Anglo-Canadian Migration into the United States and Western Canada, 1880–1920*, published by McGill-Queen's University Press.